Pupology

Raising a Well-Behaved Puppy

The Dog Way

Cat Dubber

Copyright © 2024 Cat Dubber

All rights reserved. This includes the right to reproduce any portion of this book in any form

The information in this book is intended as a guide and consists of the author's own views. It should not be considered a substitute and should not be relied on for professional advice. The author disclaims, as far as the law allows, any liability arising directly or indirectly from the use or misuse of information contained in this book.

Cover images courtesy of Cat Dubber, Jemma Price and Rosie Barrett

The names of individuals, both human and canine, mentioned in case studies have been changed to protect the identity and privacy of these individuals

ISBN: 9798336108453

For T , B and Socks

About the Author

Cat Dubber is the owner of Take The Lead Dogs, offering training and behavioural advice to dog owners in need of help in her local area and beyond. She fell into the profession by accident, having discovered that traditional reward-based/positive reinforcement methods, so widely advocated in the UK, didn't help when it came to the issues that her second puppy developed at puberty. Food or play rewards simply didn't work and she was at a loss as to what to do. Extensive research eventually led her to look at training from a completely different perspective. Dog psychology was the key. Instead of trying to control her puppy with commands, what she found she needed was to understand WHY her puppy was doing the things she was doing and find a way to effectively communicate with her that this behaviour was unwanted. Using the methods that dogs use to teach their own young provided her with the key to sorting out her puppy's problems. In time she found herself increasingly helping other owners with their dogs using these methods. This eventually led to her taking up the role professionally.

Contents

Foreword i
Chapter One – Why Do things The Dog Way? 1
Chapter Two – Let's Buy a Puppy 15
Chapter Three – Preparing Your Home 23
Chapter Four – The Big Day 33
Chapter Five – A Typical Day in the Early Weeks 39
Chapter Six – Toilet Training 49
Chapter Seven – Feeding Time and Treats 57
Chapter Eight – Playtime 69
Chapter Nine – Rest Time and Relaxation 81
Chapter 10 – Visitors To Your Home 91
Chapter 11 – First Trip to the Vet 107
Chapter 12 – First Trip in the Car 117
Chapter 13 – First Pavement Walks 125
Chapter 14 - First Walks in the Park 145
Chapter 15 – Problems When Out Walking 167
Chapter 16 – Take Your Puppy Everywhere 179
Chapter 17 – The Challenges of Puberty 185
Chapter 18 – Reading Your Puppy 195
Chapter 19 – Other Pets and Small Humans 205
Chapter 20 – Adopting a Rescue Puppy 219
Chapter 21 - First Year in the Bag! 225

Pupology

Foreword

I am a dog owner like you. I learnt the hard way with my second puppy that, despite the best intentions and doing everything by the book, puppies don't always grow up to be the dog that we envisaged owning. I saw myself doing the usual reward-based puppy training and becoming a good, responsible dog owner. I envisaged having a dog I could take anywhere - the pub, the café, the park - a dog who would be a joy to walk and loved by everyone. That worked with my first puppy, but not my second. Why? Because conventional reward-based training can work beautifully if you are lucky enough to pick the right puppy with the right temperament and put in the hard work, but it doesn't always go as planned. This can particularly be the case if the puppy you have chosen is born to lead, has very strong instincts in certain areas or is born with a nervous disposition, for instance. Owning a dog isn't simply a case of buying a puppy, taking it to training classes for a bit and then, bingo, you have a well-behaved dog. There is so much more to it than that.

My second puppy had a strong instinct to hunt and was a natural born leader, two things I didn't have a clue about when I got her. Despite being a gold-star pupil at her puppy training classes, with excellent recall initially off-lead, it all went horribly wrong when she hit around 6 months old. All her previous reward-based training went out of the window as her instinct to hunt took precedence over her willingness to listen to us. She also switched from following my older dog's lead to being the leader herself, bossing him around, taking treats and even bones out of his mouth, with him willingly capitulating. He remained a well-behaved, lovely dog, but the dynamic of our little family definitely changed once she hit her teenage spell. We tried everything to sort her out, even going so far as to send her off for two weeks residential training. And that really was the turning point for me, because my happy-go-lucky spaniel came back a broken dog, in my opinion. Yes, she was well-behaved and didn't put a foot wrong, but it was as if her personality had been totally squashed out of her. She had also lost a lot of weight, which concerned me, as she was a great eater normally. We had been desperate, so we put our faith in a trainer and took on board everything we were taught (even some techniques that didn't sit comfortably with us). We gave the methods a try for a while because we trusted the trainer and were desperate for a solution. However, we soon stopped using most of the techniques as we just wanted our happy dog back, not this cowed shadow of her. Yes, she had improved in some areas, but she had lost her spark and love for life and seemed afraid to do anything. And that is what led me to investigate other ways of sorting out our dog's issues, but that's a whole other story in itself! A story that led me down the road of dog behaviourism.

Fast forward to now when, after close to eight years working as a dog behaviourist and trainer, I see things very differently to the dog owner that I was when I got my first puppy back in the late 1990s. I wish I had known then what I know now as I would have taken a very different approach to raising my two puppies. I, like most dog owners, knew nothing about dog psychology, nothing about body language, nothing about dog instincts, nothing about dog communication. Why would I? I was under the impression that all I needed was to book into some puppy training classes and have a few puppy books to hand and a nice big bag of treats. How hard could it be? Pretty hard, as it turned out! Had I known about all these things, I would have been able to communicate effectively with my puppy from the outset in a way she understood - the dog way - and could have avoided a lot of the common pitfalls, saving myself a load of stress and money in the process! She would have done things AUTOMATICALLY for me, rather than needing to be asked with a command. And if I did have to issue her with a particular command, she would listen without question.

I want to share with you the things I have learnt in my years working as a behaviourist, what the dogs I have worked with have taught me about what a dog needs to be balanced and happy. I want to teach you the things I wish I had been taught before I started my journey with my puppy and equip you with the simple skills you need to communicate effectively with your dog. This is the foundation of everything I do - I use dog communication and a mother dog's way of teaching her young to train puppies and rehabilitate older dogs with behavioural problems. Understanding how dogs communicate with each other and teach each other is at the core of everything I do. Food rewards simply are not. Yes, I sometimes use food as a reward (recall training and winning the trust of a nervous dog spring to mind), but it plays a very small part in my approach. After all, dogs themselves don't use food to teach their young, do they? The most important thing I focus on is the <u>relationship</u> between a dog and it's owner, a relationship built on mutual trust and respect. A harmonious relationship, where the dog and owner are part of the same team. The owner is the team leader, the creator of rules and boundaries which the whole team learns to honour and respect. A good team leader will get to know his team members inside out, understanding that they are not just a pet, but also that they are a dog, with instincts and behaviours specific to their species. A good team leader will also understand and acknowledge that each member has its own personality and individual idiosyncrasies, which shouldn't be ignored. A team leader does not bully its team members into doing things for them. This is not a dictatorship based on fear and punishment. Team members willingly give their best. You and your puppy are a team and should work together in harmony. There are so many factors at play when it comes to raising a puppy, but remember, the most important one is YOU! Your puppy is just a baby, and it is down to you to teach him how to live with humans harmoniously. For the rules of living successfully in the human world are very different to living in the dog world.

Just like human beings, every dog is different. Every dog has individual characteristics, some of them inherited, some of them learnt from an early age. If only we could see inside our dogs' minds, we could understand why they do the things they do. But we can't. They can't speak, so we can't ask them either. So, where does this leave us? It leaves us hugely vulnerable to getting things wrong and ending up with behavioural issues! Not deliberately, obviously. No owner in their right mind is going to deliberately do things that will lead to their dog having issues. We all have the best of intentions when we get a puppy. However, things don't always work out the way we intended because we INADVERTENTLY get things wrong, particularly with puppies. We simply don't appreciate that there are certain things we can do when raising a puppy that can help put us on the right road from Day 1 and avoid common behavioural problems.

Of course, it is possible to raise a well-behaved dog from puppyhood without digging deep into dog psychology. There is plenty of information out there to help you do this, and with that and luck (and a massive dose, at that), we might successfully raise our puppy with just a few minor irritating habits. However, these days the guidance available is frankly overwhelming. The advent of the internet and social media has resulted in new dog owners being bombarded from every direction with different and, often conflicting, advice. Their local puppy training classes will more than likely take them down the reward-based training route, with few, if any, offering an alternative approach. Or perhaps, instead of attending training classes, they will turn to social media, the internet, books, or TV programmes for advice on how to raise their puppy successfully. And, as I said before, it may all work out fine. But if it doesn't, if the puppy starts to show unwanted behaviour, this tsunami of conflicting information, not to mention the advice of every dog owner in the local park, is going to leave those poor owners baffled, confused, and stressed when it comes to tackling these new problems emerging with their puppy. So, what can they do? Read on and perhaps I can help a little, having gleaned over the years through my work a wealth of information that I wish I had been party to when I first made that decision to become a dog owner!

Chapter One – Why Do things The Dog Way?

Before we begin, I am going to ask you a simple question. "Why did you pick up this book?" Was it the cute puppy on the cover that drew your eye? Or maybe the well-behaved bit in the subtitle? Or maybe you were just curious about how someone raises a dog "the dog way"? Us dog lovers are suckers for a cute puppy picture and we all want to raise a well-behaved dog. But many of us have this somewhat naïve idea that raising a puppy is straightforward and just involves teaching them some basic commands using tasty treats in the early months. That's what I thought when I got my first puppy. Loads of people had dogs. How hard could it be? I knew what a well-behaved dog looked like - it fitted into human life seamlessly, doing what it was told and causing no trouble to its owner or other humans and dogs. What I didn't realise was that these sorts of dogs were 'balanced'. Why would I and why would it matter? I'd never considered whether a dog was balanced or not. But what exactly is a balanced dog?

A balanced dog is one that has been raised to fit into our human world in a way that allows it to completely enjoy life as a dog without any stress or confusion over how it is supposed to behave in different situations within the human world. It will have a calm nature, but still be full of the joys of life, and will always look to its humans for direction. It will obviously still have natural instincts, but if its owner asks it to ignore these, it will. Dogs raised in the wild by their own kind (dogs!) grow up to be balanced adults. They will NOT have behavioural issues. Their behaviour is very much instinctual. They know what to do and when to do it and take direction from the dogs in charge of their group. There is no room for unbalanced dogs in a dog pack. Puppies are taught from Day 1 the rules of the pack, they understand boundaries, both behavioural and physical. They simply know what is expected of them when they live amongst their own kind.

Now, at this point, some of you may be rolling your eyes at the mention of dog packs in the wild, yes? You will read time and time again that the notion of dogs being pack animals is totally irrelevant to domesticated dogs and if that is your view (and I really hope you have done your research before reaching this conclusion, rather than just read an opinion on the internet), you may as well just give this book to a charity shop right now before reading any further. Please don't. Because after doing extensive research myself when I was an ordinary dog owner like you having problems with my second puppy, nothing <u>OTHER</u> than the behaviour of dogs in the wild came close to explaining why my perfect young puppy had turned into an adolescent nightmare. Believe me, I tried every bit of equipment and every training method out there to try to sort Molly's issues, which predominantly comprised a strong instinct to hunt and extreme pulling on lead. Walks had gone from being a pleasure to something I dreaded. I had exhausted all avenues and, in desperation, delved deeper into the behaviour of wild dogs. I had never given a thought to how dogs think and behave i.e. dog psychology. It just didn't occur to me that the way they raise their own young could be important. My research took me far and wide and opened up a whole new way of looking at dog behaviour. This approach gave me the answers I was looking for, fixed my dog's issues and eventually led me to the career I have today. THAT is why I do things the "dog way."

The work I do always starts with a client consultation. One of the questions I ask at this consultation is rarely answered correctly. I ask the owner, "What dog are you likely to come across in human society that is impeccably behaved but will likely have had little or no formal training?" Chances are you will have seen one of these dogs at some point during your lifetime, maybe on your daily commute to work or when you are out shopping or perhaps on a night out in your local town centre. Remember, this is NOT a formally trained dog, like a guide dog or a police dog. Got it yet??? It's a homeless persons' dog. "Ah", you say, "Of course!". That dog lying on an old blanket in a doorway, more often than not without a lead. Just watching the world go by, doing nothing wrong, barely looking up when a passerby throws some coins into its owner's cup. Ask yourself, why is it that this dog can sit on the pavement all day without a lead and not get run over? Could you walk along a busy shopping street with your dog off lead confidently? Ok,

Why Do Things the Dog Way?

that isn't a fair question as you have only just got your puppy, but can you envisage doing that in the future? Please don't, as you would be breaking the law! Why is it that the homeless persons' dog seems to instinctively know how to behave in this situation? Well, in my opinion, it's because it is living the closest thing to a primal pack life that you can get in the human world, the closest thing to the life its' ancestors would have led in the forest. Let's think about this. What would a typical day look like for this dog if it lived in the wild?

I am going to hugely oversimplify things here, just to get my point across. I don't pretend to be an expert on wild dogs, I simply take this loose model as a framework on which to hang my approach to training and rehabilitation because time and time again, I have found it works. Quite simply, I wouldn't have succeeded as a behaviourist if these methods didn't. In the wild, the average day for this dog might include daily activities such as patrolling the packs' territory, killing some prey, eating that prey and some social interaction/play. The patrolling of territory might sometimes include migration from one area to another. Movement of this type would be done in an organised fashion, with the dogs mentally connected to the dog or dogs in charge. What does mentally connected even mean? Well, when the lead dog stops, the others stop, when he moves, they move. The "following" dogs are tuned into this leader, always with one ear on them. This isn't a "leisure" walk. There is no playing or sniffing or zig zagging about investigating interesting smells. This is a dedicated journey from A to B which is done in something I call "travelling" mode (more of this later when we talk about teaching a puppy not to pull on the lead). If the pack were lucky enough to make a kill, the dog in charge would eat first with the others maintaining a respectful distance until he or she has had their fill. Only once this leader walks away would the other dogs move into eat their share. Lastly might come some leisure or social time, with mutual grooming or play between the dogs.

Now, let's think again about that homeless persons' dog. When that homeless person decides to get up and move to a new pitch, what does the dog do? He simply gets up and follows. No lead, no need for any talk or commands. He will simply trot behind the homeless person in "travelling" mode with his ears flat, his eyes fixed forwards and his tail in a neutral position (see Chapter 18). If the human stops, he will stop; if the human moves, he will move. He is not being taken on a leisure walk, nor is he leading the walk. He is doing a primal walk from A to B, mentally connected to the homeless person. Food resources will likely be scarce on the streets. He is unlikely to be served up a gourmet breakfast and dinner each day in a swanky china dog bowl. More likely, he will be chucked some scraps of whatever the homeless person is eating. It may be that he gets nothing at all. Life on the streets is tough, there is no time for molly coddling, endless playing and luxury toys. Life is about survival. Just like in the wild. Love and affection come last in this equation of daily life. So, you see, things happen in a different way and a different order on the streets - the homeless persons' dog isn't controlled with a bag of treats and a load of commands, he simply knows what to do and when. Why? Because he is living a life that bears a striking resemblance to the primal life he would be living in the wild with other dogs. He has bonded with the human he has chosen to spend that life with and looks to that person for direction in all situations.

This dog is unlikely to have been born on the streets. It's more likely to have been dumped somewhere by someone, or maybe has lived in a domestic environment with its current owner until they found themselves down on their luck. It doesn't really matter what the circumstances were that led him here, what matters is his genetic programming. He was born to live life as a member of a pack, whether it be a pack of two (in this case) or a pack of fifteen in the wild. So next time you see a homeless person sitting in a doorway with their dog, take a moment to observe from a polite distance and ask yourself, is this dog behaving well, is he happy and content? Is he being forced to stay where he is?

A pet dog living with humans ISN'T living anything close to a primal life and must adapt to the rules of the human world. In fact, when you think about it, the pet dog in your home is actually living in a form of captivity! He can't just go anywhere he fancies, whenever he wants. He is restrained by the four walls of your flat or house. When you are out and about on a walk with him, he will often be restrained by his lead. He doesn't get to make his own decisions, you make them for him most of the time, unless he is off the lead. The boundaries of his life with you, both physical and behavioural, are different from living in the dog world. It is not acceptable in our human society for two dogs to sort out their differences in the park through having a scrap, yet that is what they would do if they were in the wild. But imagine if you allowed your dog to do that at your local park? You would quickly become a pariah and your dog would be labelled as out of control or a nuisance. Nobody wants to be THAT dog owner, and nobody wants their dog to be labelled this way. Yet to your dog, this is perfectly natural behaviour!

So how DO you raise a well-mannered, balanced dog that can function happily within human society? There is no simple answer to this because there are several factors at play with a puppy which ultimately contribute to the kind of dog he will turn out to be. However, if you are aware of these factors BEFORE you even get the puppy and keep them in mind as he grows, you will give yourself a better chance of success in the long run.

One of the first things you should try and understand when raising a puppy is how dogs communicate with each other and other animals, including you. Once that puppy arrives you are going to be so caught up in the chaos and excitement of his arrival that you are unlikely to give dog communication a second thought. Your main concern will be getting through each day and night with your sanity and your house in one piece! You might wonder, does dog communication even matter? It absolutely does, because dogs **can't speak** and we humans rely almost exclusively on speech to communicate. Consequently, already we have two conflicting means of communication in the mix! It would be amazing if our dogs could talk back to us. Training would be so much easier, wouldn't it? But they can't because they use very different methods than us for communication, and if we fail to acknowledge this and we fail to learn about these methods, we are making the job of bringing up a well-behaved puppy so much harder for ourselves.

If you feel tempted to skip this chapter because it sounds a bit boring, please don't, as it really will help you in the long run. I know that all you really want to know is how to toilet train your puppy, how to get it to sleep all night, how to stop it nipping you with those sharp teeth and destroying your things, but if you read this chapter, you can avoid all those problems in the first place so very easily! Maybe I can persuade you with a few simple observations from my work about common things people get wrong about dogs. Wagging tails, for example. The majority of owners I have talked to think this means a dog is happy and being sociable. Not necessarily the case. Flat ears is another one. A lot of owners think this means their dog is sad. Not necessarily the case. And a heck of a lot of people think that the way to stop a dog jumping up at you is to turn your back on it! We'll get to that one later!

So, let's get back to the nitty gritty. We have already agreed that dogs can't speak English (or French or Japanese…). So how DO they communicate with each other and other animals, for that matter? I was intrigued to learn about this when I first delved into the issue of dog communication. There is an awful lot of literature out there, but the best explanation that I found was the theory that they communicate by reading body language and assessing brain energy levels. Put these two together and it tells you the <u>STATE OF MIND</u> of the animal. I will be talking a lot about the state of mind of your puppy in this book, so it might be worth folding the corner of this page over so that you can find it again quickly (unless you are reading it on a Kindle!). Think of energy levels in your puppy's brain as being on a scale of 0 to 5, where 0 is very calm and 5 is very excited. A super-excited dog has a very high level of brain activity, whereas a calm dog will have a much quieter brain. Most of us understand about body language – we can tell when other people are tense or excited from what their bodies/muscles are doing, from their posture etc. A dog, like all other animals, will constantly assess the body language and brain energy levels of another animal (including you!) and respond accordingly.

It's not just dogs who communicate this way. Other animals do it too. In fact, we are the only species whose brain has evolved sufficiently to use speech to communicate. A group of animals at a watering hole can't

TELL each other verbally when there is danger nearby from a stalking lion. Yet, they can still communicate that message to each other. How? By reading changes in each other's state of mind and reacting accordingly. If the zebra standing next to the antelope suddenly tenses up (because it has spotted the lion or even just sensed the lion's presence), the antelope is going to notice the change in the zebra and tense up too, because it has got the message that there is something to be worried about. Not a word has been spoken but the two different species have communicated! It is the same with dogs. Your puppy or dog spends every second of every day reading your body language and brain energy levels and responding accordingly. He also does this with other dogs, other humans and other animals. You don't need to speak for him to understand whether you are tense or relaxed, he can READ you!

We don't just need to understand how dogs communicate with other animals if we want to set ourselves up for success when raising our new puppy. We also need to understand how they TEACH each other. After all, you are going to be your puppy's teacher once he leaves his Mum, aren't you? You probably just think that involves teaching some basic commands, which you can either do on your own using a handy puppy training book, or perhaps learn at puppy training classes. In both cases, you will most likely be using the human approach to teaching a dog (using speech and rewards such as food). There is absolutely nothing wrong with this if it leads you to a well-behaved, well-socialised dog who fits seamlessly into the human world. But is it always enough? Sometimes it isn't, as I mentioned with my second puppy. Sometimes puppy owners find that success after this initial phase of training is followed by a deterioration in their puppy's behaviour, normally from around 4 or 5 months onwards (i.e. around the start of puberty). Puppy training concentrates on the EARLY months of raising a puppy. There are often advanced classes available which take you beyond this but, in my experience, only a handful of owners sign up for these. Their puppy is trained, right? There is no need to take things further. WRONG! It is precisely at puberty that most puppy owners start to experience behavioural issues with their puppies.

This begs the question, surely it should be possible to sort these puberty issues with the same sort of training you did earlier on with your puppy? I certainly believed this was the case with my second puppy. And yet these methods didn't work. I simply could not sort Molly's obsessive hunting and lead pulling issues using treats and commands. She wasn't interested in food in these instances, yet she would happily take treats at other times. I was missing something and I had no idea what it was. It turns out that what I was missing was two key things about dogs and their behaviour. Firstly, you CANNOT, as a human, always get through to a dog when it is in a heightened state of mind (a level 5 of brain activity!) and influence its behaviour by using speech, or even food. Secondly, a dog at puberty is genetically programmed to challenge for leadership of its pack. Now, don't despair, I'm not going to launch into a whole load more heavy stuff about psychology at this point. It IS important, but you won't need to worry about any of this if you take on board that the important thing is HOW YOU TEACH YOUR PUPPY FROM THE OUTSET. If you get it right in the early months, you are far less likely to find yourself losing influence with your puppy at puberty! Which brings us to the point that we need, as humans, to understand how dogs teach their own young when they are born.

We have touched on the fact that wild dogs live in packs when talking about the homeless persons' well-behaved dog. There are those that believe that the ancestry of our domestic dogs is completely irrelevant to training pet dogs. Whether you think this is relevant to your puppy or not is entirely up to you. The way you train is a personal choice, just like everything else to do with your dog. Before you make this decision, however, please do consider the following points. Is it fair on your dog to not even consider its heritage when you are considering bringing it into your life and providing it with a home? Isn't it a tad arrogant of us humans to think that our methods of teaching are superior to the methods the dog species uses to teach its own young? If **OUR** methods are so great and successful, why is it that there are so many dogs out there in society with behavioural issues? Why are our rescue centres full to the brim? Indeed, why do I even have a job???!!!

I would ask you to bear with me for a moment and think about how a mother dog raises her young, whether "in captivity" (which is effectively what a pet dog is) or on the streets (like a feral dog) or in the woods (like a wild dog). Street dogs manage to raise their young successfully without any human input. You don't see them queuing round the block to sign up for the latest puppy class, do you? No, the mother dog will raise her young the only way she knows how. The dog way. And those puppies will grow up to be balanced dogs, who know exactly what they should and shouldn't be doing on a daily basis. Let's look at this in a little more detail.

It is believed by many that modern day dogs are descended from grey wolves or a similar wolf-like early wild dog species which is now extinct. Whichever is the case, their ancestors, as I have said before, were genetically programmed to live in packs. Whilst the modern-day, domestic dog is a very different creature from these wild ancestors, nonetheless, they still share the same DNA and have the same instincts and natural behavioural traits. Their instincts and behavioural traits are those of a DOG, not a human. If you can accept this and learn how to provide for your dog's daily needs from your dog's point of view, your dog will be able to live a calm and happy life alongside you, its human owner. If you ignore this, and many people who think talk of the "pack" is nonsense, you may well still raise a well-behaved dog, but you might find it a heck of a lot harder!

Firstly, you need to see things through your dog's eyes. Your dog sees you and your family, no matter how large or small, as its pack. When it was born at the breeders' home, its pack consisted of its mother and its brothers and sisters. In this situation, the mother is in charge - she is the leader and the educator of the pups. When it is taken from its mother and placed in your home, YOU take the mother's place as its leader and educator in the puppy's brain. And all the other occupants of your home, even the cat, are higher up the pecking order than the puppy! Now at this point we are going to stop for a minute and pretend that your puppy has not been brought into your home, but instead has been born into the wild. I have over-simplified what happens in nature, for the purposes of making it easy to understand and absorb. You only need to know the bare bones of things to be able to apply a mother dog's methods to your puppy in your home. Bear with me on this as this is the important bit!

Firstly, let's give the puppy a name. Gino will do. So, Gino is born in the woods, along with his brothers and sisters. He is part of a large pack of wild dogs. He is born blind and deaf - he can smell and feel, but his eyes and ears don't open until he is about 12 days old. He can smell his mother, his mother's milk and his siblings. He uses his nose to find his way around the new world he has been born into, both to smell and to feel. Indeed, his nose is THE most important part of his body, and you will see later that a dog using its nose FIRST is what we want, if we want him to be balanced. An unbalanced dog will often use its eyes before it uses its nose – think of a dog reacting to the SIGHT of another dog before he has even had the chance to pick up its scent.

Gino's mother cares for him in the den and he quickly grows. His eyes open and his ears start to work. From the very first day he is born his mother will teach him when he is doing something unwanted. How else is he going to learn what is and isn't acceptable behaviour? Let's imagine he is the greedy puppy in the litter. His mother has fed her babies but now wants to rest in the cosy warmth of the den. But Gino has other ideas; he wants more milk so he keeps trying to feed. He uses his nose to sniff out where the milk source is (his mother!) and tried to latch on. Initially, his mother will warn him off with a low growl (a VERBAL intervention). He is deaf at this point, remember, but he can still FEEL the vibration that the growl creates as he presses against her body. But crucially, he doesn't know what that growl means the first time it happens, so he carries on trying to feed. So, his mother flips him away with her nose (a physical intervention). And she will repeat this process until he gets the message that he isn't getting fed! THIS IS HOW GINO LEARNS HIS BEHAVIOUR IS UNWANTED. His mother is giving him a signal; she is INTERVENING when his behaviour is unwanted. I should stress at this point that the mother dog ISN'T being mean, she is simply communicating a message "the dog way" that the pup's behaviour is unwanted. Quickly the puppies learn to use this technique on each other. If Gino nips his brothers or sisters too hard they will squeal (verbal warning) and he will immediately let go. If he doesn't let go, they will bite back but the pressure will be carefully controlled and not aimed to hurt, just warn. If he annoys his mother when she wants to sleep, she will warn him off with a low growl, and if he ignores this she will snap at him with her mouth and he will learn to leave her alone. All the things he learns are done through smell, touch, and sound.

The most important thing to remember about the dog intervention is that it is <u>subtly</u> different from a human intervention. This is absolutely KEY to teaching the dog way and is something that is often overlooked, leading to confusion as to the difference between intervention and perceived punishment. Punishment is NEVER an acceptable way to interact with an animal. When a human intervenes when a young child is doing something unwanted (e.g. drawing in red pen on the adults' nice white walls), they do it with heightened emotion, be it anger, frustration or disappointment, and they hang on to that emotion (or energy) for a good few minutes after they have told the child off. The adult remains tense with heightened brain activity in this situation. When a mother dog intervenes with her puppy, she does it for a second, then <u>immediately</u> moves on mentally and <u>relaxes</u> again. In other words, she returns to a calm state of mind. She is effectively saying "Don't do that, relax with me," which means that the puppy learns to go back to being calm immediately after the intervention. Us humans stay tense for a good few minutes (or even longer) after "intervening," so the message becomes "Don't do that, be tense with me." In other words, if we use the human way to intervene with our puppy's behaviour we fail to return the puppy to a calm state of mind after intervening; we leave his brain in a heightened state. As you will learn going forwards, we WANT our puppy's default state of mind to be **calm**. Yes, they will get excited when triggered, of course they will, and that is totally natural, but the rest of the time in their day-to-day life we want them to be calm, balanced individuals. You will only ever see unwanted behaviour from your puppy or dog when his brain is EXCITED! When he is calm he will be doing nothing wrong. We will return to this later in the book when we look at how to replicate the mother dog's behaviour in problem situations to return our puppy to a calm state of mind. Don't worry, no growling involved!

The above is a lot to take in. I have thrown an awful lot of information at you in this chapter. You may find it interesting, or you may have found your mind wandering and started thinking about what you fancy for dinner. Talk of dog psychology and wild dog packs isn't everyone's cup of tea. However, you want to raise your puppy to grow up without issues. And you want to do it in the simplest and quickest way possible, yes? Doing it the "dog way" will allow you to achieve these aims. Your puppy will learn faster if you use his language, he will learn faster if you use his species' teaching methods, he will bond with you in the way he would bond with another dog if you BEHAVE like a dog in the first place. So why not combine HIS way with YOUR way to get the results you want?

If you really are struggling to think of the whole pack approach, it may help to think of yourself and your dog as being members of a team. The sports analogy is often helpful for owners as it's something they can identify with. Are you a football fan with a favourite team? Imagine if your team didn't have a manager? If each player, when they went out on the pitch, just followed their own agenda and paid no regard to the rules of the game, or their teammates. Do you think they would prove a successful side? The manager is there to use their wisdom and experience to guide the players and encourage them to work as a cohesive unit for the greater good, in other words, to be the winning team. It simply isn't possible to be successful at sports if you don't follow the rules and boundaries of the particular sport you are doing. Dogs are programmed to live and work as part of a functioning, efficient team. Their very survival in the wild depends on this. So be a team leader for your dog. Provide his life with structure and clear rules and boundaries and I can guarantee he will live a much happier life as a result. Dogs don't like chaos. They are at their happiest when they have a clear idea of what they are expected to do in any given situation. Living with humans requires them to abide by human rules and boundaries and, on occasion, ignore their instincts and it is your job to teach them what these rules and boundaries are from a very young age. If you don't, there may be times when your dog will be forced to listen to his own instincts when making decisions and that won't necessarily result in an agreeable outcome!

Here's my final thoughts about the particular situations in which your puppy should have a clear idea as to how it is expected to behave. In the coming chapters, I will be showing you how to achieve well-mannered behaviour in these situations:

Around humans, both in and outside your home, no matter what they are doing
Around dogs, both in and outside your home, no matter what they are doing
Around other animals, both in and outside your home
Inside other people's homes
In your car or other people's cars
On public transport
On the streets
In the park
At the vet
At the groomer
At the kennels/dog boarder
In the pub/restaurant/café

The above list seems pretty obvious, when you think about it, as it's the places your puppy/dog will be going. I mean, you won't be taking it to the cinema, will you (unless you happen to live near a cinema that does dog-friendly screenings!)? Naturally, we want our puppies well-behaved in ALL situations but the above are the key ones I find clients tend to have the most issues with. If you get things right in the beginning, your puppy will behave wherever you take it.

Pupology

Chapter Two – Let's Buy a Puppy

I hope that by now, you have learnt a little bit about how dogs communicate and how they teach each other. It's now time to think about actually getting a puppy. There are a few things you need to consider before you go down this road, the two most important things being what breed of dog to choose and which puppy to choose from a litter, assuming you are lucky enough to get a choice.

Don't just assume that every type of dog is suited to every type of person! It really helps if you can match your lifestyle and energy levels to your choice of breed. It is blindingly obvious that a person living a sedentary lifestyle shouldn't be picking a breed designed for work, like a border collie or a German shepherd. Working breeds are better left to experienced dog owners, in my opinion. A dog bred to do a specific job will often find a job to do itself if you don't satisfy its in-built instincts, so do bear this in mind. A person with a sedentary lifestyle would be far better suited to a dog bred for companionship, rather than one bred to work on the hills with sheep all day long. So, think about your energy levels before choosing your breed - are you an early riser who loves nothing better than to be outside all day, walking, running, cycling, exploring the countryside? Or are you a homebody, who likes to rise at a leisurely pace, potter around the house or garden and rarely engage in regular or strenuous exercise? Obviously, these are extremes and there are plenty of people who will fall somewhere in between. But do think hard about how your dog will fit into your life and what you are prepared to endure for the sake of your dog. For a dog to be fulfilled, it does need walking every day, come rain or shine.

If you still have an active social life and are regularly out in the evening or at weekends and enjoy a long lie-in the morning after a night out, think about how your dog will fit into this lifestyle? Likewise, if you still work full-time or part-time, you are going to need to consider who is going to care for your dog whilst you are at work. This is particularly important in the first two years of your dog's life. Your puppy, in these early years, is going to need a lot of input from you. It simply isn't fair to expect a young puppy to endure long spells on its own. He needs company and stimulation throughout the day. You may feel that a daycare centre or a dog boarder is the answer. If you go down this route, do your homework; talk to owners that already use the facility and make sure that the place you choose is suitable for a young puppy.

Another thing to think about is fur, or what we often refer to as dog hair. Are you a very fastidious person who can't bear the sight of dog hair on your clothes? You might want to investigate how much different dog breeds shed. The dog hair that comes off a husky or a golden retriever is very different from the dog hair coming off a collie or a long coat chihuahua. I speak from experience! I have the latter two and my clothes are not perpetually covered in visible dog hair. Instead, my two shed their undercoats subtly. It gathers in wispy furballs underneath the furniture! The type of coat a breed has will also determine the amount of time it will have to spend at the groomers. Some breeds need regular clipping, whilst others need none at all. Similarly, some dog breeds need a lot of washing after a muddy walk, whilst with others the mud simply drops out if you let it dry. Whilst the smell of a fragrant dog shampoo may be a pleasure to our noses, your dog is less likely to enjoy the smell of perfume and may do his best to rid himself of the smell by rolling in something unpleasant such as fox poo! So, think about how much time and effort you are prepared to put into keeping your dog's coat clean and in good condition.

Finally, don't make your breed choice based on your previous experience with dogs or because other people are telling you their views on breed choices. This could potentially backfire further down the line. Just because you had border collies in the family growing up, doesn't mean that your current lifestyle and home situation is suited to having a border collie puppy now. Your parents likely did most of the training and care of that dog, remember. How much did you actually contribute back then? Similarly, you may hear about certain breeds making great family dogs from other people whose advice you ask. Just remember that ANY breed can develop behavioural problems and you might be surprised to hear that some of the most commonly chosen breeds can be the ones keeping the behaviourists in work! That is certainly the case with me when I look at the breeds I get called to help with the most. A puppy's genetic line, the conditions in which it has been bred and how it is raised once you bring it home can all play a part in determining the type of dog it turns out to be.

Yes, certain breeds will have breed traits that need to be taken into consideration - sight hounds are more likely to chase small, moving furry animals, border collies are more likely to try to herd everything in sight (including your children!) and spaniels and retrievers are more likely to bring you offerings of your underwear and shoes when you step in the door after work. This is because these breeds have been bred over generations for a specific purpose, whether retrieving game, herding sheep, or running alongside carriages (dalmatians!), to name but a few occupations dogs have been bred for. Our domestic pets are the descendants of these ancestors so, naturally, will be more inclined to show the behaviours they were originally bred for. Educate yourself thoroughly before you settle on a breed. Talk to your friends about their dogs, but make sure you push them on any negatives and don't just fall for the positive blurb. Talk to local trainers or behaviourists and question them about the breeds they are most commonly asked to help with. Ask them their views on which breeds have particular problems. You may be surprised by their answers!

Once you have decided that, yes, a dog WILL fit into your lifestyle and make the decision to purchase a particular breed of puppy (or indeed give a home to a crossbreed puppy), it is time to put some thought into which puppy to choose from the litter, should you be lucky enough to have a choice. Naturally, the first step is to find a reputable breeder who will allow you to meet the mother (and preferably the father, if it isn't a stud dog) before the litter is even born. Sometimes this isn't practical, if they live far away, but I would strongly recommend that you try to find someone within driving distance and do your research. Read reviews about the breeder first before you commit to going to view a litter. Ask the breeder if they mind you having a chat with other owners who have bought puppies from them in the past. A good breeder won't mind you doing this. Beware of any breeder who refuses to hook you up with an existing client for a chat or won't let you meet the mother dog.

Case Study 1: A Pack of Lies

I was asked by a friend who was considering buying a puppy to take a look at the one they had found advertised online. They were very excited about getting a new dog, as their former dog had passed away and they missed her hugely. They had waited an appropriate amount of time to get over their loss and were now on the lookout for a new dog. They were keen to buy local and noticed an advert for puppies not far from where they lived. The breeder sounded nice when they communicated by email, so they set up a meeting with them to view the puppy. In the meantime, they asked me to have a quick look at the advert and give them my opinion. I duly did this and asked them a few questions about what the breeder had told them. The first thing that struck alarm bells for me was the fact that the breeder said the puppies were not with their mum anymore. They said the puppies had been born in this country when the mum was visiting, but that she had now gone back to France. This sounded suspect, but my friend went ahead and booked an appointment to see the puppy. As soon as they were given an address, I checked this online. It turned out to be a rental property. Another red flag. In the meantime, another friend was doing a google search on the image of the puppy posted online. It turned out this was a library image that had been used to advertise different litters of puppies. By now we had three red flags, so my friend alerted the RSPCA of their suspicions that this address was being used as a front by a puppy farmer. They cancelled their appointment and didn't buy the puppy. Thankfully, they did, in the end, get a puppy from a reputable breeder.

When you do come to view a litter, there are a few things to keep in mind which will help you go home with the right puppy for you. You may already have an idea from seeing pictures as to which puppy you would like to buy. STOP RIGHT THERE! Do not choose a puppy based on looks or colour! The single most important thing you should be considering is the puppy's personality and energy levels. A simple way of thinking about this is to match YOUR general energy levels with that of the puppy - if you are quite a lively person who is always on the go, by all means, choose the lively puppy. But if you are a calm, sedate sort of person, DON'T choose the lively joker of the litter. You want to be choosing a puppy who has similar or LOWER energy to yourself to have the best chance of success. The ideal pup to choose is the one who is curious and friendly when you first arrive and then wanders off and does its own thing after saying hello. Avoid choosing a puppy who seems unduly nervous and shy of human interaction. You may feel sorry for him, but if you are a first-time dog owner, he isn't the one for you and may be better suited to someone with more experience, because a nervous disposition in a puppy can prove challenging further down the line. Similarly, avoid choosing the puppy who seems super excited and is charging about like a lunatic. Again, leave this one for the more experienced dog owners. Finally, watch the puppies closely as they play. If you spot one who looks like a bit of a bully, maybe being more dominant than the others, avoid this one too unless you already have experience dealing with dogs with a dominant nature. The breeder may try to push you towards certain puppies but trust your instincts and stay firm when making your choice. You will be living with this dog for the rest of its life, remember, so you want to set yourself up for success from the outset.

Case Study 2 – Choosing the Wrong Breed for You

Janet was an experienced dog owner who had owned many different breeds throughout her life, predominantly those on the larger side. She was close to retirement and had young grandchildren. Her previous elderly dog had passed away and she felt that the time had come to get a new companion. She had considered a rescue but felt buying a puppy would avoid the problem of dealing with any pre-existing behavioural issues. Her new puppy would be a blank canvas that she could raise as she saw fit. She was experienced, after all, so didn't foresee any issues. Being a fan of larger breeds, she chose to buy a labradoodle puppy, a mixed breed created from crossing a labrador with a standard poodle. She had read that these dogs were great family dogs, good with children, enjoyed plenty of exercise and were hypoallergenic to boot. Janet was a keen walker and an early riser and looked forward to having a dog that she could take on long walks every day, keeping her fit and youthful as her retirement years approached.

She went ahead and purchased a lovely male labradoodle puppy, whom she called Ernie. All went well in the beginning, but Ernie grew at an alarming rate and was soon a very big dog. He was also incredibly boisterous and demanding. Janet had dealt with large dogs before, but what she had forgotten to take into consideration was that she was no longer the young woman she used to be. She was also continuing to work, albeit from home, so there were periods of the day when she simply could not interact with the puppy and needed him to happily rest and be quiet. Ernie had a very different personality to her previous dogs. He was very bouncy, very demanding and very intelligent! When owners choose a poodle cross, they are usually thinking that the poodle element of the dog is all about being hypoallergenic. What they often forget to consider is the fact that poodles are also a very intelligent breed and can be quite highly strung. It hadn't occurred to Janet that the puppy she had purchased would need a lot of stimulation mentally, as well as physical exercise. Soon he was proving too much for Janet to handle, particularly when he hit puberty and his hormones began to rage. Janet found herself being knocked over, grabbed and humped by young Ernie. He also started to try to control her with his teeth, which was very alarming. She had simply taken on too much.

This was a classic case of choosing the wrong breed for her circumstances. In hindsight, Janet realised that she would have been better off choosing a dog bred for companionship, which would have still been perfectly capable of accompanying her on her daily walks but would also have been quite happy to snooze all day on the sofa next to her or lie in a dog bed whilst she worked at her desk. You may be wondering how this situation ended up? Janet realised that she was not able to provide for Ernie's needs and that he wasn't the right dog for her. It was a difficult decision, but Ernie was eventually rehomed with a more suitable owner and, after a break from dog ownership for a while, Janet eventually took on a much more suitable, older dog. He was still a large breed but much calmer and proved to be a perfect fit for her and her lifestyle. They quickly became soul mates and she now has a perfect companion for her retirement years.

Case Study 3 – Buying without Seeing

Another case study I am going to share with you is my own! Once upon a time I was just an ordinary dog owner, with a lovely male cocker spaniel who was friendly and well-behaved. We could have just stuck with the one dog, but I had always hankered after a particular colour of cocker spaniel, an orange roan (orange and white). Why orange and white, I can't tell you, other than that I found this colouring particularly appealing. The first cocker spaniel puppy was a blue roan because there simply weren't any litters available at the time with orange roan puppies. With a landmark birthday approaching, I decided this was the perfect opportunity to finally get my orange and white cocker. Reading this now, I can see how ridiculous this sounds. What was I thinking, choosing a puppy based on colour? To make matters worse, the only puppy of this colour available at the time was with a breeder some distance from where we lived, so we couldn't visit prior to buying the puppy. I did lots of background checks to ensure the breeder had a good reputation and we decided to go ahead with the purchase of an orange roan bitch. We'd already raised one well-behaved dog so thought we had it sussed. The new puppy would follow the lead of our existing dog, surely? We would do all the same training and everything would be great.

Oh, how wrong we were! Not viewing the puppy prior to picking her up meant that we didn't have the opportunity to watch how she behaved with her siblings. We had no clues as to what sort of personality she had. No clues as to whether she was confident or nervous, a natural leader or a natural follower. Basically, our lack of understanding about how important it was to view a puppy with its mum and siblings meant that we bought a dog without any inkling of the troubles we were going to encounter further down the line due the personality she was born with. She was a wonderful dog, of that there is no doubt, but boy did we struggle with her for a while, from puberty onwards. The approach we took to training that worked with our first puppy worked brilliantly at first, but it all went out the window when Molly's hormones kicked in at around 6 months old. She simply stopped listening and we found ourselves unable to influence her when her hunting instinct kicked in. We were clueless as to why this was happening and could have avoided a lot of these issues if we had chosen a different puppy from the litter. She was BORN to lead; she was very dominant and we were totally unequipped for dealing with a puppy with this nature. Luckily, as I have already mentioned, I eventually stumbled upon an approach to dog training that allowed me to tackle the issues that had developed during Molly's puberty. It took a little while, as I was learning myself, but eventually I got through to Molly that it was MY walk, not hers and that I expected her to be mentally connected to me throughout! This totally changed our lives, because we now had a dog who listened to us, but a dog who still hugely enjoyed life.

Pupology

Chapter Three – Preparing Your Home

The excitement that comes with the prospect of having a new puppy in your home can trigger a shopping frenzy! The puppy industry is massive and the array of items available to buy for a new puppy is, frankly, mind-boggling. But do you really need all this stuff? In short, no you don't, but it's a personal choice and if you really want to splash the cash and have all the latest gadgets and gizmos, by all means, knock yourself out! It's not for me to lecture you on what you should and shouldn't buy for your puppy, but let's go back to something I mentioned at the start…… Your puppy is first and foremost a DOG. Not a baby, not a princess, not a little human in a furry suit. Your puppy is an animal and has basic animal needs – food, warmth, and a safe, cosy space in which to curl up and rest. My advice would be to address these needs first before you start satisfying your HUMAN need to provide for your little one with lots of cute puppy stuff. Keeping it simple in the beginning will not only save your wallet but will also minimise the risk of your young puppy coming to harm. Once your puppy has settled into a regular routine, you can start thinking about adding to his personal belongings!

Think back to when you viewed your puppy with its litter. The breeder will likely have had the mother in a purpose-made, functional whelping enclosure which is easy to clean and safe for the puppies. You can rest assured this will not have been kitted out with expensive beds. It's more likely that it will have been furnished with a pile of old towels and blankets! The breeder may also have created a separate play area for the young pups with some suitable toys, where the puppies are put to exercise and explore, and for mealtimes once weaned. This play area may well have had puppy pads in it, to encourage the puppies to wee on these. It is highly likely that the puppies were confined to just one room in your breeders' house, with easy access to an outside area. Mimicking these environments will help your puppy settle in quickly to your home and keep him safe. With any luck your breeder will have started toilet training the pups, but if not, don't worry, this is very easy to do if you approach things right (see Chapter 6).

One of the biggest mistakes new puppy owners make is to give their new puppy free rein of their whole house. Your puppy will not have had this at the breeders - imagine having eight puppies charging around the home peeing and pooing everywhere! That simply will not have happened. It is much more likely they will have been confined to one room. So do yourself a favour and choose a suitable room to keep your puppy in initially, preferably one with easy access to some outside space (although this is not essential). Don't feel guilty about doing this, it is what your puppy has been used to after all! Keeping your puppy safe in the early weeks should be your number one priority, as like young children, puppies are inquisitive but inexperienced in life and can come to harm quickly in a domestic environment if not supervised properly.

The easiest way to keep your puppy safe, allow you to carry on everyday life with minimal disruption and get your puppy toilet-trained as quickly as possible, is to have a crate with a puppy pen securely attached to it. There are numerous pens available to buy - just make sure the one you choose is suitable for the size of your dog! No point in buying one with low sides, if your puppy is going to be able to jump over it within a week or two because it is a larger breed. Whilst some owners think of crates as being a "cage" for a dog, and therefore cruel, try to think of it from your puppy's point of view. Your puppy is used to snuggling into a big pile of its brothers and sisters to sleep at night. Up until now it has felt safe and secure in this nice cosy environment. An effective way of recreating that nice safe, cosy feeling is to create a "den" for your puppy. Think of the den your puppy would have been born into if it was in the wild. You can recreate this "den" by buying a crate with an accompanying purpose-made cover, or simply cover a crate with a large towel or blanket, tucked securely under the bottom to ensure the puppy can't grab a corner, pull it into the crate and chew it. Your puppy will initially be very small in relation to the crate, so this also allows you to provide a ready-made "ensuite" toileting area within the crate that is away from the puppy's bedding. This allows your puppy to toilet if he wakes up in the night, without causing him huge distress, as dogs hate to soil in their own beds. This also gives you the option to teach your pup to sleep alone all night from Day 1, without you having to get up in the middle of the night (more about that shortly when we think about your puppy's first night).

The crate also allows you to avoid separation anxiety further down the line. If you teach your puppy from Day 1 that the crate is his private space where he naps when tired or can rest without sleeping whilst you are busy doing other things, this helps hugely when it comes to leaving him. Getting him used to going into his crate to settle with the door closed whilst you move about the house is by far the quickest way to teach him to cope when you aren't there. One word of caution about the crate - do make sure you make it clear to your puppy from the outset that, whilst the crate is his den, you and any other humans or animals are allowed to touch it, put your hands in it and even get in it (if it is big enough!). What you absolutely do not want happening is for your puppy to become territorial about his crate or even his bed.

Attaching a puppy pen securely to your crate will give your puppy a secure area to be placed in during the day when you need to get on with other things. Puppies are by nature curious and will get into everything and anything given the chance. They explore the world using their mouths (dogs don't have hands, remember!), so it is hugely important to have a safe space to put them when you can't watch them like a hawk. The puppy pen will give you that safe space. The ideal place to have your pen and crate set up is the room that you intend the puppy to sleep in from Day 1. This may be your kitchen, a utility room or your living room. It really doesn't matter but, if you can, choose a room that has access to your outside space, for ease of toilet training. It's not essential, but it does make it a little easier to get outside quickly when your puppy starts circling for a poo! To recap, securely attach the puppy pen to your crate in such a way that the crate door opens into the secure pen. Make sure the pen isn't pushed up against a radiator. If you are getting your puppy in the summer, this won't matter, but in the winter you don't want your puppy getting too hot because his crate and pen are next to a radiator that is on full blast! Place a sturdy water bowl in the pen, along with a few indestructible puppy toys. You can put a smaller sturdy water bowl into his crate away from his bedding. Place a puppy pad in the pen, well away from the water bowl. You may find that your puppy is the type to chew puppy pads. If this is the case, dispense with them altogether!

Using the puppy pen and crate set-up allows you to keep the rest of your house the same during those first early weeks. If you don't provide this safe space for your puppy, you will need to spend some time ensuring that your home is free of hazards. Your home is filled with countless hazards for a young puppy, from electrical cables (that can cause electrocution) to your cat's food (which can cause an upset tummy). As you will see in further chapters, we will be teaching our puppy NOT to touch these items from the very beginning and we will be doing that each time we take our puppy out of it's pen to play, to the toilet and to explore each room of the house one at a time.

If you don't want to use a crate or a pen for your puppy, I would strongly recommend confining them to one room initially, the kitchen being the obvious choice (if it has access to the garden), or the utility room if you are lucky enough to have one. Don't forget these are recommendations to make the first few weeks of your puppy's life with you as easy as possible. Not everyone who gets a dog has access to a garden. If you don't have a garden, you will need to work out how best to manage the issue of toilet training for your particular circumstances, but all the rest of the above suggestions still apply.

If you DO have a garden, preparing it BEFORE your puppy arrives will save you a lot of headaches going forwards. Our gardens are full of all sorts of hazards for young puppies. Even the smallest patio may have items on it that could cause a puppy harm should he swallow them – from small stones to slug pellets in your flowerpots. By far the simplest way to keep your new arrival safe from garden hazards is to have ANOTHER enclosure outside in which you will teach your puppy to wee and poo. This may be another puppy pen, or you could simply use some chicken wire, or anything else you have handy, to create some impenetrable boundaries (just make sure they are sturdy and safe as you don't want them falling onto your puppy and squishing him). Having an area cordoned off that you can keep free of ALL hazards and interesting things will speed up the toilet training process hugely. It is a little unfair to expect a young pup to ignore interesting things like leaves, snails, and stones when you take him outside to wee. He will naturally be drawn to explore and the thought of weeing will be far from his mind! Making an enclosure which is SUPER BORING will make it easier for you to encourage him to go to the toilet (more of that later!). Having this space right by your back door is the best plan, so you can open the door and let your puppy straight into it. However, if it isn't possible to do this, the next best thing is an enclosure near the back door that you can either carry your puppy to when he is tiny or take him to on lead when he is bigger. If you live in a flat, you can create a toileting area using artificial grass (glued or nailed onto a piece of board). I have seen this done successfully several times!

If you don't want to create a dedicated enclosure for your new puppy, you MUST ensure that as many hazards as possible are removed from your garden or temporarily blocked from access. If you don't do this, you will need to keep your puppy on a lead whenever you take him outside to go to the toilet until he has learnt not to touch things in your garden. As he grows, you can train him not to go in your flowerbeds or pick up objects off the ground (using a technique I will explain later on), but this will take time and effort and you want to keep him safe from Day 1.

There are some things that you won't be able to remove, for example, a pond. It is also impractical to remove all the poisonous plants from a garden and really, there is no need but, again, this is entirely your choice. A few canes and some chicken wire are enough to keep a young puppy away from these hazards if you don't want to use a pen/home-made enclosure. As the puppy grows and learns, you can simply remove the barriers and teach him not to go in the pond or in your precious flowerbeds. After all, you are going to have to teach him to ignore hazardous objects when out on a walk, so what better place to start than in your own garden. If your garden is totally laid to lawn, you have nothing to worry about, but do check the lawn over before you let him loose for anything he could pick up in his mouth and swallow. Keeping the grass short in the summer will help you spot hazards. Likewise, check your fencing for any foxholes or broken panels that he could squeeze through. Safety is your responsibility. Get everything sorted BEFORE he arrives (and periodically re-check), and you will have no need to worry!

Your house/flat is ready, your garden is ready, and you are now counting down the days until you collect your new puppy. There are several other things worth considering before you bring your puppy home. The whereabouts of a veterinary surgery is one thing to think about. If you have friends with dogs, ask them for recommendations or do some research online. If your chosen vet will let you register your puppy in advance of pick up, great. But if not, at least have their number stored in your phone or handy at home. Some puppies do find the car journey from the breeders a bit stressful, so it's always best to have that number to hand BEFORE bringing your puppy home, just in case he is poorly on his first night with you! Another thing to consider is insurance. Not insuring your puppy from the outset could leave a big hole in your bank balance, particularly if you are unlucky enough to have a puppy who becomes ill in the first few weeks, or God forbid, has an accident of some sort, such as a fracture. Vet bills can quickly mount up, so do bear this in mind and make sure that if you do get pet insurance, you get adequate cover with an affordable excess from the outset. Public liability insurance is also something to consider – whilst it won't occur to you when your puppy is tiny, as he grows there is always the possibility that he might knock someone over, or trip someone up and hurt them.

Another handy thing to do is make a list of house rules that will apply to your puppy, particularly if there are multiple occupants. You may think there is no need at this point, but I believe that having a set of house rules BEFORE your puppy arrives makes life a lot easier for all family members and will be a massive aid in raising a well-behaved dog. Time and time again, the feedback I get from clients about their puppy's early days is that they started off with good intentions with their puppy but quickly let the rules slip, or only some family members stuck to them. How on earth can you expect your puppy to know what you do and don't want him to do in the house if you don't stick to a clear set of rules from the start? Here are the rules I have for my dogs in my house. My two current dogs (a long coat chihuahua and a border collie) are both rescues and I have had neither from a very young age, so they had to learn these rules after they came to me. These rules don't just apply to our house, they apply to any house we visit with our dogs, which allows us to take them anywhere with us:

Only allowed on furniture when invited (that includes beds, chairs, sofas, and garden furniture).
No touching things on the floor, except your own toys unless you are given permission.
No touching ANY food, no matter where it is, without permission.
If you pick something up and I don't want you to have it, you let me take it off you without fuss.
Come in from the garden as soon as I tell you to.
No coming in from the garden without getting your paws wiped first if they are likely to be dirty.
No going through the open front door without permission.
No jumping up at visitors. Greet them with all four paws on the ground!
Please alert me when the doorbell rings but stop barking when I ask you to and return to a calm state.
Don't chase the cats. They are part of our family and not prey!
A sleeping human must be left in peace! No scratching at the bed to try to wake me up or thrusting a wet nose in my face! When I sleep, you sleep, no matter what time of the day or night it is.
When I go out, settle quietly where I leave you and sleep until I return.

You may have a different set of rules. The rules and boundaries you set for your puppy are entirely up to you, but before you set them think about the things that annoy you about other people's dogs. That will help you decide what matters to you and what isn't welcome behaviour! Make a list and stick it on your fridge!

On a final note, we haven't mentioned the presence of existing pets in your household. You may already have a dog but are thinking of adding a puppy to the mix. Or you may have other non-canine pets in the house, whether it be cats, birds, rabbits, Guinea pigs, hamsters or even reptiles. Other pets are going to fascinate your puppy, so it is best to be aware of how you should deal with these interactions so that ALL your pets can live in harmony together. As a behaviourist, I have been to many homes with stair gates all over the place, put there to keep the resident cat safe. I have, in some cases, come across resident cats that have been forced to live upstairs (often with a litter tray) because of the appearance of a puppy. Trust me, if you get it right from the outset, your new puppy can live quite happily alongside a resident cat! There is no need for loads of barriers and changes to your household set up, provided you introduce them in a controlled manner from the outset and teach the puppy some clear rules about interacting with the other pets. As an owner of two cats and two dogs who live happily together, I can assure you that it is possible. If you do have a cat or other pets, please refer to the dedicated chapter on integrating your puppy with existing family pets (Chapter 19). If you have opted for the puppy pen/crate set-up, you have no need to worry about your puppy meeting the cat for the first time, as your puppy will be in the pen from the outset and will be unable to chase your cat.

Case Study 1: Keep Things Simple for Success

Alan thought he had considered everything necessary before bringing his new puppy home. He called me in to help with some house-training issues, as his puppy, Foxy, even at 6 months old, was still toileting inside the house, despite his best efforts. What quickly became apparent was that, although Alan had set up a crate for Foxy to sleep in, he had allowed the puppy to have free range of his kitchen from Day 1 and hadn't set up his garden to maximise the chances of his puppy toileting outside. He had put a puppy pad down in his kitchen, but it was a long way from his back door. What Foxy had learnt to do was toilet on this pad, but whenever Alan took the puppy outside, he simply wouldn't go. The garden was far too interesting, and Foxy was distracted by all the smells and interesting objects as soon as he went outside. To get around this problem, Alan put the puppy on the lead whenever he took him out, but still Foxy wouldn't perform, instead choosing to continue to investigate things, albeit closer to the house!

Why wouldn't the puppy toilet outside? Well, firstly, Alan had taught Foxy that he could toilet in one particular corner of the kitchen. The door to the garden was some distance from this and there was no way that Alan would be able to get the puppy outside quick enough to result in an outside wee. Furthermore, the outside space was simply TOO interesting for Foxy. His brain had learnt that the inside kitchen corner was for toileting and that the garden was for exploring. To sort this problem, I advised Alan to create a dedicated fenced off toileting area right outside the back door and to rub some wee from Foxy's next accident in this space, to ensure the scent of the wee was present next time he took the puppy to this area. Next, I suggested that over a period of a few days, he gradually move the puppy pad away from the "toilet" corner and closer to the back door. He should also clean this corner thoroughly using a diluted solution of biological clothes washing liquid (which apparently breaks down the enzymes in dog pee!), and once dry, place a large piece of furniture or a sturdy cardboard box over this area to prevent Foxy returning to it for toileting. He should encourage the use of the puppy pad as he gradually moved it towards the back door, but simultaneously be taking Foxy out to the new BORING toilet area and give him a chance to wee or poo. If he persisted in doing this over a week, with the puppy pad ultimately being right next to the back door, Foxy would quickly learn that he should head for the back door when he felt the urge to toilet. Once the puppy had successfully performed in the outside toilet area a few times, Alan would be able to remove the indoor puppy pad and dispose of puppy pads entirely. Foxy soon got the hang of the new regime and toileting outside became a quick and functional visit, with other times in the garden being the time for fun.

Pupology

Chapter Four – The Big Day

The big day has arrived, the day you will collect your new puppy from the breeder. No matter how long or short that journey is going to be, make sure you run through your checklist before you set off. Decide on a number of key things to avoid arguments when you get there. Imagine being a young pup, being removed from your mum and siblings and finding yourself in a car full of arguing humans! Ok, it's not the end of the world and won't damage the puppy for life, but do try to agree that from now on, you are all going to be nice and calm around the puppy, to help it settle in as quickly as possible. I know this goes against your human nature because you, and your kids if you have them, are going to be super excited about this whole business, but as you will find out later on, excitement is your enemy when it comes to raising a well-balanced, confident dog!

Back to that checklist. In terms of items to take with you, I would suggest the following:

A soft washable blanket/towel to carry the puppy to the car and hold him in during your journey or a small cardboard box in which to have him on your lap
A couple of puppy pads (if your breeder has already started this process, or you intend to use them)
A small bowl and a bottle of cold water (if the journey is long)
Poo bags!
A spray disinfectant and some kitchen roll in case your puppy is sick or has an accident en-route
A tiny collar and puppy lead (if your breeder hasn't already put a collar on your pup)

With regards to the puppy lead and collar, your puppy will likely be too small for a harness at the moment, although that depends on the breed. Having a puppy collar and lead on him will give you extra peace of mind from a safety point of view. He won't be going down on the ground as he hasn't been inoculated, but if you need to stop at a service station on the journey to let him wee (more of that in a moment), having him on the lead gives you extra security - a wriggling puppy can be hard to hold onto, so do make sure an adult is holding the puppy when you are outside the car. The cardboard box is to use if you don't want to hold the puppy on your lap, or one of your children wants to hold him on the journey. Popping a blanket in a small cardboard box that you/your kids can hold on their knee is a nice safe way for the puppy to travel and is particularly handy should the puppy be sick!

The above should see you through the car journey. Oh, and don't wear your best clothes - it won't be the puppy's fault if he ruins your favourite jumper by being sick on it. If the journey is a long one, plan a break at a service station. If the puppy isn't stressed by the travel, he may need a wee or a poo. The simplest way to let him do this is to open your boot and pop a puppy pad down in it. Be very careful that the puppy can't jump out (particularly if he is a larger breed!). Having him on a collar and lead will ensure he can't do this. Give him the opportunity to empty his bladder or poo if he wants to. Chances are, he won't, but it is good to give him the option, rather than him weeing on you in the car! He will most likely sleep for most of the journey anyway, so the above is just for those longer journeys from breeder to home.

When you get home, carry him into the house straight to the room where he will be starting off life in your family. If he has a pen and a crate set up, pop him in there, ALL step back and let him have a good sniff around. Put the blanket you used in the car into his crate (provided he hasn't soiled it!). And pop into the crate any blanket or toys that the breeder has given you, as these will smell of his Mum and litter mates. ONLY PUT SAFE TOYS IN HIS CRATE/PEN. Do not put anything in there that he could potentially bite chunks off and swallow! Rope toys are particularly hazardous, so keep them out of his pen/crate.

Leaving his Mum and siblings is a really big deal for your new puppy, and he will likely be very tired after the car journey and possibly feeling a bit sick! Let him have a little explore of his area on his own and then make yourself a cup of tea and quietly sit down somewhere nearby, leaving him be. Try really hard not to overwhelm him with excited play if he appears a bit sleepy. And don't feel like you need to feed him either. Just think of how you feel after a long journey when you arrive home. Would you want someone throwing you a full-scale party? Perhaps you would! But rest assured, the best way to get your new puppy to settle into your family home and get through his first night successfully is to keep everything calm and low key. Let him explore, let him nap, let him have some quiet time and then when he wakes up, that is the time to offer him some food and start your journey of bonding properly with him.

Don't be alarmed if he is a little sick or has an upset tummy when you get him home Many puppies feel a little under the weather after a car journey and the stress of leaving their Mum. So long as he is drinking and seems happy otherwise, this is not something to worry about too much. If he is repeatedly sick and has bad diarrhoea, you do need to keep an eye on him, as puppies can dehydrate very quickly (hence me saying have a vet's number to hand). If in doubt, phone the vet for some advice!

Let's fast forward to the end of your puppy's first day with you. First-time puppy owners are often quite nervous about their puppy's first night, having no doubt read or heard lots of horror stories about crying/barking puppies and bleary-eyed owners who have gotten little sleep or slept on the floor for weeks beside their puppy. The first night with your new puppy can go several ways and you can take several approaches. There are no guarantees with any of these approaches that you will have a good first night, but like everything else, you want to give yourself the best chance of success, so think long and hard as to which approach you intend to take and stick to it for at least a couple of nights if you can. If after a couple of nights your puppy is still very distressed at night and keeping the whole family awake, regroup and consider another approach.

My personal favoured approach that I adopted with both of my new puppies successfully was to have them downstairs on their first night in their covered crate with the crate door locked shut. Crates come with a plastic removable tray that is easy to keep clean. I put a pile of soft towels, along with the blanket the breeder had given me, at the far end of the crate away from the door and left the remainder of the plastic tray at the other end of the crate uncovered, with a very small bowl of water tucked in the corner by the door. This allowed the puppy to snuggle down at one end, but also gave him a place away from his bed to toilet if he woke in the night. I would strongly recommend that you try this. It's not an approach that everyone is happy with, but I felt that it would be the quickest way to get the puppy to sleep alone at night and allow us to have a decent sleep too. Some people like to invest in a heartbeat toy, which aims to mimic the sound/feeling of the mother's heartbeat to provide comfort. Obviously, it won't EXACTLY mimic her heartbeat, but anecdotal reports from some clients suggest that this device has helped soothe some puppies on their first nights away from their mum. Other people have reported success leaving a radio/YouTube/Spotify playing soothing music at a low volume.

If you choose to have your puppy downstairs in a crate on this first night, alert your neighbours that you have a new puppy and that there might be a night or two of noise disruption whilst the puppy adjusts to being alone without its siblings. If you are a light sleeper, earplugs are a must. Spend time with the puppy in the late evening, playing for a while to drain his excess energy then, as late as possible (and hopefully straight after he has had a wee), pop him in his crate without fuss, shut the door, switch off the light and leave him. He will likely whine/bark for a little while initially. This is hard for some people to bear, but if you can, try REALLY hard not to respond to this or you will teach him that if he whines/barks you will reappear. Hopefully, he will settle down after a little while and go to sleep. He may wake in the night needing a wee, and once awake may whine and bark again. Again, try REALLY HARD not to go down to him. He has an area to toilet in and access to water, so he will come to no harm. It may be that he whines and barks all night – this does sometimes happen, but again, try very hard to resist the urge to go down to him. You need to try at least one more night, in my opinion, to see if he copes a little better on the second night. If he is a little better on this second night, carry on with this method. If he still whines and barks all night on the second night, it is time for a rethink.

Whatever happens, when the morning arrives, I would encourage you to get up nice and early, go down to the room he is in and enter it WITH MINIMUM FUSS AND EXCITEMENT. If he is in the kitchen, walk in, ignore him and head straight for the kettle. Pop the kettle on and then, and only then, go over and open his crate door and QUIETLY interact with him. Don't be tempted to go in making a huge fuss and open the door when he is whining/barking or clawing at the door of the crate. If you do this, you are teaching him that this is what he should do whenever you appear whilst he is shut in the crate. WE ABSOLUTELY DO NOT WANT THIS!!! Why? Because it can lead to issues further down the line. The crate needs to be a place of calmness and relaxation. Maximise your chances of your puppy understanding this, by getting into the habit of initially ignoring him when you first come into the room when he is in his crate.

It normally takes around 2 nights of doing the above for the puppy to realise that he is expected to sleep alone at night. Switching off the lights in the room is his cue to settle down and go to sleep. As he gets older, he will be woken less and less by his bladder, until eventually he is sleeping through the whole night without needing to toilet. However, do remember that this will take time and if you put him to bed at 9 pm, you really can't expect him to hold his bladder until 7 am the next morning. You should be aiming to put him to bed at 11/11.30 pm with this method and be getting up at around 6/6.30 am to take him out to the garden/patio. As he grows and starts to be able to hold his bladder for longer, you can push your wake-up time in the morning forward by about 10 mins every day. If he whines during these 10 minutes, ignore him and only go down when he has taken a break from whining. Or you can put him to bed a bit earlier if that is your preference.

I must stress that this approach doesn't work for every puppy. There are some puppies that really struggle with being on their own on that first night. You will hear stories of puppies barking and whining all night. Some owners will tell you how they slept on the sofa for weeks next to their puppy and got up several times in the night to take them out for a wee. It really is a case of trial and error, and luck. Similarly, there are owners who simply can't bear the thought of leaving the puppy on its own to cry for a bit. Nothing wrong with that, you are human after all. If you DO decide to have the puppy in your bedroom, or sleep downstairs with the puppy and let him out to go to the toilet whenever he wakes up in the night (whether on a puppy pad or outside in your garden), I would still advise you to crate him, rather than let him sleep with you. And, more importantly, I would strongly advise you to do the following if he wakes up in the night - KEEP YOUR ENERGY LOW AND YOUR TALK TO AN ABSOLUTE MINIMUM. Also keep the light off. Use your phone torch if you can't see what you are doing! Your puppy needs to learn that the middle of the night is NOT playtime! Just because he has woken up, doesn't mean that you want to be awake too. Make it very clear by being very quiet, calm, and relaxed, showing him that when it is dark it is REST time. Open his crate, pick him up (you will only be doing this when he is tiny) and take him outside to the toileting area. Let him toilet. Allow him around 5 minutes to sniff around. If he starts to play with anything (and remember, there should be NOTHING interesting in this area), take him straight back inside without talking and calmly pop him back in his crate and shut the door. Go back to bed. If he successfully toilets when you take him outside, don't give him a treat or lots of excited praise. Just pop him back in the crate as above. Remember, we want to keep him calm, as we want him to go straight back to sleep. A calm, soft "good boy" is praise enough for doing a wee or a poo.

Dogs are very clever at picking up verbal queues if you repeat them enough, so get into the habit when it is bedtime of saying "Bedtime" or a similar phrase to your puppy when you are asking him to settle down for the night. Later, I will be mentioning the "Settle" command, which is another thing your dog should learn to do, as there will be times when you want him to sleep during the day, or simply chill out, and it is perfectly possible to ask him to do this when you tell him.

Chapter Five – A Typical Day in the Early Weeks

You made it through the night (just about!), and it is now your puppy's first full day in your home. It is entirely up to you how you structure your day with your puppy. No two people's daily routines are the same, after all. Just try to make sure you follow a consistent timetable in the early weeks, with your main goal being to get him toilet-trained as quickly as possible. Your second goal is to teach him from the outset to rest on his own without you there. This is something that a lot of owners forget to do at the beginning. It is very easy to get caught up in the sheer delight of having a new cute puppy in your life and spend virtually all your time with him initially and forget to teach him that it is absolutely fine for you NOT to be there with him! Being alone is one of the hardest things for a puppy to learn as it simply isn't natural to him. In the wild, he would always be in the company of other dogs at this young age.

There are certain routines that you should stick to that make things as simple as possible for yourself, and give your puppy the best possible chance of settling into a manageable routine within your household. In the early weeks, before he is fully vaccinated and allowed outside on the ground, there are four main things you should be thinking about in the house: toilet training, feeding time, playtime, and rest time. But before we look at each of these in more detail, let's look at what your typical day is going to look like over the next few months until your puppy reaches around 5 or 6 months old when puberty sets in.

At this point, I would like to put into your mind a mantra that I think will help you enormously on your journey with your puppy. That mantra is "It's all about the 'C's!". I will be referring back to these repeatedly throughout this book. The 'C's that you should keep in mind are calm, confident, consistent, commanding, and the final one, take

CHARGE. These are all things that you should be doing when interacting with your puppy.

Let's get back to a typical day with your puppy. You have woken up and your day will start with you entering the room he has been sleeping in (assuming he hasn't been sleeping in your room!). You will be tempted to rush straight up to him, cooing your head off and give him a nice big cuddle. Harsh as this may seem, I would strongly encourage you NOT to do this, but instead to walk straight past his crate (or pen if he isn't crated) and pop the kettle on, like I mentioned before. If you have decided not to use a pen or a crate, simply walk past him as you enter the room and head for the kettle - he will just trot along behind you. If he is in a crate or pen, he may whine a little as you walk past, but stay firm and ignore him until you have popped the kettle on and then, and only then, quietly, and calmly go up to him to say "Hello" and let him out of his crate. DO NOT OPEN THE CRATE DOOR UNTIL HE IS CALM AND HAS BACKED AWAY FROM IT. If he is clawing at the door and you open it, you will simply teach him that this behaviour results in you opening the door, and we don't want that! If he is just in a pen, wait for him to be calm then lift him out and take him straight to the back door to his outside toileting area. Pop him down, stand back and let him do his first wee of the day. He is far more likely to do this if you haven't already whipped him into a frenzy of excitement. Go down to him all noisy and excited, talking to him as soon as you go in the room, and I can pretty much guarantee that it will take you longer to get him to do that first wee! If you follow the advice above, your puppy will quickly learn to wait patiently until you turn towards him and let him out and will also quickly learn that the first thing you expect him to do in the morning is wee outside. If you have set everything up as I have advised, this should be a simple process. There is no need to put a lead on him if you have a secure outside area ready for him. Just lift him up and take him to the back door. Once he has got the hang of weeing outside first thing, you can start letting him walk to the back door, but initially, carrying him is the quickest way to get him out there without an accident.

Once he has done his wee, he can have his breakfast, either in his pen, or at a chosen spot in the room he is primarily living in. Some puppies are big eaters, others aren't. If he isn't hungry first thing, don't force him to eat, just wait until he shows signs of being interested in food. Follow the feeding guidelines in Chapter 7 on how to give him his meals. Whilst he has his breakfast, potter around the room, but occasionally pop back and pop your hand in his bowl, maybe adding a bit more kibble or picking it up temporarily and then putting it down again. This is to ensure from the start that he doesn't become territorial around his bowl.

When he has finished eating, lift his bowl and put it out of reach. This is a good time to give it a wash, ready for his next meal. It's then time for a quick play, and then back outside again to do his first poo of the day (this often comes around half an hour after eating, but every puppy is different). You can then play with him again for a little bit. Finish this play, pop him outside again to see if he will wee again, and then it's back in the pen with the crate door open. Now is the perfect time to teach him it is YOUR turn to eat. Make your breakfast and sit down and eat it somewhere in the room, but not right next to him. Ignore him whilst you are doing this. He should be ready for a little rest by now, and what you want him to learn is that when you pop him back in his pen you expect him to relax and let you get on with whatever you are doing. If he is still full of beans at this point, pop a couple of toys in his pen so that he can play by himself. If he conks out again, great.

Your day has now started in earnest, so you need to think about how you are going to fit in all the things you need to do, whilst at the same time taking care of the needs of your puppy. When he is very young he is going to sleep a lot. In-between those sleeps he is going to want to play, so think about arranging your schedule of human jobs around his nap times. Don't feel you need to be quiet whilst he is napping; it is better for him to learn to sleep through any noise, so do your hoovering, pop your tumble dryer on, get those dishes done. All these noises should be ignored by your puppy. You will need to factor in play time with him (see Chapter 8), and then will take the opportunity when it is time for him to rest to get on with your human jobs. This is how he will learn to rest on his own whilst you are still in the house. What you shouldn't be doing is letting him fall asleep on you all the time and having him rest on you. He must learn to rest on his own, otherwise you are going to find it hard to leave him when you need to go out of the house without him.

Can you see the pattern emerging? Playtime, followed by outside for a wee, followed by rest time in his pen/crate, followed by a wee when he wakes up, followed by playtime, followed by a wee, followed by rest time in his pen/crate. You get the picture! We want him to choose to fall asleep in his crate, rather than force him to do this. If you have followed my advice and had him in there from the first night, he should automatically choose to nap in his crate, but some puppies do prefer to simply stretch out on the floor of their pen. This isn't a problem as such, but if he doesn't choose the crate and chooses the pen floor to fall asleep on, do then move him into the crate and shut the door. He will be sleepy, and you want him to get used to you placing him in his crate for a nap, as well as letting him choose to go in there independently. Having the door latched is another thing we want him to accept, so get into this habit from the very start. He is most likely to accept this when he is sleepy, so don't try to do this when is still in an excitable state. The sound of the crate being latched should mean NOTHING to him. This is very important. We absolutely don't want the sound of the latch to equal stress!

Your day will progress as I have mentioned above. Factor in his lunchtime feed, and then his dinner time, and by now it will be early evening. This is when he is likely to go a little crazy! It is normal for puppies to have the zoomies after their evening meal. It is hilarious to watch and there is no need to stop him doing this. What I would say is that don't make yourself part of this ritual. You aren't a toy, remember, and if you let him grab you or chase you when he is having the zoomies, it may be funny when he is tiny, but it will very quickly stop being funny as he grows and gets his adult teeth. He will be perfectly happy having the zoomies on his own with you watching. If you let him do this uninterrupted, he will eventually grow out of it. This is one of the few behaviours dogs do seem to grow out of! Making it a game involving you, could result in it becoming a problem behaviour that he doesn't grow out of.

After the zoomies, he must go out for another wee and, indeed, is likely to need a poo too as he will have recently had his dinner. He may well nap again in the evening. This is the perfect time to let him have a cuddle on your lap/nap on you. You can carry him into the living room with you to have a cuddle on your lap on the sofa, but do remember that he is very little, so don't put him down on the floor to wander around or he may wee/poo on your carpet/floor! Having a cuddle on your lap is fine when he is tiny, but going forwards, he needs to learn some manners around the sofa and chairs, so I will be suggesting that as he gets older you teach him to only go on furniture when invited. After he wakes up from this nap, I suggest you have another play with him in the kitchen, or wherever is appropriate, then put him out for his last wee before bedtime. Make it clear to him that it is bedtime, by saying "Bedtime" when you pop him into his crate for the night, shut the crate door and switch off the light. Giving him a verbal cue that the day is over and everyone is going to bed to sleep will help him settle quickly every night going forwards. It will also mean that when he is older, he will be able to sleep anywhere, whether at a dog minder, in a kennels, on holiday or even in a tent as he knows exactly what "bedtime" means.

The above routine gives you an example of a typical day in the life of a very young puppy. It won't necessarily pan out this way, as every puppy is different, so you may find that your puppy doesn't sleep as much as I have suggested and seems to need more playtime. Even if he is like this, do make sure you set aside periods during the day when you expect him to be in his pen on his own amusing himself whilst you get on with other things. Once you have passed the final vaccination point, your day will also involve several walks with your puppy, both on the pavement and in the park. Again, decide what times are most suitable for you to do this and try to stick to them in the early months whilst you are mastering toilet training. It really doesn't matter when your dog is fully grown what time you walk it (although a morning walk is a must after your dog has been asleep all night!), but it is much easier for you and your puppy to master all aspects of dog ownership if you have a regular schedule in that first year. Taking your puppy out for a short walk in the morning and again in the afternoon is a good idea. Some owners like to do an additional evening stroll or even a pre-bedtime stroll, to allow their puppy to do its final toileting, but that is entirely up to you. We will be talking in more depth about pavement walks in Chapter 13.

A good habit to get into after each walk, which will also avoid separation anxiety, is to pop your puppy back in his pen or chosen room after the walk for a rest. It may be summer when you get your puppy so you won't initially be dealing with a wet, soggy dog, but I can guarantee there will be days when you come back from you walk with a muddy pup. Having him learn that after a walk comes a rest on his own makes things a lot easier further down the line when you want to keep him out of the rest of the house when he is damp. If you don't do this from the start and just let your puppy straight off lead when you get back into the house to do as he pleases, don't be surprised if things go a little pear-shaped later on. Imagine getting back from a muddy walk, washing him off and then having a wet puppy loose in the house? Imagine the same situation with you trying to shut him in a separate room until he is dry, but him not wanting to be alone? He may cry, bark or scratch at the door. Is this his fault? No, absolutely not. You haven't taught him from an early age that you expect him to rest on his own wherever you put him after a walk.

You should factor in some grooming time into each day, if you have time, or every couple of days. Grooming and checking him over for any injuries should be a regular habit. It gets him used to being touched all over and having all parts of his body inspected. I have come across many owners who have found it impossible to pull thorns out of their dog's paw or remove a tick effectively because their dog simply won't tolerate having anything done to it that might result in pain. It you teach your puppy from the outset to trust you, no matter what you are doing to him, he will let you help him when the need arises. Having you gently feel between his toes, look in his ears, wipe his eyes, part his fur in all sorts of places and lift and move his limbs around from when he is tiny is the way to build this trust. Once you have checked him over to make sure that everything is fine, you can give him a brush or a comb all over. Familiarise yourself with the kind of things that will attach to his fur when out walking and check him over for them when you are at home. Some things, like sticky buds, are easy to remove from a coat, but burrs can be a little bit tricker, so you may need to resort to the scissors with these (use safe dog grooming scissors!). A tick stick is the best way to remove a tick from your puppy. Familiarise yourself with what a tick looks like at different stages of its lifecycle (from a tiny spider-like dot to a big grey lump of sweetcorn!). Grooming should be an activity he looks forward to, not something he fears. Being calm, patient and pausing for a second or two if he seems to be getting stressed, will show him that you can be trusted when handling him. Don't rush things, take it at his pace.

Once he has settled into the room he is predominantly living in, you can start introducing him to other rooms in the house one by one. Don't forget that he is in the early stages of toilet training, so only take him into another room to explore right after he has done a wee or a poo, to avoid accidents in this new room. Also watch him like a hawk when you pop him on the floor to explore, making sure that you don't allow him to touch anything that is dangerous, like cables and wires. If he does try to sniff something like this, say a quick "Ah, Ah" or "Leave" in a firm voice to show him this object is not for touching. Only stay in the new room for a short time, before returning to his usual area. If you intend never to let him go up the stairs, make sure when you are letting him explore the hallway that you don't allow him to climb on that first step of the staircase. In later chapters I will be explaining how to create invisible exclusions zones around areas that you don't want him to go, but initially when he is tiny, just remove him from the first step and encourage him to go in another direction. If you are going to allow him upstairs, you will need to watch him closely as he attempts to go up and down. Puppies are pretty clumsy when they are little, so teach him to go up slowly and carefully. As he grows you will be teaching him to follow you calmly up and downstairs and not barge past you in an excited way. You can use the "blocking & claiming" technique described in Chapter 7 to teach him manners on the stairs. He needs to learn to walk a few steps behind you in a calm manner when going up or down.

Case Study 1: Unable to Cope Alone

Cairo was a lively cocker spaniel puppy. He was a lovely boy, very friendly and affectionate, but his owner was struggling to get on with her day as he was glued to her side all the time. It hadn't mattered too much in the beginning, as she just took the puppy everywhere with her in the house, even the bathroom, but now that he was older and being walked outside, she needed to leave him in the kitchen to dry off after a walk and get on with her housework. She had tried shutting the door and leaving him, but he would bark and whine. She then tried a stairgate across the kitchen door so that he could see her as she moved about downstairs, but again that didn't work and he would be very distressed at not being able to be by her side. She had just assumed that as he got a bit bigger, he would go to sleep after a walk as he would be tired. But he was unable to go to sleep as he was so anxious every time she left him in the room on his own.

The first job was to get him to stay in one spot and relax whilst his owner moved around the kitchen. I showed his owner how to invite him to lie in his bed then share a relaxed state of mind with him until he too became very relaxed. Once he was totally chilled, she could then take a step away from him, intervening verbally if his brain activity increased (a sign he was getting anxious). What she was doing was telling him that she didn't want him coming out of a relaxed state when she moved. She was asking him to exhibit self-control and resist his instincts. Working at his pace, she was gradually able to step further and further away from him without him sitting up in the bed. I taught her how to spot when his brain was elevating and to step in at that precise moment with a gentle verbal intervention and then IMMEDIATELY relax again herself. Working at his pace was absolutely essential, as he started to trust that nothing bad was going to happen when she moved away from him. He was learning to maintain his calm state of mind, DESPITE her moving.

At this point we added in a "Settle" command. We needed Cairo to associate the word "Settle" with lying in his bed and relaxing. He didn't need to be asleep, he just needed to be relaxed and not moving. If he did move out of his bed, he was calmly led back to it (note, NOT dragged back to it!) and the exercise was repeated.

A Typical Day in the Early Weeks

His owner put in a lot of work getting him to settle whilst she was in the kitchen and she was soon pottering around doing jobs without him batting an eyelid. Next up came actually leaving the room. Because Cairo had learnt what was wanted of him when asked to "Settle" and was entering into the right frame of mind (calm & relaxed) and maintaining it, he didn't stress when she left the room momentarily. She only left for a second and then returned calmly and walked back into the kitchen without making a fuss. It was important for Cairo to learn that she will always return if she goes out of sight. She then built up the time she was out of sight, and I am happy to report that Cairo's issue with being asked to stay in the kitchen after a walk disappeared.

Pupology

Toilet Training

Chapter Six – Toilet Training

One thing we all want to get sorted quickly as new puppy owners is getting our dogs clean in our house. Anyone who has stepped on a soft poo in bare feet at 3 am knows how totally disgusting this is and will want to avoid this happening at all costs! By the time your dog is 6 months old, the only accidents he should be having indoors are ones caused by a dodgy tummy. He should have bladder and bowel control by this age and it is actually very common for puppies to master this within the first 3 months of their lives, if their humans know how to set them up for success. We have touched a little on toilet training already, but in this chapter, we will look at things in more detail.

Back in the olden days (I'll let you decide when this might have been!), people trained puppies to toilet on old newspapers. Nowadays, actual newspapers are a less common item in the home, with the dog industry promoting the use of puppy pads to toilet train puppies. This got me thinking. Could it possibly be that these quite pricey items might slow down the toilet training process if left lying around too long? With newspaper, once the puppy toileted, the soiled bit was lifted and thrown out, so there was no wee or poo left lying around. With puppy pads, owners often want to get their money's worth, so leave the pad down until it has been used several times, so the puppy gets used to the smell lingering in a particular place. This is just speculation on my part, but if you ARE having issues getting your pup to wee outside, maybe think about how often you replace that pad or whether to use them at all.

The key things to remember when toilet training is that puppies are most likely to wee right after waking up from a nap, after play and after eating a meal. Pooing generally comes within an hour of eating, although obviously there is no hard and fast rule - some pups poo more than others! You increase your chances of success with the poo training if you give your puppy meals at dedicated times and take his bowl away when he seems full. I would strongly advise NOT leaving the food in the bowl for him to graze on throughout the day. You have far less chance of predicting his poo routine if you do this, not to mention the issue of potential resource guarding further down the line. Whilst some puppies will clear their bowl in seconds, there are others who may leave a bit of food and walk away. Do bear in mind that wet food and raw food can go off in warm temperatures, or that flies might lay their eggs on it!

I like to train puppies to go to the toilet on command. Whilst many people have told me it isn't possible to train a dog to poo on command, I strongly disagree, having trained all four of my dogs to do this. If I ask them to poo, and there is a poo in there, they will do it! If I ask them and there is no poo ready to be jettisoned, they will sniff about for a bit, and may even try to squat, but then will trot back to me without performing! Teaching a puppy to toilet on command is very simple. All you must do is choose your word (e.g. "wee wee," "poo poo" or whatever charming phrase you are happy to say without being mortally embarrassed in front of other people) and say it at the **PRECISE** moment your puppy is weeing or pooing. Don't make the mistake of saying it in advance or too late. This is where most owners go wrong in training. It takes many repetitions at the precise time of an action before a dog's brain will automatically associate the word with the action. Some dogs get it after just a few repetitions, whilst others may take much longer. You will know when your puppy knows what "wee wee" means when you try saying it in advance and he actually does go! If you say it in advance and he doesn't go, he has not yet learnt what the command means, so you need to keep on repeating whilst he is ACTUALLY weeing for a bit longer before trying to say it in advance again. Don't give up. He will get it eventually, I promise you. You can speed things up by giving him a tiny treat each time he successfully performs, but phase these out once he has learnt what the command means. There is absolutely no need to keep treating your puppy once the command has been learnt.

Toilet training is a perfect time to start teaching your puppy to come in from the garden as soon as you tell him. Do this right from the start and you will avoid the problem many owners have of a dog who ignores them when they want to call them inside! The simplest way to teach this is to say a firm "In" at **exactly** the moment your puppy crosses over your door threshold to enter your house. As with all command training, DON'T say the word in advance of him coming over the threshold until you are absolutely sure he has learnt what this word means (in his brain it must mean cross the ACTUAL threshold)! REPEAT, REPEAT, REPEAT whilst he is actually doing the action, then test by saying it in advance to see if he has learnt its meaning.

Start toilet training from Day 1 of your puppy's arrival. If the breeder has already started putting puppy pads down, your puppy may already know that this is where he is supposed to toilet. However, he is still likely to empty his bladder elsewhere indiscriminately as he has very little control when he is tiny, so it is your job to keep your beady eyes on him AT ALL TIMES whenever he is outside of his puppy pen or dedicated room. Let's imagine a typical day and how you would go about toilet training. You wake up and come downstairs. Go into the kitchen quietly and pop the kettle on. If your puppy is scrabbling to get out of the crate, try VERY HARD not to give him eye contact or go over to him but do watch him out of the corner of your eye. The second he stops scrabbling and pauses to watch you, go over and CALMLY unlatch the crate door so that he can come out into his pen. Walk away again, giving him the chance to sniff around and have a wee on the pad you have left in the puppy pen. Say your chosen phrase, such as "wee wee" as he does this. I don't advise putting a pad in the crate at night as he may decide to chew it and we absolutely DON'T want that! If he has had a wee during the night (or pooed) in the part of the crate away from his bed, remove the poo and mop up the wee with a piece of kitchen roll and rub this onto a clean pad in the pen. Clean up the soiled crate floor with a solution of diluted biological clothes washing liquid. Mopping up the accidental wee gives you the opportunity to transfer his wee scent on the pad where you want him to toilet during the day when he is unsupervised. You could skip this phase and take him straight outside the moment he wakes up and make this your daily routine. This is a personal choice. Having an intermediary phase, however, where he is allowed to toilet in his pen on a puppy pad gives you a bit more freedom and makes the whole process a little less intense. This can be particularly useful if you have a busy household and find it hard to watch him like a hawk every minute for signs that he is needing to go to the toilet. You will be dismantling the pen/crate arrangement further down the line once he gets the hang of toileting outside, but in the early weeks this arrangement takes a lot of the stress out of toilet training.

He may have trodden in his wee or poo, so now is the perfect time for you to get him used to having his paws washed (or his whole body, if it has got elsewhere in his fur!). It won't do him any harm to wait until you have made your cup of tea and woken up, but you probably don't want to be cuddling him before you have given him a clean! So, he's woken up, you have let him out of his crate, he has peed on his puppy pad in the pen area or outside, depending on which method you have chosen to follow (with you saying, "wee wee" and "good boy", when he is doing it) and it is now time to give him his breakfast.

Continue the routine of putting him outside for a wee after each nap, playtime or meal. In between these times, you should also be putting him outside every couple of hours. Chances are a lot of these times, he won't go to the toilet, but don't worry about that. It is very much hit and miss in the early days! If you are choosing to have a puppy pad in his pen, he may opt for this instead. The key thing for you is NOT to get stressed about the whole business of toilet training and particularly not to get upset if he has an accident. He is a baby, remember, he can't control his bladder and his bowels yet. In the wild, his mother would be cleaning up his mess in the den. Admonishing him or getting annoyed with him is simply unfair and will also be counter productive. We want toileting to be associated with a relaxed state of mind, NOT an anxious state of mind. If you allow yourself to become impatient with him, or worse, annoyed, he is going to pick up on the fact that you are feeling this way and this may make him tense up. Do you find it easy to go to the toilet when you are tense? I thought not. Let me explain why this matters.

Having worked with dogs for many years now it has become apparent to me that dogs develop equations for different situations based on experience. We have already touched upon the fact that puppies follow the lead of the older dogs when they are young. They learn appropriate responses from those older dogs to different situations, with those older dogs' behaviour being determined by instinct and by what they themselves have been taught when younger. The puppies learn what state of mind is associated with different situations. They develop an equation for that situation. So, let's now talk about what happens when your puppy poos on your best rug for the first time. We will break it down into two different scenarios - one where you catch the puppy in the actual act of pooing and one where you discover the poo after the deed has been done. Your response is likely to be one of two in either scenario. You will either be totally cool with it and just say "oh dear", quietly chuckle to yourself and get a poo bag and some cleaning spray to clear up the mess. Alternatively you will be annoyed, tell your puppy off, and huff and puff whilst clearing up the mess. Two very different states of mind. It's human nature, right?

Let's look at the scenario where you catch him in the act. If you catch him as he starts to circle and quickly verbally intervene with a sharp "Ah, Ah" or "No!", you may just stop him going ahead because his bowel will tense up. This may give you time to scoop him up and get him outside, but it is still incredibly important for you to immediately relax after the verbal intervention so that he doesn't develop an equation where preparing to poo equals an anxious state of mind. Intervening, relaxing and relocating him won't be detrimental to his toilet training. BUT if you catch him about to poo, shout at him and get angry, grab him and then thrust him outside, remaining in an annoyed state of mind yourself whilst doing it, you will put a new equation in his brain for preparing to poo. And that equation will be preparing to poo equals a tense state of mind. He follows your lead at this age, remember. You may think that telling the puppy off and being annoyed is going to give him the message that this is something he shouldn't do again. But do you seriously think he is capable of that sort of analytical thought? If you tell him off for having an accident in your home, you are going to run the risk of teaching him that toileting equals stress, particularly when you are present. This is why dogs sometimes sneak away from their owners and toilet behind pieces of furniture! Or won't go when you put them outside and stand watching them, but then immediately poo or wee the minute you bring them back indoors and stop watching them. Why? Because they are relaxed again once your attention is no longer on them!

There is no hard and fast rule as to how long it takes a puppy to become fully house-trained. Every puppy is different. You will get there, I promise you. The calmer and more relaxed about it, the simpler you make things for your puppy and the quicker everything will fall into place. It may be that you feel that you are making good progress but then your puppy starts to regress with his toileting. Don't be alarmed, the path to a "clean" puppy is rarely a steady upward trajectory. You are likely to have some setbacks, but don't despair. Just ensure that you don't allow your puppy to create a new routine on his own. For example, it may be that as he grows and finds the outside environment increasingly interesting, he spends all his time outside sniffing around and then as soon as you bring him inside again he toilets. If you allow this to continue, this could become a new routine in his brain – explore outside, then toilet when I come back inside! If this starts to happen, you are going to have to put some more work in to break this pattern. Take him outside, give him the chance to toilet and if, after 5 minutes, he doesn't do a wee or poo, take him back inside but watch him like a hawk, and don't put him back in his pen if you are using one. If he shows ANY sign of being about to toilet, it's straight back outside again for another try. REPEAT, REPEAT, REPEAT UNTIL HE GOES! Then, and only then, pop him back in his pen or let him potter around the room. Once he can go outside on a walk, things become much easier too, so hang in there in those early weeks!

Case Study 1: Puppy Pads Everywhere!

I was called to help an owner who was struggling with toilet training. The puppy, Max, was weeing and pooing seemingly indiscriminately throughout the house and refusing to go in the garden. The owner would take him out and stand for ages outside waiting for him to toilet, but he simply wouldn't go. It was winter, so cold and wet, and his owner was getting very fed up. Max would spend all his time sniffing around, picking up leaves and whatever else looked interesting. The last thing he seemed to be thinking about was having a wee or a poo. Yet, as soon as she took him back indoors, he would inevitably 'go' somewhere in the house. I asked the owner to show me the places where the puppy was toileting indoors. A quick tour, both upstairs and downstairs, revealed a plethora of puppy pads all over the place! Not only was there one in each room in the house, but they were also on the landing and in the hallway. Basically everywhere. Now, if I was that puppy and had the choice of toileting in the warmth, rather than in the cold, wet garden, I know which I would choose.

I advised the owner to fence off an area just outside the back door and to remove ALL interesting objects from the area, including leaves and snails! Next, we cleared the house of all puppy pads, except one near the back door. We also rubbed some mopped up wee on the paving in the outside toileting area. Keeping this area TOO clean and dousing it in disinfectant all the time will actually backfire, as it won't smell like a toilet to your puppy. Think how strong bleach smells to us. Imagine how it must smell to a puppy, whose sense of smell is so much more sensitive than ours! The puppy was old enough by this point to be able to hold his wee, if need be, so I didn't allow puppy pads anywhere else in the house and advised that the staingate be kept shut at all times, so that the puppy couldn't sneak upstairs to have a wee in private. I suggested to the owner that they mount dedicated surveillance for a whole week i.e. not let the puppy out of their sight at any time to avoid him toileting when they weren't watching. It was their responsibility to watch him like a hawk and ensure that they took him out regularly to his outside toilet area to give him a chance to 'go', giving him calm praise and a treat whenever he successfully did so. If they noticed him circling or pausing indoors (signs that he needed to toilet), they should quickly but without massive fuss, lead him to the outside toileting area. Usually, interrupting this "preparation" to go to the toilet is enough to stop a puppy actually weeing or pooing, particularly if it is a little older. Changing their approach to toilet training did the trick and the puppy was soon happily toileting outside all the time and puppy pads became a thing of the past.

Case Study 2: Held Back by Fear

My next example of a puppy who failed to master toilet training shows the importance of understanding what your puppy is telling you about how he feels in different situations. In this case, it was fear that was stopping the puppy toileting outside. Little Jinx had reached 6 months old and was still not toileting outside for his owner. His owner had done everything he thought he should. He was going out on pavements walks and the park and happily toileting but was still having accidents in the house. After some head scratching, I noticed that Jinx kept well away from the steps that led to the conservatory where the back door was. I asked the owner about this, and he told me that Jinx didn't like going down the steps, so they carried him to the back door when putting him outside. Having tried to persuade Jinx myself to walk down the steps, it became apparent that he would get as far as the top of the steps then freeze. Fear was behind the problem! Jinx was too scared to walk down the steps, and consequently always reverted to toileting somewhere in the house. He would get to the top of the steps when heading for the garden but would be unable to go any further because he was scared.

All I had to do was show Jinx that nothing bad would happen to him when he walked down the steps. Fear makes us shut down mentally. In order to overcome fear, we need to be led gently and carefully through a situation we fear by someone we trust. That is what I had to do with Jinx. Once I had gently persuaded him to come down one step at a time under his own momentum, he was soon happily trotting up and down the whole set of steps without a care in the world, and the toilet training could start again.

Chapter Seven – Feeding Time and Treats

Teaching your puppy how to be around food is incredibly important, whether it be his own food or yours. No-one wants a dog that guards food or shows any signs of aggression around food, or even a puppy that grabs treats rudely from your fingers. You have the perfect opportunity to avoid these problems occurring if you put some work in at the very start with your puppy and his relationship with food. You want him to be well-mannered at his mealtimes, take treats gently from people and to understand that he is not allowed to touch any food, except that which is given to him. Your puppy's mealtimes are the ideal time to start this work.

A good breeder will brief you on how often and how much your puppy is being fed when he is handed over to you. They will also likely send you home with a pack of the brand of food your puppy has been weaned onto. CAVEAT: DO NOT TAKE A PUPPY HOME WITH YOU WHO HASN'T BEEN WEANED. QUITE SIMPLY HE IS TOO YOUNG TO LEAVE HIS MOTHER. You can continue on the brand that your breeder has given you for the duration of your puppy's life, switching to adult versions of the type of food you have chosen as he matures. Or should you wish, you can change him to another brand, but do take care to gradually do this over a period of time to avoid upsetting your puppy's tummy. Stick to the feeding routine your breeder has been using initially. As he grows, that will change, obviously, but to start with, mimic the breeder.

As, I mentioned in Chapter 5, I would advise you to have dedicated mealtimes, rather than to leave food down for him all the time to graze on. Puppies usually poo within an hour of having dinner, so you will increase your chances massively of catching him at the right time if you know exactly when he had his last meal. Some food can spoil if left down or may attract flies. Obviously, fresh water should be available to your puppy at all times. On another note, food is an incredibly valuable resource to a dog and if you want to build a healthy relationship around it and avoid resource guarding issues, being TOTALLY in charge of his access to food will cement in your puppy's brain that food only comes from YOU and is not a resource that he can access willy nilly without your consent. Why does this matter? Well, us behaviourists repeatedly get asked to help with issues surrounding food, whether it be counter-surfing, stealing, food aggression or eating unsavoury items when out on walks (and that includes dog and cat poo, which we might not think of as food, but your puppy might!). A puppy who is taught from an early age that food only ever comes via the human hand is much less likely to end up with these sorts of issues, as he understands that there is a hierarchy when it comes to food, just like in the wild. In the wild the leader eats first and the followers don't get to tuck in until the leader has finished. This doesn't apply to water, generally. Fresh water should be available at all times to your puppy but do watch out for any signs that he is guarding his water bowl in the house (or indeed his water on walks) from other dogs or family pets. If he does show signs of this, you are going to need to put in a bit of extra work around water. However, this is a fairly rare occurrence, and I can pretty much guarantee that a dog guarding water has other issues too!

Your puppy will likely be starting off on three meals a day – breakfast, lunch and dinner. I would advise feeding him in his puppy pen on all these occasions, or at a specific spot where you intend to keep his food and water bowl going forwards. Prepare his breakfast and give it to him to eat. Now is the perfect opportunity to start teaching him to wait for permission before tucking into his food and for you to teach him that food is <u>not</u> about EXCITEMENT. You will see later that excitement can become your enemy when it comes to raising a well-mannered dog, and it often starts with how an owner feeds their puppy from Day 1. Excitement is behind so many issues dog behaviourists are called to help with, so let's start with getting mealtimes right, by being calm and relaxed from the outset. This will be hugely helpful further down the line with his training. We will also take this opportunity to introduce the concept of OWNERSHIP of food. Food is one of **<u>the</u>** most important resources to a dog, so it is crucial to get this right.

Naturally, I am now going to advise you NOT to make a huge song and dance about your puppy's mealtimes. If an owner leaps about crying "Dinner time, do you want your dinner!?" at a young puppy, they quickly learn that meals = excitement. The key to a well-behaved dog is CALMNESS! So, start as you mean to go on by making as little fuss as possible when you feed your puppy. He will naturally become a bit more excited at the smell of food, which is fine, just try not to ADD to this natural excitement by whipping him into a frenzy. Yes, it may be cute to see him spinning and grinning, jumping up and down, and whining for his breakfast/lunch/dinner, but remember it is YOU who is finding this cute and you may live to regret it further down the line when he is much bigger and totally focussed on the food rather than you at mealtimes. Fast forward to taking him to the pub or a café or having friends round to dinner. Fast forward to trying to find a dog boarder to have him when you go on holiday. Do you really want your dog to be in a frenzy of excitement on these occasions? Your dog boarder won't thank you, I can promise you that!

Back to the nitty gritty, then. Get his bowl, measure out his food and take it to his chosen spot (don't get hung up on how much you feed him – remember, the recommended amounts on puppy food are a GUIDE). If you have a puppy pen set up, get in the pen with him. Stand facing him and lower the food bowl to the floor BEHIND you (so that your body is between your puppy and the food bowl). Imagine in your mind that you are placing his food bowl into an EXCLUSION ZONE. This can be a bit tricky if he is really tiny, so you could kneel on the floor to make it a bit easier. The key is your body position in relation to the food and him – you MUST be blocking his access to the food with your body. As you are lowering the food bowl to the floor, if he rushes forward towards it, use a verbal intervention and lift the bowl upwards out of his reach. Your verbal intervention must be a short, sharp sound that your puppy notices. You must deliver it with confidence and you must relax <u>immediately</u> after you have made the noise. It will be your go-to sound going forwards that makes your puppy sit up and take notice of you. You are replicating the first noise his mother would make when she is signalling that her puppy is doing something unwanted, although in her case it would be a low growl! I personally tend to use "Ah, Ah" or a sharp "Shh" sound. Repeat, repeat, repeat until he gets the message that the food bowl isn't going onto the ground when he is rushing forwards. Puppies pick this up really quickly and will often automatically go into a polite SIT without being told once you have done this a couple of times.

What you are teaching him is that, if he displays unwanted behaviour (i.e. excitement/rushing forwards), you will be intervening with a noise, and when he hears this noise, he should pause, put his attention back on you and relax. It doesn't matter what noise you use, just use whatever sound makes you feel confident and in charge. If it helps, place your hands on your hips to improve your stance. There is no need to say "wait" or "stay." He is a tiny puppy after all and we must remember he CANT SPEAK ENGLISH! But he does understand dog language - if a more senior dog has food it doesn't want to share yet, it will block access to that food by standing in front of it and give a verbal warning to the junior dog that approaches (a low grumble in the chest). If the junior dog ignores this warning and continues to approach, the senior dog will physically intervene (e.g. with an air snap). The message is, don't approach, stop and be respectful. This is MY food and I am not sharing it with you yet. So, you are replicating an older dog by asking him to wait politely before you share the food with him. Why do I suggest not issuing commands at this point? The reason is, we want our puppy to do everything automatically without being told. We want calmness around food to be his default behaviour, not something we have to instruct him to do. Once he has backed off from you and made eye contact (and preferably sat or laid down without being told), you can move to the side and beckon him towards the food bowl OR gently push the food bowl towards him. Either way, you are giving him the message that you are sharing the food with him, and it is time to eat.

A puppy who ISN'T taught manners around food from an early age is far more likely to have issues further down the line with bad manners, either towards humans or dogs, or in the worst-case scenario, resource guarding and food aggression. Avoid this by making it clear to your new puppy that the food belongs to YOU and you will choose when to share it with him. Because you are the provider of this important resource to

Feeding Time and Treats

your puppy and want to avoid resource guarding behaviour, I would strongly advise that you REMOVE his bowl after he has finished eating. Give him a chance to eat it and when you are sure he has had enough, pick it up and wash it out, ready for his next meal. Remember, we want to AVOID the possibility of problems like resource guarding arising so removing the bowl reduces the risk of your puppy becoming territorial around this object and the food inside it.

I mentioned that we want the puppy to automatically have good manners around food. Another reason I prefer not to issue commands such as "Sit" and "Stay" or "Wait" when it comes to putting food in front of puppy is that if you issue a command to a dog when it is in an excited state of mind (and dogs generally ARE excited where food is concerned), you are effectively teaching them to be in an excited state of mind around food, whereas it is much safer and also more pleasant all round to teach your dog to be CALM AND RESPECTFUL around food, rather than be poised in a state of excitement for a release so they can rush forwards and grab the food. This will also come into play when we are teaching the puppy recall (more of that later).

Once your puppy has learnt that food equals calmness you can progress to the core technique I teach dog owners to communicate ownership of objects (such as food) and territory to their dogs. This is a technique called "Blocking & Claiming" and it will be referred to in other chapters in the book. It is a technique dogs use on each other all the time and the simplest way for you to learn how to use it with your puppy is by starting with his mealtimes. I have explained the basic way of blocking his food. The more advanced method involves standing calmly in front of his food bowl ("blocking" him from access to it with your body) then walking towards him until he turns fully and walks away (you are "claiming" it as yours). The second he walks away he has conceded that the food belongs to you, not him. THIS IS DOG BEHAVIOUR/DOG LANGUAGE! He must walk away the first few times you do this. You must only move forwards or sideways along a horizontal line when interacting with him, keeping the food behind you. DO NOT MOVE BACKWARDS, as in a dog's brain, this means you are retreating and conceding territory, so the food becomes fair game again! If he simply stops and sits down, keep moving towards him, particularly the first few times you do this exercise. Dogs are very good at pretending that they have given something up to another dog (sometimes called dummying), which goes back to their behaviour in the wild when competing with rivals. You can test whether he really has acknowledged the food is yours by doing what I call THE TEST (surprise, surprise). Step to the side and let him have a full view of the food bowl. If he immediately moves towards it you have not got the message across that the food bowl belongs to you and will have to repeat the "block & claim" again. If, on the other hand, he stays stationary and is CAMLY giving you full eye contact, despite the fact that there is nothing between him and the food bowl, you have a FULL MENTAL CONNECTION with him and he has acknowledged that the food belongs to you. Well done! Give him a thumbs up and say a low "Nice" to show him that this is the desired behaviour. You can now go to pick the food bowl up, place it in front of him and tell him "Ok" so he knows he is now allowed to eat it.

It is a good idea at this early stage of his development to let him eat a little then lean down and take the bowl away for a few seconds or pop your hand in it and rummage around. This should elicit NO reaction from a young puppy. I can't stress enough how important it is for you to be doing this from Day 1 with your puppy. Being able to take food of any sort out of your dog's mouth is essential for safety, whether it be their dinner, an old chicken bone they have found on the street, or a nice juicy bone you have given them. Do this from puppyhood and you will be fine. Leave it too late and all sorts of issues can arise.

Here's a quick recap again on **BLOCKING & CLAIMING**:

Place the item on the floor (e.g. food bowl) behind you, with you facing your puppy.

Walk calmly and confidently towards him. Pop your hands on your hips if this makes you feel more confident. Make sure you aren't bending forwards. Stand up tall!

If he tries to nip past you, block his route by moving sideways but don't step backwards!

Keep moving towards him until he turns and walks away from you.

The moment he turns away, mentally disconnect from him, return to your spot in front of the object and face him again.

*If he has given up ownership of the food bowl, he will stop some distance away from you (most likely where he turned) and make eye contact with you. He may even sit down. Give him a thumbs up and give **calm** praise (such as "Nice") in a low voice.*

Step to the side so that he can see the object fully to check whether he has truly given up ownership. If he moves forwards, block again and move towards him again until he turns and walks away.

Keep repeating this exercise until you are sure he isn't going to move forwards and maintains full eye contact, rather than looking at the object. Once you are confident you have full control the exercise is over and you can either give him gentle praise or give him the object if appropriate.

Practice with different objects to perfect this skill – dog treats, his toys, shoes, your underwear, the TV remote! Some things he will be allowed, other he won't.

Whilst the above may seem a bit of a palaver when it comes to feeding your puppy, rest assured, establishing this relationship with him over food at a very young age is going to help leaps and bounds when it comes to raising a well-mannered dog. You are making it clear from the outset that food resources come from you. Using his own "dog language" to convey this message not only makes it quicker for him to learn, but also ensures that you are building from Day 1 the foundations of a beautiful relationship with your dog, where he looks to you for direction in all situations.

<u>CAVEAT</u>: DO **NOT** USE THIS METHOD ON ANY DOG OTHER THAN <u>YOUR NEW YOUNG **PRE-PUBESCENT PUPPY**,</u> WITHOUT CONSULTING A PROFESSIONAL

BEHAVIOURIST FIRST. A VERY YOUNG PUPPY WILL NATURALLY FOLLOW HIS MOTHER'S LEAD AND YOU ARE REPLICATING HER. THIS IS NOT THE CASE WITH A DOG ENTERING PUBERTY AND BEYOND, WHO MAY WELL CHALLENGE YOU FOR THE FOOD.

Case Study 1: The Devil Incarnate

When I met Joey's owners, he was a lovely puppy by all accounts. With one big exception. If he got hold of any food he became a vicious monster if you tried to take it off him. His owner had the bite marks to prove it and she had been forced to "trade" Joey for anything he stole, by swapping the item for a dog treat. She had become scared of him when he had food in his mouth. I asked her what her usual routine was with respect to feeding him, right from the outset, and she told me she had simply filled his bowl, popped it on the ground and let him eat in peace. She hadn't been aware that it was a good idea to take the bowl away or put her hand in it from time to time, believing that he should be allowed the space to eat his dinner on his own. She had noticed that he growled at the cat when it walked past him whilst he was eating but hadn't thought much more about this. As Joey grew, she noticed that he was becoming increasingly territorial around his food bowl. If she did happen to pass near when he was eating, he would stiffen and pause in his munching, giving her the side-eye until she had passed by, before resuming his meal. He also seemed to be eating faster and faster, as he got older. When she first gave him a dog chew for his teeth, he would run off with it and eat it under the table. Again, she let him do this in peace and didn't attempt to take it back off him. But then one day, she accidentally dropped two on the floor and he grabbed both of them and ran off. She went to get the second one back and he growled and snarled at her. Naturally, she backed off when he growled, as he sounded pretty scary. She didn't have the confidence to just go up and take it out of his mouth, because she was afraid (quite rightly) of getting bitten. Instead, she got another dog treat and persuaded Joey to drop both chews in return for the treat. This worked, naturally, and became her default way of getting things off Joey.

Whilst you may think this was a perfectly sensible solution, unfortunately for Joey's owner, his aggression around food became much worse and she found it very distressing seeing this unpleasant side to his character. She was also worried about what might happen if someone else tried to take food from his mouth without her knowledge, particularly if it was a child. I explained to her that as far as he was concerned, any food he had in his mouth was rightfully his, and what he was doing was completely natural to a dog in a dominant state of mind. This behaviour had started right back at the very beginning when he was a little puppy – he had been allowed to "own" his food. He had guarded it from the cat, and also from his owner (remember the side-eye and the tense body language?) and allowing him to do this had simply cemented in his brain that food was his and not the humans (or the cats or anyone else's). He had become very powerful around food through showing aggression when challenged and that would not have happened had he been shown as a very young puppy that ALL food resources belonged to the humans. After some intensive work with Joey that involved removing all food (including treats) from his control and starting from scratch with some ownership work, Joey's owner was able to redress the balance and take charge of food once again.

Most new puppy owners consider puppy treats to be an essential part of their shopping list. They are incredibly handy when teaching dogs commands quickly. Dogs are very clever. It doesn't take them long to work out that certain actions will result in a tasty treat being dispatched but do take care when using this method of training that you don't create a monster when it comes to food. As I said above in relation to your puppy's mealtimes, calmness is the key to good manners around food going forwards, and the same should apply to treats. If you teach your puppy to be like a coiled spring around that treat packet, you are potentially going to have issues going forwards when it comes to other food, and this can be particularly annoying for other people! I have come across plenty of cases of dogs who are so over-stimulated by the sound of a treat bag, or the scent of a dog treat, that they rush up to other dog owners and jump at them for a treat, or even worse, steal another dog owner's treat packet and run off with it. Do you want your puppy to grow up to be that dog? I doubt it. Likewise, do you want your puppy to be a complete nightmare when you are in a café or a pub enjoying lunch or dinner? Or do you want him to be lying quietly under the table because he isn't stimulated into excitement by the smell of food.

Snatching treats from a human is a common problem that develops with puppies. No-one likes a grabber! This type of behaviour usually develops when someone who isn't confident around dogs gives the puppy a treat. They hold the treat in their fingers and dangle it above the puppy and let go as the puppy opens its mouth and reaches up for it. This is a bit like feeding penguins fish at the zoo. The penguin's default action is to open its beak and catch the food as it drops. If treats are delivered to your puppy in this way, he too will learn to "catch" the treat. The trouble is, he may also catch fingers in the process. This can be a particular issue with children, who then become wary of giving the puppy a treat. Anyone who has had their fingers accidently caught by a dog's teeth is naturally going to be a bit cautious the next time they are in this situation and won't be approaching treat dispensing with calm confidence. The dog will pick up on this nervous energy and itself will be more alert as a consequence. The dog learns to grab at treats, to make sure he gets them! To avoid this issue with your puppy and to stop other people's dogs snatching treats off you, put the treat in your hand and close your fingers over it. Now turn your wrist, so that your curled fingers are facing upwards. Offer the treat to your puppy – he will scrabble and snuffle at it in an excited way. Just be patient. Don't open your hand! Wait until he backs off a little or calms down. This is the perfect time to unfurl your hand and let him take the treat GENTLY from it. If he does it nicely, say "Gentle" as he takes it. If he tries to grab it as you unfurl, calmly close your hand and start again. You can use "Gentle" as a verbal cue going forwards if he is a little excited when a treat comes out.

One final word on food. Some puppies may appear to be fussy eaters and owners worry that they aren't getting enough food. An animal will not eat when it is stressed and anxious, so don't be too alarmed if your puppy isn't keen on his food when he first arrives. If he does seem a bit reluctant, try to work out why he might not be eating. Does he look a little anxious? Perhaps there are too many people crowding around him and he is feeling a little overwhelmed. Try to give him space and ask the family to leave him in peace whilst he has his dinner but only do this a few times until he is relaxed at mealtimes. You don't want another Joey! It could be that he has a tummy upset. A quick test to see if a dog is really feeling unwell, rather than being hampered by fear, is to rub a little wet food (or mashed up kibble) on his gums. This can help the brain kick into eating mode. You would be surprised by the number of times I have got a fussy eater to instantly tuck in by using this method! If he is feeling poorly, this won't trigger him to eat up his dinner. Dealing with a poorly tummy will be dealt with later on in Chapter 11.

Case Study 2: Food Obsession

I was called in to help Archie because the owners were having trouble with him being food obsessed. They were unable to leave any food lying around on tables or kitchen counters without the dog trying to steal it. If he did manage to steal it, he point blank refused to give it up, instead swallowing it as fast as he could if the owners approached. Naturally, they were very worried about him stealing something that could be potentially harmful to him and were also worried about him growling at them whenever he had managed to steal something and they tried to retrieve it. They were very dedicated owners and had spent months training their puppy with puppy treats. He was very good at his basic commands and would sit, stay, leave, wait etc when told. He was also fantastic at doing tricks! The problem was that if he WASN'T given a command, he just helped himself and they didn't know how to overcome this problem.

It was clear to me from the outset that food = excitement to the puppy. Just the mere rustle of a treat packet sent him into a frenzy, with wide staring eyes and excitable behaviour. He was like a coiled spring waiting for his reward. Quite simply, he had become food obsessed. His equation was "food = excitement". The first thing I did was ask the owners to remove all treats from his daily life for the time being and to start from scratch, teaching him that to get a reward he needed to be in a CALM, FOLLOWING state of mind i.e. calmly following his OWNER and not focussing on the food. His default around food should be to look to his owner first to see what he is supposed to do and do this in a CALM STATE OF MIND. To do this, I first asked the owner to put a treat in their hand and hold their arm out to the side. Naturally, the puppy just stared at the outstretched hand with the treat in it! I then told the owner to wait patiently until the puppy started to calm down (which would be obvious by his body language, his eyes, his tail etc). Even then, Archie would not be given the treat. He would only be given the treat once he had calmed down AND given FULL eye contact to his owner. Not just a quick glance, FULL HOLDING EYE CONTACT. Owners can find this quite hard initially as it takes a lot of patience and they too must be calm and relaxed during the exercise, but if you hold your nerve, relax your face, drop your shoulders and remember to breathe, your puppy will eventually learn exactly what state of mind you want him to be in before he receives the treat. Give up too soon and you will simply be teaching him that he can remain in a heightened mental state around food.

Initially, Archie spun round, sat and offered a paw and whined, but once he realised that none of these behaviours resulted in him being given the treat, you could almost see the cogs turning in his brain whilst he tried to work out what is was the humans wanted! And he did learn. He realised that all that was wanted of him was calm, following behaviour. As soon as he gave this, he was calmly given the treat. We then moved on to teaching him that ALL food required this same behaviour. We also taught him that, just because he gave us this state of mind and full eye contact, it DIDN'T mean he would always be given the food at the end. This is where showing your puppy clear boundaries as to what he can and can't touch comes in. A puppy should be taught from the outset that ALL food belongs to YOU. Whether that be a packet of dog treats, a sandwich on the kitchen counter or a discarded bit of burger on the ground in the park. This also extends to OTHER PEOPLE'S food, so treats belonging to other dog owners, or the food on the table of the couple sitting next to you in the café! Rebooting Archie's brain around food helped enormously, and when I last heard, he was well on the road to having food manners!

Chapter Eight – Playtime

Young puppies are great fun. You will find you have never smiled and laughed so much as in those first few weeks and months with your puppy. Just like toddlers, puppies want to play, play, play and, believe me, they would play 24/7 if you let them (in-between naps)! However, there are some things you ought to bear in mind when it comes to playing with your puppy, because puppies also LEARN through play and if you get it wrong in the early days, you could be setting yourself up for some issues further down the line.

I really do advise not playing with your puppy endlessly at random times. In the beginning, whilst he is learning HOW to play nicely with humans, it is much easier to teach him if you are completely in charge of when playtime starts and when it ends. This also lays a good foundation for skills you are going to need in the local park when it comes to playing with other dogs and leaving other humans (particularly those that don't like dogs) alone. I know what you are probably thinking right now. For goodness' sake, this woman is the fun police! I'm not, honestly. Of course you must play with your puppy lots, but just add some structure to it. Giving him a clear signal that it is time to play and also a clear signal that playtime is OVER is very handy. One of the common problems us behaviourists get asked about is how to stop their puppy/dog charging up to every dog and human in the park wanting to play. Teaching him when he can play with another dog and when he must stop is really important, so do it from the outset.

Back to play in your house - he is likely to want to play in the morning (he's been alone all night, after all), after his naps throughout the day (he would normally play with his siblings at this point) and especially in the evening after having his dinner (a time when puppies generally go a bit nuts and have the zoomies!). I am going to be a little controversial here by suggesting that you consider NOT leaving toys lying around all over the place in your house. The reasoning behind this goes back to teaching your puppy when it is playtime and when playtime is over, but also feeds into teaching him what he can and can't touch in your home and other people's homes. To teach him playtime manners, get the toy basket out and say to your puppy "Do you want to play?". This is his signal that playtime has started. Play with him for a little while and then when you decide it is time to stop, collect up the toys in a matter-of-fact way and calmly say "Game Over" whilst walking away from your puppy and putting the toy basket out of reach. You are giving your puppy a clear message that playtime is over. You are DISENGAGING with him physically and mentally, and you expect him to disengage too. It doesn't take a puppy long to pick this up and it is hugely helpful when you get to the park and need to influence his behaviour around other dogs, particularly if they have toys with them. DO NOT USE TREATS WHEN YOU ARE TEACHING YOUR PUPPY TO STOP PLAYING WITH TOYS.

Keeping your puppy's toys out of the way in a toy basket is also helpful in teaching your puppy what is a toy and what isn't. If you leave toys lying around and also leave your shoes, your mobile phone or your medication lying around, how on earth is your puppy supposed to know that he is allowed to touch some of these but not the others? Yes, it will initially be funny when he keeps running off with your shoes or your underwear, but your patience will start to wear thin, particularly if he uses them to relieve his teething pains. Again, DO NOT GIVE YOUR PUPPY A TREAT IN EXCHANGE FOR YOUR PRECIOUS ITEMS. We don't want to teach him to steal in order to get a food reward. It is quite simple to teach a puppy what he can and can't touch in terms of objects. We have already talked about the technique with relation to feeding time. I will revisit this in a little while, but let's get back to toys and playtime first.

It is a good idea to have two baskets of toys that are kept out of reach of your puppy. Having two ensures he won't get bored of them quickly and if you keep them in different locations, it also means you are more likely to have some toys handy when you need a distraction from mouthing/nipping. You can leave a couple of indestructible toys in the puppy pen for him to play with when you are busy doing other things, as we do want him to learn to amuse himself when you are busy, but again, rotate these regularly so he doesn't get bored with them. Why indestructible? To keep him safe. Do NOT put rope toys in his pen or soft toys that he could easily destroy. It is very easy for a young puppy to pull the fibres out of rope toys, particularly if the toy is fairly cheap and poorly made. I have heard several reports of sick puppies being found to have a load of these fibres from rope toys stuck in their bowels. You can play with these toys with him when supervised but keep them out of reach the rest of the time. Squeaky toys are another type of toy you need to give a bit more thought to. There are some dogs who will quite happily play with a squeaky toy without doing their utmost to get to the squeaker, destroying the toy in the process. But others, particularly breeds bred for hunting vermin, will "kill" anything that squeaks, given the chance. It really is down to you whether or not you teach your puppy not to destroy his toys. Obviously, from a safety point of view, stopping your puppy before he disembowels his favourite teddy is preferable, but if he doesn't actually eat the stuffing or the squeaker, it isn't such a big issue. If you are the cautious type and want to ensure you keep vet visits to a minimum, take his toy away if it looks like he is starting to make headway on the stitches. A simple "Enough" command when he is getting too frenzied, followed by the toy's removal will indicate to him that he shouldn't take things any further.

Another thing we want to avoid is your puppy becoming possessive over toys. Possessive behaviour is something dog behaviourists get asked to help with a lot. We have talked about ensuring that your puppy doesn't become possessive around food, and you should adopt the same approach to his toys. The simplest way to do this is to make it clear that his toys are actually YOUR toys. You are sharing these toys with him and not the other way round! It may be that your puppy quite happily shares all toys, and if that is the case you have nothing to worry about. But do keep an eye out for any signs that he might be becoming a bit obsessed about one particular toy, as this can easily escalate into possessive behaviour. To avoid this, simply block and claim each new toy you introduce to him in the way I have explained in earlier chapters. This lets your puppy know that the toy is yours, first and foremost, and that you are sharing it with him. Regularly take toys from him with no fuss and then give them back to him.

Naturally, he will want to chew some of his toys, particularly when his adult teeth start to come through. Make sure you have plenty of suitable, strong toys to hand when the chewing phases are happening. Do not let him chew either you or your furniture to relieve teething pain! A frozen carrot or a frozen toy will help his sore gums. I have even heard of people twisting up tea-towels and sticking them in the freezer to help relieve teething pain! If you catch him eyeing up the chair leg, "block & claim" the chair and give him one of his own toys to grind on. If he is persistent, you can try spraying an anti-chew product on tempting items of furniture, but this won't always work. Similarly, popping him in the puppy pen with a suitable toy is another option if he makes a beeline for your chair or table legs. Whatever you do, do not let him chew things that belong to you. You need to make it very clear to him that furniture is out of bounds. Again, do not try to tempt him away from chewing your items with a tasty treat as you will simply teach him to go and touch those items in order to receive a treat! He will grow out of this phase eventually, but if you have let him have a chew on stuff he shouldn't, it could become an annoying habit. Worse still, he could do it round other people's houses, so your invites might dry up!

Now let's get down to the fun. Learning through play is one of the delights of having a young puppy. Your puppy has a great time and you get to teach him new behaviours. For example, playing fetch gives everyone lots of pleasure and is very handy when you start going to the park and you want him to bring things back to you. You can start teaching him these games from the minute you bring him home. Throw a toy for him a little distance from you. Don't say anything (particularly not FETCH!). See if he goes after it and then turns to bring it back to you. If he does bring it back, at the moment he reaches you say "FETCH" and good boy (no need for a treat). You must get your timing right with commands. If you say Fetch when he is a little distance from you, he may learn to only bring it that close! I have seen many owners throwing balls in the park, only for the dog to leave it miles away from them! What has happened is that at some point they have got the timing of the command wrong, and the dog has learnt to drop the ball nowhere near them. The owner then walks over to collect the ball and then throws it again. What has happened is that the dog has effectively taught the owner to fetch the ball for them! With your puppy, just keep repeating "FETCH" every time he brings the ball all the way back to you. He will soon get the message. There is absolutely no need to be giving him a treat for this. More of this in a minute.

Next up you can teach him "DROP". Whether you say "DROP", "DROP IT" or "LEAVE" is up to you, but I prefer to keep "LEAVE" for when I don't want him to focus on an object/dog/person, but instead focus on me. This is a personal preference, obviously. All I would say is once you have chosen a command for a particular action STICK TO IT, do not change it e.g. from "DROP" to "DROP IT", as this may confuse your dog. With some dogs, it won't matter, but why make things difficult for your puppy. Keep it simple!

To teach your puppy "DROP", first of all teach him "FETCH". When he brings the toy back, he may automatically drop it on the floor in front of you. If he does, say "DROP" at the **precise** moment he lets it go. Not a few seconds before or a few seconds after. You are probably getting the message by now about teaching commands. IT'S ALL ABOUT TIMING! If you are struggling to teach your puppy something, it will not be because he is stupid, stubborn or being "naughty", it will be because YOU are getting something wrong, most likely the timing of the command. So, with the "DROP" command, keep saying it at the precise moment he drops it and then say "Good Boy" or "Nice" in a calm voice. There is no need to get excited with your praise, no need to touch your puppy and no need to use treats. You want him to learn that being with you is all about calm cooperation. Save your excited praise for when you really need it i.e. recall out in the park when he spots a squirrel out of the corner of his eye! Why no treats, you may ask? There is a very good reason for this, other than that they can cause over-excitement. I don't want you to teach your puppy to steal for a treat! If you teach him "Fetch" and "Drop" using treats, you run the risk of him fetching and dropping other dogs' balls when you are out in the park. He's not daft. If he knows that if he picks up a ball and gives it back to you, he is going to get a treat, this can massively backfire later on in this way! I'm not saying it will definitely happen, it will depend on the individual dog, but it COULD happen, and I have seen it happen many times with dogs that have learnt to steal things in order to be given a treat. They won't just fetch their own ball for a treat in the park, they will also fetch any other ball they happen to see getting thrown. Teach your puppy from the outset to fetch HIS ball, the ball thrown by YOU alone, and you will avoid this scenario going forwards. If he does head for another dog's ball, start right away teaching him that he must not touch other dog's toys in the park. Do your verbal intervention (see earlier chapters) as he approaches the ball (e.g. "Ah, Ah") and if he looks at you when you make this noise, say "Not Yours" and call him towards you informally. Give him gentle verbal praise. Repeat this whenever you see him looking at another dog's ball or toy. If he does manage to get hold of it and run off, don't chase him as you will simply teach him to steal for a chase! Ignore him, walk away and call for him to follow you. When he arrives simply take the ball out of his mouth and return it to its owner. If he is a persistent thief, you will need to pop him on a short training line and do the verbal intervention training above, using the line to stop him actually reaching the ball. He should soon get the message.

Going back to the "DROP" command, if your puppy brings you the toy back after you ask him to fetch it and DOESN'T immediately drop it at your feet, do NOTHING. Don't try to negotiate with him or take it out of his mouth at this point (I will advise you how to remove things from your puppy's mouth safely in Chapter 13). Simply wait calmly and do nothing. You want your puppy to work out for himself what he needs to do in order for the game to be repeated. Trust me, he will work it out, even though it may take him a little while. Patience, as ever, is the key here. Calmly wait. If he walks away and drops the ball elsewhere, do nothing, just end the game mentally and move on to doing something else with him, surreptitiously picking the ball up when you next pass it. If he stays by you and eventually releases the ball, say "DROP" at the moment of release, as above, and throw it again. It won't take him long to work out that bringing the ball back and dropping it at your feet is how he gets another turn to fetch! You may find you have the kind of puppy who simply runs off with the ball/toy every time you throw it. DON'T chase him if this is the case. As I mentioned above, the last thing you want to do is teach your puppy a game where he picks something up and then gets chased, as this will backfire on you further down the line, particularly in the park, if he picks up a bit of dangerous rubbish.

On the subject of chasing, I would strongly discourage you from playing chase with your puppy when he is little. This is particularly the case if you have young children. It is unfair of you to expect your young puppy to know that YOUR children don't mind being chased around the dining room table by him but that a young child in the park DOES mind being chased and is actually really scared! Clear boundaries are important to a puppy, but a boundary that YOU understand isn't necessarily one that he is going to understand, so put yourself in his shoes before you encourage a game that may prove problematic further down the line. Your puppy will get plenty of opportunities to play chase with other dogs once he starts going to the park. Again, when you do get to that stage, he will need to learn to stop playing chase with a dog when you tell him, NOT when he chooses!

One of the most common things new puppy owners have a problem with is mouthing and nipping. Whilst this isn't a big issue when the puppy is teeny tiny, as the puppy grows it can become a painful problem, particularly if you don't have a clue how to stop it or you are a household with children. Your puppy doesn't have hands – he uses his nose, eyes and mouth to explore the world and that mouth comes with a set of needle-sharp baby teeth. If your puppy was growing up in the wild with his mother and siblings, he would be using his mouth for various functions, including eating, picking things up and COMMUNICATING with his fellow dogs. We don't think of dogs' mouths as a means of communication, but they use it on each other all the time. Just watch a bunch of puppies playing together. They will be opening and closing their mouths at each other, grabbing each other, nipping each other and yet, not generally upsetting each other, unless one of them grabs a little too hard. If that happens, the disgruntled puppy will yelp, causing the aggressor to let go, and they will carry on with their game again as if nothing happened. Puppies are taught very early on by their elders something called "bite inhibition". You may well have heard of this already and know that it is the amount of pressure a dog can put on another dog's skin without causing it real pain. The key thing to be aware of with bite inhibition is that the amount of pressure applied without pain relates to a **dog with fur**! Us humans don't have fur, we have delicate skin with no added protection, so the same pressure that wouldn't hurt a fellow pup or adult dog, DOES hurt us and is very unwelcome!

So, how to get around this issue without curbing your puppy's instinct to play and explore with his mouth? I find that the simplest thing to do is to teach a puppy from Day 1 that no contact between puppy teeth and human skin is allowed. To do this you need a ready supply of interesting toys nearby at playtime. Why? Because we don't want humans to be viewed as an extra big toy in the puppy's brain. Think about it. He puts pressure on your skin, you yelp and get agitated and wave your arms around. You have just become a massive squeaky toy and fuelled excitement in your puppy's brain, so he is likely to come back for more! Far better to teach your puppy that human skin is for gentle licking only. Much better to be licked and then wash your hands after playing, than to be constantly trying to fight off an over-excited puppy who keeps nipping you. If you have a major issue with dogs licking your skin, it's not the end of the world, just find another alternative to teach your pup when he opens his mouth near bare skin.

To teach your pup to lick rather than bite, simply smear something tasty on your hand (peanut butter is a good one or some wet puppy food) and as he starts licking it off, say "Nice licking" or "Lickies" or another chosen command. Repeat this a few times and then try again with clean hands. If he immediately licks, you know he has learnt what "lickies" means. If he doesn't, you need to repeat a bit more whilst he is ACTUALLY licking. If he licks you accidently at any point, reinforce that this behaviour is allowed by saying "Lickies" at this moment. Your aim is to be able to convert a nip into a lick. The mouthing stage of puppyhood doesn't last forever, it is normally temporary, but if you get

Playtime

this wrong at the start, your dog could LEARN to mouth and nip. Instead of growing out of the behaviour as he matures, it is likely to become worse. Mouthing and nipping usually happens when the puppy gets too excited during play. Teach him to focus on his toys, not your body, by putting a toy in his mouth whenever he reaches for your skin and then carrying on playing with him. If he simply won't do this and keeps coming back for you, calmly stop play and walk away. If he STILL comes after you, nipping at your heels, don't be tempted to yell at him and get cross. This will achieve nothing other than feeding his excited state. Stand still, take a nice deep breath, and make sure your whole body is relaxed, and see if this influences him at all. Changing your STATE OF MIND is often enough to get a puppy to change its state of mind, but if it doesn't, you need to find something to distract him temporarily, such as another toy, and then pick him up with this toy and pop him in his pen. The message you are giving is this: if you persist in using ME as a toy, I will stop playing with you and you can play on your own until you are a bit calmer. Keeping your cool when a puppy is getting over-excited and nippy is essential. If he was bugging his mum like this in the den, she would growl at him as a warning and if he ignored it, snap at him or even nip him. You can't go around biting your puppy, so you need to find another way of getting the message across to him that this is unwanted behaviour.

If you are unlucky enough to have a really determined, quite dominant puppy who simply won't take these cues from you that you no longer wish to play, you can try popping him on an indoor puppy line attached to a little puppy harness. What this does is give you the opportunity to keep him AWAY from your body whilst you get him to calm down and stop targeting you. Keep him away from your body by having your arm fully outstretched whilst you fetch another toy to distract him with. As soon as his focus moves off you, you can drop the puppy line again. Remember, you must stay calm and keep breathing whilst holding the puppy line. Try very hard not to be tense. Tension is your enemy!

I often get asked if it is a good idea to encourage a puppy to play tug-of-war. There are varying opinions about this, and you must decide for yourself which approach you consider to be the most sensible.

Personally, I think there is no harm in playing tug with your puppy, so long as he learns to take it in turns to win and stops when you ask him (use "Game Over"). If you watch two dogs playing "nicely" together, you will notice that they take it in turns during play - sometimes one will be on top, sometimes the other, sometimes one will be the chaser, sometimes the other. You want to replicate this with your puppy, as you don't want to encourage domineering behaviour. No-one likes a bully, and this is very much the case out in the park. If your dog is constantly dominating other dogs, this can be an issue and you can avoid that by teaching your puppy from a young age to 'play nicely'. Do this by ensuring that you sometimes win the tug of war, and sometimes he does. If he gets over-excited and growly during play, cease playing with him and walk away. That is what a sibling puppy would do. Teach him that you will play with him when he is happy, friendly and co-operative but NOT when he is dominant or aggressive. When he starts mixing with other puppies, you want to continue this work, ensuring that you step in and halt play if your puppy is starting to dominate or intimidate the other one.

Case Study: When Playtime Goes Wrong

Jerry's family got him as a companion for their children. They felt that the kids were old enough to have the responsibility of a pet dog and, whilst the mum wasn't a big fan of dogs and was actually a bit scared of them, she put her desire to encourage her children to care for a pet above her own misgivings about having a dog in the house. Her husband needed help from carers so she felt that a puppy would be a welcome addition to the household, giving her children a pet to raise and her husband a companion. At first everything went well. The children were delighted with the new puppy, who was a small breed and incredibly cute. One of their favourite games was encouraging the puppy to do zoomies around the top of the two sofas they had in their lounge. They would whip him into a frenzy until he was charging around barking madly, jumping from one sofa to the other. The son, in particular, loved to do this when his friends were around and the boys took great delight in the puppy's antics. Mum was a little less sure about encouraging the wild behaviour, but the kids and the puppy seemed happy, so she didn't step in to stop it. The puppy settled into family life and was adored by all.

However, some worrying behaviours did start to appear as he grew. This culminated in a call for help to me. The puppy was becoming increasingly aggressive and had started biting family members. He had also started biting the husband's daily carers and had given himself the job of protecting the husband from anyone who approached his wheelchair. The mum was in despair - their cute little puppy had turned into an aggressive little devil and they couldn't understand why. I explained to them that what appeared to have happened was that the wild play at the start of the puppy's life had cemented in his brain that humans = excitement. There was no control involved in the play. The dog was simply allowed to wind itself up into a frenzy and was never taught when to stop or encouraged to calm down. The kids just waited until he conked out of his own accord. A lack of any rules or boundaries in the household as to what the puppy was and wasn't allowed to do resulted in the puppy setting his own rules. As puberty kicked in and the puppy started to change into an adult dog, the lack of leadership in the house resulted in Jerry stepping up into that role. In Jerry's brain it was his job to control the humans, not the other way round! And he did that in the only way he knew how - with his teeth!

The situation was so bad that it was agreed that Jerry needed to be removed from the home. As an emergency measure, I brought him to my own home as there was nowhere else he could go in a hurry. I then set about "rebooting" him, by teaching him from scratch how to live side-by-side with humans (and my dog) in a harmonious way. He did bite me that first week that we had him, but that was the one and only time. As he began to trust us and to understand the rules of living in our household - no charging around like a lunatic, fun but structured play, loose lead walking, pack walking off-lead and general manners indoors and out - Jerry flourished. Once the excitement abated, he was a lovely, loyal little dog. I rehomed him with some friends once I felt he was ready, and he has lived out his days ever since, a treasured and well-behaved little dog.

Pupology

Chapter Nine – Rest Time and Relaxation

It is incredibly important for your puppy to learn to rest when you ask him to. Not only does this ensure he doesn't become over-tired and cranky, but it also helps you avoid the issue of separation anxiety further down the line. If your puppy doesn't learn to switch off and go to sleep when you ask, you are going to be at his mercy in these early weeks and find yourself only getting things done when he conks out naturally. Learning to switch off and rest on demand is an important skill for a young puppy to learn. Fail to teach him this and you could encounter lots of problems later on, most notably separation anxiety! We touched on this subject in Chapter Five, when talking about teaching your puppy to rest after a walk, but we will revisit it again, as it is such an important issue.

Before we get to teaching him how to rest when we ask, let's just think about noise in the household and how it affects your puppy. It may be there is just you and the pup, so your household is pretty quiet on the whole, or it may be you are a big family with a number of kids of different ages, coming and going at different times. Either way, I would strongly advise taking the same approach to being noisy around your puppy, whatever your circumstances. DON'T modify your noise in any way, no matter what the puppy is doing, keep it natural. In particular, don't creep around the house when your puppy is resting! Having a dog that can switch off no matter what is going on is far preferable to having a dog who is disturbed by every little noise. So, get into the habit of acting normally no matter what your puppy is doing. You want your puppy to be bomb-proof, so if you drop something on the floor or slam a door by accident your puppy learns that it is no big deal. He might lift his head to take a look, but he should go back to resting again right away. DON'T make a big fuss of your puppy if he seems alarmed at a sudden noise. Yes, the noise will initially startle him, but if YOU act as if it isn't a big deal and stay relaxed, he will learn to view sudden noises that way too. Think ahead to Bonfire Night, New Year's Eve, Diwali or even a loud thunderstorm. These events can be a nightmare for owners with noise-sensitive dogs.

The absolute WRONG thing to do when your puppy is startled by a loud noise is molly-coddle him, saying in a baby voice "It's ok, there's nothing to be scared of". This is HUMAN INSTINCT not dog instinct! You want to reassure him and tell him it's ok. Yes, that is what you MEAN, but in his brain you are sharing what we dog behaviourists call "weak energy" with him in a moment of stress. Pity, guilt and anxiety are all weak energies in nature and a puppy is not programmed genetically to follow weak energy, he is programmed to follow calm, confident energy, so if you want him to follow your lead when something scares him, it is important to be calm and confident and show him YOU AREN'T BOTHERED by the sudden noise and if HE is bothered, he needn't worry because you are there to take charge of the situation. It will become apparent that adopting this mindset is vital to raising a confident, balanced dog. If you share weak energy at a time he is stressed AND shower him with affection, not only are you showing him you aren't fit to lead (which means HE will have to step up and lead himself and follow his instincts to fight or to flee), but you are also telling him it is OK to be in this state of mind when he is worried about something. Think of that team captain analogy. You wouldn't want your team captain to be falling apart in a crisis, would you? No, you would respond far better to calm, confident leadership when it really matters! You should adopt this approach in any situation where your puppy is scared or unsure, not just with loud noises. Remember, giving him affection or pity when he is scared will not help him. He needs calm support in these moments.

Case Study 1: Yapping at Every Sound!

Herbie's owners contacted me because their young puppy was driving them mad with his constant barking. Every little sound seemed to trigger him, whether it be someone talking in the street, the bin-men emptying bins, the postman or a thump from the neighbours next door (their house was semi-detached). He never seemed to fully relax, even when he appeared to be asleep. The slightest sound would have him jumping up and reacting vocally. As you can imagine, this was putting a lot of stress on the family. They had tried distracting him with treats and keeping the curtains closed during the day but nothing was working. They kept finding themselves losing their temper in frustration and would then feel guilty at doing this!

He hadn't always been like this. His owners told me that when he was a very young puppy, he had been fine. Yes, he would bark a little at the doorbell or when the post came through the letterbox, but he stopped quickly when told to. The problem had escalated when he hit 5 months or so and progressively got worse from then onwards. The reactivity to noise struck me as a guarding problem. Herbie was alerting his owners of perceived danger outside the house. It is completely natural for a dog to alert its pack to danger and I personally think it is a good thing that our dogs alert us when someone is at our front door or appears unexpectedly in our back garden! So long as they stop barking when asked! Herbie's owners had not taught him which noises to react to and which noises to ignore. You might think there is no need to do this, and with some dogs there isn't, but in Herbie's case, the inconsistent approach to dealing with his unwanted barking (first treats, then hiding the threat behind curtains and sometimes shouting in frustration) simply confused the puppy. There wasn't a calm, consistent approach to handling unexpected noise. Herbie was not being given clear leadership when he perceived a threat, and consequently his default reaction each time was to deal with the threat himself. In other words, his dog instinct kicked in - GET RID OF IT! His humans weren't dealing with it, so he had to.

If Herbie had been taught from a young puppy to alert his owners when he heard the doorbell with a couple of barks and then be quiet, but NOT to alert his owners to any other noises he hears whilst in the house, he would have quickly learnt to ignore external noises. So that is what I had to do - I had to take him back to the beginning. I commonly call this rebooting the dog, as I am teaching him a new equation for situations that replaces the old unwanted equation. Firstly, I taught him that he could bark a couple of times when he heard the doorbell or a knock on the door, but when I said "Thank You", he had to be quiet. I did this using the Blocking & Claiming technique explained previously in Chapter 7. As usual with my training, no treats were involved. Putting an exclusion zone in front of the front door area meant that Herbie could run into this area when he heard the bell or a knock, but as soon as I entered it and asked him to leave with my body, he would enter a calm state of mind and acknowledge that the area and anything beyond it belonged to me. If he didn't calm down and he resumed barking, I could intervene with a verbal cue (e.g. "Ah, Ah"), praising him calmly when he stopped. I would then go back to *answering the door. Work started with him on a puppy line so that I could easily keep control of where he went and make sure he didn't rush from the front door to the sofa by the window. Then as he got the hang of what I wanted, the line was dropped on the floor and eventually removed altogether, when I felt the new equation for the front door was fully embedded.*

This exercise was then repeated in other areas where he was triggered to bark - the front windows of the house, the wall adjoining the neighbours, the back windows, and the back door of the house, except this time there was no "Thank You" involved - I didn't thank him for alerting me because I didn't want to be alerted when he heard noises in these areas. Instead, I calmly blocked & claimed each area until he moved away from it and ceased barking. The equation I was putting in his brain was that it was not his job to guard these locations. Similarly, if he wasn't anywhere near any of these places, but still barked at a noise outside, I would quickly intervene with a verbal cue, and praise him calmly as soon as he stopped the noise. All these practices ensured that Herbie's default equation for outside noise changed from excitement and barking to quiet acknowledgement. It's a bit like living next to a railway line. You really notice the sound of the trains going past when you first move in, but your brain soon learns to filter out the noise until you don't notice it at all. All I was asking Herbie to do was filter out external noises because it wasn't his job to react to them, it was mine/his owners!

Most puppies are, by nature, excitable. And we love them for it. It's why they are incredibly cute and so much fun to be around. But there will be times when you wish your puppy would just switch off and relax for a bit. Many owners believe that the only way to ensure that their puppy will relax and give them some much needed time off, is to give their puppy a load of exercise so that they conk out for a while. This does indeed work for many dogs, but we do have to be careful in our puppy's early years about exercising too much, particularly in the first year when their bones are still growing. If you over-exercise your puppy this could lead to joint issues further down the line. Walking isn't the only way to tire him out, remember. Doing activities with him that require him to use his brain are also very tiring for him.

Being able to induce a state of calmness and relaxation in your dog whenever <u>you want</u> is a useful skill to have. This is a bit different from teaching your puppy to rest on his own in your home, like we talked about earlier. This is a skill that can be utilised in all sorts of different situations, particularly when your puppy or older dog becomes stressed by something. It is something I teach owners of anxious dogs who find it difficult to totally switch off, and I believe it to be a really useful skill for all dog owners to have. It is also very good for the human too! Indeed, this technique is used by many human therapists! I am going to share with you a version of this technique that I teach to induce a calm, relaxed mind in your puppy. However, before we get to this, let's think a little bit about OUR minds. We humans do have very busy minds on the whole. We are always thinking about things, whether it be mulling over the past or wondering about the future. Depending on our particular nature, we may be someone who worries a lot about stuff, or we might be a super-chilled individual who is fazed by very little. You may think this doesn't matter with respect to your puppy, but actually it does. Your puppy can't help but tune in to your mood, so if we are to induce a state of relaxation in our puppy, we first need to create a state of relaxation in ourselves. We need to quieten our mind.

You may be thinking I'm going to now start telling you to meditate and burn some smelly candles. Far from it! The method I teach involves using three of your key senses – sight, sound, and touch. We will get onto how in a moment. What we are aiming to do is to stop your brain having an active thought. It is very hard to have a conscious thought if you are concentrating on staring at something, whilst listening to a sound and also being aware of the feeling of touch. Your mind will simply be empty of thought when you are doing all three and your puppy will become aware of this and, no matter how lively a personality he is, he will find himself relaxing with you. This may take some time. Some puppies will relax very quickly, whilst some may take quite a while. Be patient and don't give up!

Your puppy will go through several stages of relaxation before he becomes fully relaxed. If, when you start the exercise, he is walking around, the first thing he will do is stop and sit down. He will then lie down but have his head up and his eyes open. Next, his eyes will get soft and sleepy and start to close. He will then place his head on the floor, and may open his eyes a little, but this will be followed by sleepy eyes. He will then roll onto his side, stretch out and appear to be asleep. Throughout this process he may lick his lips, yawn, scratch, twitch or even pace around the room, depending on how much pent-up energy he has in his body. But by the time he is fully "gone", there will be no tension left. You will know for sure when he has entered this state as you will be able to lift one of his legs and it will drop like a dead weight when you let it go, without him stirring!

So, let's get to the nitty gritty and teach you how to do this-relaxation exercise, which I call the Zen Technique. Firstly, find somewhere quiet where you aren't likely to be disturbed. Sit yourself down somewhere comfortable. It can be on the floor or on the sofa, it doesn't really matter. The first few times you give this a try, make sure your puppy is somewhere else – either asleep or with another member of the family somewhere else in the house. You don't want any distractions. Start the exercise by taking a nice deep breath and releasing it, dropping your shoulders and relaxing your facial muscles. You are going to be breathing calmly throughout and NOT holding your breath! Now find something small to stare at intently, preferably on the floor. It might be a speck of dirt, or a mark on your floor. It really doesn't matter. All that matters is that you stare at this tiny mark with laser-beam eyes and DON'T move your eyeballs! Keep staring and now listen to the sounds around you and pick one out to focus on. It may be that you can hear birdsong outside, or the hum of a radiator, or the ticking of a clock. Again, it doesn't matter what it is, all that matters is that you listen to that one sound intently. If there are no sounds in the room where you are, focus on the white noise you hear in your ear. Finally, you are going to lay your hand on your leg and be very aware of the feeling of that hand touching your leg. Focus on that sensation of touch intently. Keep breathing calmly throughout. If you are managing to do all three at once (or even just two, if it's easier), you should start to feel really relaxed, and maybe even a little tingly. If you are struggling, try half closing your eyes whilst you are staring. Some people find this helps. If a thought does pop into your head whilst you are doing the above, don't worry, just try to refocus on your senses. Practice this a few times on your own without your puppy. You only need to do it for a few minutes, your aim being to induce deep relaxation in yourself.

Now that you have mastered this, do it with your puppy in the room. He can be walking around freely when you start. It may be that if you are on the floor, he comes over and climbs on you, as he will be curious about what you are doing. Gently push him off. Don't look at him or talk to him. If he comes back on you again, keep repeating until he gets the message. Keep focussing on your three senses. What should happen is that he chooses to join you in this relaxation after some initially pacing or curiosity. See if he goes through the different stages I mentioned above. Enjoy the fact that you have created this lovely relaxing environment for him and are sharing mutual relaxation with him. If he goes right down to the stretching out on the floor, leave him like this for a few minutes, then move slightly so that he wakes up and looks at you (but stay nice and relaxed). This shows him that it is YOU that is creating this peacefulness! This is a really powerful thing for him to learn.

The first few times you try this, only do it for a very short time and then bring the exercise to a formal end by calmly placing your hand on his back (without stroking!) and say, "Well done, Buddy" (or whatever his name is). Then get up and act normally. This is the marker that the exercise is over. Why mark the end? Well, if you mark the start (with your deep breath and perhaps a chosen command, such as "Let's Relax" or "Let's Zen") and then mark the end, there will be no confusion in your puppy's mind as to what he should be doing.

As I mentioned above, I use this technique to teach owners who have dogs who find it very difficult to totally switch off. For whatever reason, they have learnt to always be on guard mentally. Being able to induce a state of calmness in a dog increases your chance of the dog actually listening to you in stressful situations. A dog can't listen to anything but its instincts when it is fearful or worried. Think about all those places where your puppy might get agitated or fearful. If you can master this relaxation technique, you can induce a state of calm in him quite easily wherever you are and he will be able to view the situation with different eyes, rather than panic. The key to mastering the Zen Technique is to take things nice and slow. Make sure you, the human, can easily induce this state in yourself first before trying it with your puppy. If you are struggling at all, the chances are that you are not fully emptying your mind. It does take a bit of practice to be able to do this. You may, indeed, find yourself trying to work out what stage your puppy has reached while you are doing the Zen, which obviously involves thinking! Don't worry about what your puppy is doing, just keep focussing on your three senses and you will get there. Once you have got the hang of the Zen Technique, try using it when you are out and about with your puppy whenever he seems a little unsure or stressed.

Case Study 2: Trauma At the Vets

One of my own dogs, my little chihuahua, is very nervous at the vet. The minute we get out of the car he is on alert, as he has already picked up the scent left by other nervous dogs who have been encouraged to pee before their appointment. He has also smelt the chemical smells emanating from the vets itself. Whilst over the years he has learnt to trust me to take care of him in this environment and no longer whines or barks in the waiting room, or bites the vet, he still can't help but be a slave to his fear and will start trembling violently as soon as we take a seat in the waiting room. He is a rescue so I don't know the history of his experience at the vet, but whatever happened, it has left him with a fear so deep that, although he does try, he can't stop the physical reaction to the environment. This is where the above relaxation technique comes into play. If I give him the signal that I am going to go into a deeply calm state (as described above, by taking a nice deep breath), within a minute or so he starts to calm too and the shaking lessens gradually until it stops completely. Once this happens, he starts to become curious about the environment, rather than being consumed by the trembling. He still doesn't exactly enjoy the experience, but his body is no longer flooded with adrenaline, which can only be a good thing!

One of the most common problems I get asked about as a behaviourist, and one of the hardest problems to fix is separation anxiety. I have touched on separation anxiety a number of times in earlier chapters, advising on ways in which to AVOID separation anxiety occurring in the first place with your puppy by teaching him how to relax on his own. If you are an owner of an older puppy who has already developed separation anxiety and have picked up this book in the hope that it will have the answer to solving this problem, you can try the relaxation techniques described above to help your puppy overcome this issue. You will only be able to master the issue of separation anxiety if your puppy is in a calm state of mind when you leave him on his own. He has to be calm when you leave and trust that you will return. Leave him in an anxious state and he will find it very hard to calm down naturally. His brain will be energised and he will have a lot of tension in his body. To relieve that tension he may chew objects, lick obsessively or bark. He definitely won't be calm and relaxed, and being without you will be horrible for him.

To help him with this, you will need to set aside a block of time to implement a phased approach to teaching your puppy to be comfortable with his own company. This may take some time, depending on how severe the problem is, but here's how the Zen Technique could be used in this situation. Send your puppy to his bed, stand next to him facing him and then say your chosen phrase (such as "Let's Zen"). Enter a Zen state yourself. If he tries to move off his bed, calmly guide him back to it and start again. Once he has fully relaxed in his bed (and this may take quite some time!), take a step back whilst maintaining your Zen state. If he moves, calmly return him to his bed without saying anything and start again. You can see why I say this can take a lot of time! Your aim is to show him that when you put him in his bed and ask him to Zen, you expect him to stay there in a calm state **NO MATTER WHERE YOU ARE IN THE ROOM** until you finish the exercise (by touching his back and saying "Well Done"),. You will start off small, by just moving a few steps away, and then as he gets the hang of what you want, you can move a little further away and start doing things in the room whilst he stays in his bed. You are working up to moving around the house and finally opening and shutting the front door without him leaving his bed. You are teaching him to relax in his bed when you ask him to and to trust you that you will come back if you move away from him, even if that means you have left the house!

Pupology

Chapter 10 – Visitors To Your Home

Your puppy is now settled in, and you have told all your friends and family that he has arrived. They can't wait to meet him and are lapping up all the pictures you are sharing of him. How you introduce him to people is entirely up to you, but there are some things you should bear in mind when you start letting people pet and cuddle him. First and foremost, has he shown any signs of being a little nervous around new people? If the answer is "No", then you have absolutely nothing to worry about, he is naturally trusting and inquisitive and will be fine being handled and petted by all your friends and family. But if the answer is "Yes", you want to take a little bit more care when making introductions, as thrusting a young puppy into the arms of strangers (remember, they are STRANGERS to him) could prove a bit overwhelming for him. Get it wrong and it could cause problems further down the line as he grows. Fear is behind most reactivity in dogs, in my experience, so it is very important to recognize early on if your puppy is a little shy. Take your time and ensure these initial introductions are done in a controlled way and you will help him develop into a balanced dog who trusts humans.

How can you tell if he is a bit nervous or highly strung at a young age? The obvious sign is if he backs off from being touched by a new person. Less obvious signs of nervousness are lip licking, yawning, a tense body and big wide eyes. Most puppies are quite happy to be stroked and fussed by anybody, but there are always exceptions to the rule. If your puppy is looking a little reluctant to be touched by a new person, ask the visitor to bunch their hand into a relaxed fist (i.e. roll up their fingers!), approach the puppy side-on and hold that hand a little distance away from the puppy. If he moves towards their hand, he is curious about their scent and they should let him have a sniff. They can then tickle him gently under the chin. However, if he moves away from their hand, they should NOT attempt to touch him, as he is a little unsure of them. They shouldn't take it personally; he is just a little shy.

Best thing to do is to ask them to sit down on the floor near the puppy, make sure they are fully relaxed and just observe him potter about. He can then approach in his own time, maybe just initially for a sniff of their feet or legs. Ask them to pop a puppy treat or two on the floor next to them and see if he will come to pick it up. Again, don't put any pressure on him. They can then hold one on their flat palm, as it rests on the floor and see if he takes it. Before you know it, he will be coming right up for a treat and they can now start gently stroking him with a finger under his chin or on his back. Tell all your visitors NOT to put their hand over his head, as this can scare a nervous puppy.

It really is a good idea to teach everyone you know, and particularly all children, that offering a relaxed hand to a dog sideways on, as described above, is the best way to say "Hello", no matter what age the dog is. It is not fair to put an animal under pressure by invading its space when, in its eyes, you are a complete stranger. Treat all animals with this sort of respect - offer your hand for a sniff and if they are unsure they will give you clear signals. Don't just thrust your hand at a dog, a cat, a horse or whatever and expect it to be happy about your attention!

Let's get back to visitors and your puppy. Another common thing behaviourists are asked to help with is excitement in the home, predominantly with regards to visitors. This might be the postman, the parcel delivery man or someone actually coming inside your home. It isn't surprising that puppies quickly learn that people coming through the front door equal excitement because visitors THEMSELVES are usually excited by the sight of a cute little puppy! Us owners are also excited to share our new arrival with the visitors and revel in the positive glow we feel when introducing our puppy for the first time to people. However, what starts as an innocent introduction in the early days, can quickly escalate into an annoying problem further down the line as the puppy grows. It's hardly the puppy's fault, is it? I mean, the humans actually fed the excitement by being excited themselves and giving the puppy loads of love and attention whilst it was bounding around beneath their feet and jumping up at them in an excited state of mind. So, the puppy is absolutely NOT TO BLAME for learning that humans visiting the house equal excitement. Your puppy is not being "naughty". Naughty is a human concept. So often I hear about a puppy

Visitors to Your Home

or dog being naughty, when in fact all it is doing is acting naturally in the circumstances.

To avoid this common problem of visitor excitement, you need to put a little effort in at the start when you first get the puppy. We will look at several scenarios in a minute and how to deal with them, but before we do that, let's remind ourselves how things look through the puppy's eyes (and ears!) The puppy hears a knock at the door or the ring of a bell. This noise alone will cause an escalation in activity in his brain. It may be that he has already learnt at the breeders that this noise equals bark, simply because his mother barked when she heard the doorbell at the breeder's house. On the other hand, if you are lucky, the puppy may not have learnt this yet and the noise simply grabs his attention at this point and he does nothing, other than look up, or perhaps trot to the door to investigate if he is loose in the house (another reason for using the puppy pen!). What happens next with the human is VERY IMPORTANT. When the human hears the knock/ring, their brain activity also increases i.e. they become alert to the sound. Their default response is to move towards the sound, often in a hurried way, and to open the door and say "Hi!" in an excited voice (if they know the person) or perhaps "Thank You" if it's the postman or delivery man with a parcel. A young puppy will FOLLOW THIS LEAD – if the human responds to the knock in a calm, leisurely way and simply saunters to the door without fuss, the puppy will calmly follow. If the human rushes to the door in an excited or worried manner, their puppy will be given the signal that there is something exciting (or potentially dangerous, if it has a nervous disposition) on the other side of the door. The puppy's state of mind will become more excited and the ultimate outcome of this is often a bark.

Let's take a brief moment to think about barking. Dogs don't just have one bark; they have many different types of barks. I am not going to delve into these here, because, hopefully, if you follow my advice, you won't end up with a dog that barks excessively. What I would say is that you should consider the fact that barking is often triggered by conflict within the dog's brain. A conflict could be a situation where the dog is trying to get rid of a perceived threat but is restrained by a lead, or get rid of a potential intruder, but is prevented from doing so by the presence of a solid barrier, such as a window or a door. Alerting a pack member to potential threats is instinctual to a dog and your puppy is no different. However, when it is VERY young the puppy relies on the older pack members to deal with these threats (we will talk about what happens to older puppies later on). YOU are that older pack member when your puppy first comes to live with you. If you are not bothered by that knock on the door, or that person walking past your house, your young puppy will get the message that people knocking or walking past your house aren't a threat. YOUR behaviour in these situations is what matters with a very young puppy, as he will learn from you what to do in different scenarios. So, let's consider some different scenarios where people are coming into your home.

Welcoming Visitors

We all want visitors to enjoy coming to our house, whether they are dog lovers or not. No-one wants to be that person whose friends avoid visiting because they are scared of the dog or hate having their clothes dirtied by them. Having a polite dog is easy to achieve if you start teaching your puppy from Day 1 that visitors should be treated with impeccable manners! Your puppy is welcome to mill around their feet when they arrive, but it is NOT allowed to put his paws on them. He must wait until he is invited for a pat or a cuddle before approaching the visitor. It is your job to teach your puppy this. You can't expect him to work this out for himself. He is a dog, remember, not a human!

The simplest way to teach this behaviour is to initially have your puppy on a lead when people come to your door. Alternatively, you can leave him in his puppy pen, but I prefer to teach puppies from a young age the front door protocol, rather than having to add an extra step in their education. Your front door is a very high value area to your puppy and becomes even more so once you start going for walks, and it is incredibly important for both safety and manners to teach your puppy that he must stay away from this door when it is open. You should be able to leave your front door open and go out to your rubbish bins or your car or to chat to a neighbour in the front garden and your dog stays inside without being told. This is very easy to do if you understand how dogs delineate territory. We have discussed this in Chapter 7 when talking about food and will use this to teach your puppy to stay back when the front door is opened. It is VERY hard for a young puppy to resist moving forwards towards a human on your doorstep who is cooing and exclaiming in delight at the sight of your cute puppy, so please make it easier for him by asking ALL visitors to IGNORE your puppy when you open the door and ask them to concentrate on you alone! If need be, put a sign on your front door to remind them! Make it clear to them that if they don't help with your puppy's training, they are the ones who are going to suffer in the end (along with the puppy!) when he has grown to full size and is jumping up at them every time they visit. Promise them that they will get their cuddles and play once they are inside the house, but that they must ignore the puppy at the front door and as they walk through your hallway.

I strongly suggest that you practise this exercise with a family member posing as the visitor a number of times BEFORE you start taking your puppy to the front door to meet real visitors. You may also find it easier to practise on a few internal doorways first, if you are worried about safety. Internal doors are easter to master as they are not as high value to a puppy as the doors that lead to the outside world. Using a family member initially at the front door will make it much easier for you, trust me. Your puppy needs to learn the physical actions and invisible boundaries before you put a real visitor into the mix. Later in this chapter, I will outline how to teach your puppy to behave around visitors when they are in the house. Here are the steps that you need to take to teach this door protocol.

Keep a slip/gundog lead (a lead that you can quickly drop over your puppy's head without having to faff around clipping it to his collar) by the front door out of reach of your puppy.

When the doorbell rings, calmly walk to the door without making any fuss. If your puppy is out of his pen at this moment, he will instinctively follow you to the door.

Take the slip lead and drop it over your puppy's head, securing the stopper so that it is held in place and he doesn't end up getting into a pickle with the lead. It doesn't need to be tight; you are simply going to be using this lead to guide him initially. You can now drop the lead on the floor. He may play with it, but don't worry too much about that for now.

In your mind, delineate an exclusion zone in your hallway IN FRONT OF THE DOOR. It may be that you have a handy radiator to use as the point beyond which the puppy ISN'T allowed. Or perhaps, the bannister post, or maybe a large doormat. The key is to make sure this imaginary line that the puppy must not cross is far back enough from the door to allow you to still have time to catch the puppy, should he make the wrong decision and run for the door. Whilst you will be starting with a lead on so that he can't run out, you will eventually be removing the lead and TRUSTING the puppy not to enter the exclusion zone.

Handy Hint – if you drive, think of the exclusion zone as being like the yellow box you get at some junctions. As a driver, you are only allowed to enter that box if the exit is clear. I like to use the yellow box analogy and get owners to imagine a yellow cross-hatched box on their floor. Their puppy will only be allowed to enter/pass through this box IF he has made eye contact with his owner, is in a calm state of mind **and** been given permission. If you struggle to imagine a yellow box, you could always go the whole hog and tape one out on your floor (if you haven't got carpet!).

Your puppy may well beat you to the front door and enter the exclusion zone in front of you. This is fine. What you are about to teach him is that he is allowed to go up to the front door when it is closed, but once YOU arrive at the door and move in front of him, you will expect him to move backwards to a respectful distance OUTSIDE of the exclusion zone and NOT re-enter it unless he is given permission. This may seem like a big ask but trust me, dogs do this all the time to each other, it is natural behaviour for them! They **claim** territory!

Once you arrive at the front door, pick up the lead and slide your body in front of your puppy so that you are between him and the door, using the lead to gently guide him back if he doesn't move of his own free will. DON'T USE YOUR HANDS. Remember, dogs don't have hands, they use their bodies to claim territory. If your puppy is very tiny, you may worry about standing on him, which is why we have the lead on to safely guide him back a little to allow you to get in between him and the front door.

Whilst you are doing all this, shout (not too dramatically, obviously) through the front door that you are just coming and are sorting out the dog! Again, you may want to put a notice on the front door, alerting any visitors that you are puppy training and ask them to be patient.

You now need to move calmly and confidently (with upright posture!) towards your puppy, using your body and the lead to move him backwards until he is outside the exclusion zone. Make sure he turns and WALKS AWAY from you the first few times you do this. If you are doing this correctly, he will turn eventually, even if you have to back him down the full length of the hall. If you run out of space, simply stand your ground until he sits and relaxes. Keeping one eye on him, return to the edge of your exclusion zone <u>the second</u> he turns and walks away. You are still holding the lead at this point. He should naturally stay back and be watching you by now.

If he takes a step forward, step towards him again to indicate that you don't want this, giving him a verbal warning such as "Ah, Ah" at the same time. He will quickly learn to stay where he is. If he doesn't stay where he is and re-enters the exclusion zone, you MUST keep repeating these actions until he gets the message that he isn't allowed in the zone. REMEMBER <u>NO TALKING</u> AT ANY TIME TO YOUR PUPPY, EXCEPT PERHAPS AN "Ah, Ah". YOU ARE DOING EVERYTHING WITH YOUR BODY!

Some puppies get it right away, others take a little longer. The calmer he is, the quicker he will get it, so remember to stay CALM AND CONFIDENT yourself. If you get frustrated and tense you won't succeed, as you will not be in a calm frame of mind and he will mirror this, as all young puppies do.

Once you are confident that he understands that you want him to stay back, you can drop the lead. If you aren't confident, DON'T drop the lead, as the last thing you want is the puppy running out of your open front door.

Now, I know what you are thinking at this point: "Flippin' heck, this seems like an awful lot of complicated work to get a puppy to stay away from a door". It DOES seem like a lot of work, but it really isn't, believe me, and it will bear MASSIVE fruits for you. Remember that homeless persons' dog? The one that didn't need to be given any direction or be kept on lead on that busy street? He learnt the "dog way" about what he could and couldn't do. Not because that homeless person is a skilled dog behaviourist. No. Because that homeless person inadvertently replicated the way the dogs communicate with each other about ownership of objects and territory. If that dog tried to crawl into the sleeping bag with wet paws, I can guarantee that he would have been moved out by the homeless person pretty swiftly and blocked from re-entering it, with no doubt some verbal noises going on during the process. The sleeping bag would be effectively "yellow-boxed". Same with any food sitting around. I can pretty much guarantee that there wouldn't have been any expensive dog treats involved - just simple body language and verbal interventions to get the message across. That is what you are doing with your puppy at the front door. You are saying "this is my territory and you don't enter it until I say so". But in order to teach him this, you have to ACT LIKE A DOG initially. You aren't a dog, remember, and he isn't expecting you to behave like one. Replicate the dog behaviour and he will soon realise that you are a DOG IN HUMAN FORM! This method translates to all sorts of situations (food, furniture, precious items, dangerous items, people, other dogs), so practice, practice, practice until you get it right!

You have now taught your puppy to stay out of the exclusion zone by the front door. Hopefully, your visitor hasn't given up the ghost and gone away.

Put your hand on the latch and open the door, keeping one eye on your puppy. As I mentioned before, if you don't fully trust him yet, keep a hold of the lead as you open the door. If he moves forward into the exclusion zone, swing back towards him with your body and move him out of the box. Your front door will be open by now, but you are still policing it!

If your puppy has remained back, calmly invite your visitor in and shut the front door, making sure that you keep your body in between your visitor and the puppy. Your visitor is now in the exclusion zone! The message to your puppy is simple - it doesn't matter who is in the exclusion zone, if he has been asked to stay out of it, he must.

Now lead your visitor past the puppy, asking them to walk straight past without making eye contact or talking to him, whilst you close the front door and walk down the hallway. Your puppy should just calmly follow you both, picking up the scent of the visitors as he does.

Practice with the lead on until you are sure you have full control of your puppy, then try the exercise with the lead trailing on the ground and eventually no lead at all.

Initially you will be using your body movements to teach your puppy to stay back from the door and your visitors. Once you are confident that he has learnt where he is supposed to be, you can start to add a noise cue (a verbal intervention) such as "Ah, Ah" or "Hey" at the same time as physically blocking & claiming. This allows you to eventually drop the physical movements and simply influence your puppy with a verbal intervention alone.

If you tried the technique and the above didn't happen, look at each of the steps and work out where you went wrong. Were you acting too jerkily and rushing? Remember, calm confidence at all times. Slow things down if necessary. Practice with a family member until you can do all of the above in a nice, unhurried fluid way. It may be that you feel the urge to issue commands to your puppy whilst doing all the above. I would strongly urge you to leave speech out of things to begin with. The timing of commands is very important, and it is easy to get it wrong and teach your puppy the WRONG behaviour without meaning to. Dogs can't talk, so dropping speech and using SOUNDS instead, gives you a better chance of success. You can put speech back in once your puppy understands what you are asking of him physically (i.e. once you have imprinted the physical boundaries of the exclusion zone in his brain).

I find when teaching this method that whilst the puppy learns very fast, the owner takes an awful lot longer! Why? Because it isn't natural for us humans to behave in this way, but it IS natural for dogs. This is why it is so important for the owner to replicate <u>exactly</u> what a dog would do in this situation. A dog would BLOCK the other dog from entering the space or CLAIM IT BACK if the other dog had already entered it. If you can master this way of getting visitors into your house, your puppy will NOT learn to jump up at them when they come through the front door. He will learn to calmly follow you and your visitors down the hallway into your house/flat. So next, we want to look at introducing your puppy to these visitors in a polite way once they are inside the house. No point in getting your visitors through the door and then your puppy leaping all over them once you have got into the living room! You want your puppy to learn to have manners wherever people are in the house.

Introducing Your Puppy to Visitors Inside the House

It's time to let your puppy meet your visitors. Let's look at two different scenarios, the first with the puppy loose in the house and the second with the puppy contained in a room/puppy pen.

Once your visitors are through your door and everyone has walked into the room where the introductions are to take place, whether it be the living room or the kitchen, ask everyone to sit down somewhere (but not on the floor at this point). The puppy should be milling around in the room with the humans. The puppy shouldn't be super excited – you have avoided creating that state of mind by dealing with the front door the correct way – just curious and happy to be amongst the humans. Get one person at a time to tap their leg and call him over, asking the person NOT to touch his head for a pat, but instead to pat him on the side of his body once he has had a sniff of their hand. This will encourage him to lean against their legs for affection and NOT JUMP UP. THIS is the behaviour we want to teach your puppy for new visitors – calmly go up to them, lean against their legs, and they will give you a stroke on your side.

The main reason puppies learn to jump up at people is that people bend forwards over the puppy with their arm outstretched to touch the puppy's head. This causes the puppy to look up and often reach up to the incoming hand, by putting its paws on the person's leg. It is much better to teach a puppy to come in sideways to a human and be patted on the side. Dogs meet each other side on. Yes, they give a quick glance at the other dog's face but then they immediately go to its bottom for a sniff. This is TOTALLY NATURAL INSTINCTIVE BEHAVIOUR! If you think it is disgusting, then you may struggle to be a dog owner and may end up causing issues with your dog. It is the most natural thing in the world for a dog to do when it meets another dog. They are checking out the other dog's scent. If you prevent him doing this, he will be unable to make an accurate assessment of the other dog and consequently won't necessarily trust him. This can be a big problem with naturally anxious puppies, as the knee jerk reaction of not trusting is to tell the other dog to stay away and that is often shown with a growl or a snap. You do not want your puppy to learn to do this.

Visitors to Your Home

You want your puppy to learn to be balanced and social with other dogs.

Once the puppy has met a person and been rewarded for his polite, calm approach with a nice pat on the side, the person can then get down on the floor and play with the puppy, should they so wish. A polite introduction is rewarded by some playtime. Try very hard to ensure that your visitors don't charge into your house and start playing excitable games with the puppy from the minute they arrive. You do not want your puppy to get the equation into his brain that "visitors = excitement". If you teach your puppy that visitors equal excitement from the minute they arrive, you are more likely to have issues further down the line with unwanted behaviour such as jumping up, mouthing visitors, sticking their nose in handbags, stealing their shoes etc. Similarly, don't give your visitors handfuls of treats to feed to the puppy. There is absolutely no need for that and, again, it may create issues going forwards, particularly with very greedy dogs. You don't want the equation in your puppy's brain to be that "visitors = food" or you may create a food pest. Manners are essential around visitors and it is your job to teach your puppy this by getting introductions right from the outset.

If your puppy is in his own room or in a puppy pen when someone comes into the house, the protocol is very similar. Ask your visitor to sit down before you let the puppy out of his pen or his room. Then follow the above advice. It may be you have a particularly excitable puppy and once let loose he charges at your visitors. If this is the case, pop him on a lead and keep him back from your visitor until he has calmed down, no matter how long this takes. You can "block & claim" your visitor (i.e. put them in a "yellow box" exclusion zone!) to speed things up, but this is entirely up to you. Whatever you choose to do, DO NOT let your puppy go towards the visitor until he has calmed right down. Wait without saying anything until he looks up at you and then calmly say "On you go" or "Go say hello," or whatever comes to mind. A dog that doesn't look at you to see what he is supposed to do in a situation isn't mentally connected to you. If you start from Day 1 with your puppy showing him that you expect him to check with you before he does something, you will find the whole journey of raising him so much easier.

One last word on visitors. It is useful to know how to deal with your puppy if you have someone visiting who is scared of dogs. In addition to doing all of the above, you can help a nervous guest by giving them a little helpful guidance. It's easier said than done to relax around animals when you are scared of them, so telling your guest to just relax and ignore your puppy may not always help. Try asking them to do this instead, no matter how daft it may sound. This is advice you can also give to visiting children or, indeed, children you come across in the park. Ask them to pretend they are an invisible super-hero. Sound bonkers!? Trust me, it works, particularly with kids. It can be a bit harder to get an adult to embrace this idea but give it a try!

Case Study 1: No Rules means Unruly!

Lola was a very friendly puppy and fairly well-behaved. Her owners got in touch because as she grew bigger and bigger, her excitement when visitors came to the house meant that they had been forced to install stair gates across various doorways in order to enable friends to enter the house without being mugged by Lola! If she heard the doorbell, she would rush barking to the front door and had to be forced aside in order for her owners to get the door open. No sooner were the visitors in the house than she was leaping up at them and scratching their legs. Bruises and scratches became such an issue as Lola got bigger, that her owners had taken to locking her behind the stairgate whenever someone arrived at the house.

Lola's bad manners around visitors had happened because when she was a tiny puppy, no rules and boundaries had been put in place as to how to greet visitors. Naturally, her cuteness meant that everyone who came in bent down and cooed at her, touching her, and marvelling at how gorgeous she was. She got used to pushing her face into human faces and having her head patted. Her owners basked in unbridled pride whilst this was happening. Who wouldn't? By the time the behaviour had become a serious issue, Lola had an equation firmly engraved in her brain; visitors equal excitement and getting up on my back legs! The staircase did prevent this happening, allowing visitors to enter the house safely, but as soon as she was set free to meet them, the old behaviour resurfaced. All the stair gate was doing was keeping her away from the visitors, it wasn't fixing the underlying problem that visitors equalled excitement. It was also creating a physical barrier that was making her even more frustrated.

We had to start again by teaching Lola a new equation for visitors. Visitors must equal a calm, sociable but polite greeting. As with all behavioural resets, the first step was to deal with the initial trigger, the doorbell. Lola needed to learn that the doorbell equalled "let me know someone is there but then calm down". With Lola behind her stairgate, we started work on returning her to a calm state once she had acknowledged the doorbell ringing. We didn't mind her barking, as that is a useful alert for the owner and a deterrent for potential burglars, but we did want her quietening down as soon as we asked. The blocking & claiming technique was used to move her back from the stairgate into a calm state after a couple of initial barks. Once she had learnt this reaction, the stair gate was left open and she was allowed to approach the front door whenever the doorbell rang. However, as soon as her owners claimed the space in front of that door, she was expected to calm down again and wait at a respectful distance. This was all done without issuing commands, by the way, or using treats as a reward. We needed Lola to be maintaining a calm state of mind when asked, not have her waiting in a pent-up state for a release or a treat! Repetition of this new protocol, which involved staying back and staying calm whilst the door was opened put a new equation in Lola's brain for the doorbell ringing and people entering the house. Guests were asked to walk right past her as they entered (effectively ignoring her) and she was then welcome to calmly follow the humans into a room in the house, without being told. At this point, the guests were invited to say a calm "Hello" by patting their leg and inviting Lola to move in next to them for a pat on her side, or even lie down for a tummy tickle. Removing her desire to reach up towards human faces and instead lean into their legs for affection, removed Lola's desire to get up onto her back legs when a visitor was present. I can report that she happily adopted this new behaviour, and the stair gates were removed.

Case Study 2: Child Scarer!

Lance was a lovely dog, but he was big breed and very bouncy. He was also a greedy fellow and having been raised in a household with several young children, had learnt early on as a puppy that small humans equalled a ready supply of food, whether deliberately shared or dropped. He had also been reward-based trained using dog treats. It was clear that food was a major source of excitement to Lance. Whilst this wasn't a big issue when he was a small puppy, it became increasingly problematic as he grew. Lance not only viewed the family children as a food source, but also viewed any visiting children in the same way! And his ever-increasing size meant that some of the visiting children had become scared of him. Lance had to be shut away when visiting kids came around to play or for tea as, whenever the children were eating any food, he would loiter, drool and sometimes even snatch the food out of the children's hands, particularly the younger ones. Whilst this was scary enough when he had his tiny puppy teeth, once he got his big adult teeth this became even more alarming for the children and some, in particular, became very scared of him. Lance needed to learn manners around both the family children and any visiting children.

My first step was to teach Lance some basic food protocol. It didn't matter WHAT food he was around, whether dog food or human food, he was expected to remain calm and not touch it without permission. Again, I used the blocking & claiming technique to show him that I owned all food in the house, whether it was a treat in my hand, a sandwich on a plate on the coffee table, a piece of biscuit on the floor that the kids had dropped, or a piece of cheese on the side in the kitchen. EVERYTHING EDIBLE WAS OUT OF BOUNDS FOR LANCE! As well as showing him that all food belonged to me, I also did some work with him to change the equation in his brain that food equalled excitement. I needed him to learn that food equalled calm respect. This is simple to do. Pop a dog treat in your closed hand and hold your arm out to the side so that the treat is far away from you. If your dog is food obsessed and excited, he will stare at your hand in an excited state of mind. Do nothing. Wait patiently until he realises staring at the hand isn't going to make the food appear. We are waiting for him to give you full eye contact. He may start with the odd glance at you but hold firm and still do nothing. You want him to work out for himself that he needs to come all the way down the excitement ladder to calm respect before he gets the treat. He needs to have a relaxed body, soft eyes, relaxed ears and if he sits down and pushes his hips out to the side, even better. He doesn't need to lie down, but if he does, that's great, although his body must still be fully relaxed. When he is calmly looking you in the eye with a totally relaxed body, you can CALMLY give him the treat. REPEAT, REPEAT, REPEAT!

Back to Lance. I taught him to be respectful around food and calm around food and then I showed his owner how to "claim" any children in the house, both the family members and visiting kids (again by "yellow boxing" them). It was the owners' job to advocate for the children as they were of various ages, with some still quite young. I showed the older children how to advocate for themselves by claiming their personal space, so that they too could communicate effectively with Lance if they were eating.

They simply had to move towards him if he came too close. Remember, this was done under my supervision when I deemed it safe to do so. He soon got the message and was able to be trusted around food and children and no longer scared anyone.

Pupology

Chapter 11 – First Trip to the Vet

One of the first big outings your puppy will have will be his trip to the vet to have his next set of inoculations and to be microchipped. Having your puppy vaccinated is something I would strongly recommend. Whilst this is, obviously, a personal choice and there will be some dog owners that don't agree with vaccination, I am personally of the mind that vaccination is a good thing. Most dog sitters and kennels will not board a dog who is not fully vaccinated, as it puts other dogs in their care at risk. You should have been informed by your breeder what vaccination course your puppy is on and how many more vaccines he needs and when. You should book this next vaccination with your chosen vet as soon as you get your puppy home. Your puppy SHOULD NOT walk on the ground outside your home until he is fully vaccinated. This is to protect him from diseases passed on by other dogs. However, it is fine for him to associate with your existing dog if you have one, provided that dog is fully vaccinated. His early vaccinations should give him enough protection from animals that enter your garden, such as foxes, so it is fine to take him outside into your garden supervised.

I can't stress enough that this first visit to the vet is going to set the tone for future visits so you need to try as hard as possible to get it right! A young puppy is protected initially from disease in his first few weeks of life by immunity passed onto him through his mother's milk. At between 6 to 9 weeks old, he will need to start his vaccinations and the breeder will likely start this process, so he should have already been to the vet by the time you get him. However, he will have been quite young and will have been with his littermates at the time, so there will have been lots of distractions for him. It is unlikely that this visit will have set him up to be fearful of vets. We want this to continue, so what happens on YOUR first visit to the vet with him is very important.

Let's stop and think about this for a moment. Why do so many dogs become fearful of a trip to the vet? Is it inevitable? The answer is, no, it isn't. Your dog may not necessarily enjoy visiting the vet, but it is perfectly possible to get him to tolerate it and not turn into a Tasmanian devil or a gibbering wreck every time you take him. It is we humans who create problems with vet visits by OUR reactions when our puppy shows signs of stress.

On that first visit a number of things are going to happen which will have an impact on future visits. For starters, let's remember that he interprets the world through his NOSE initially, and even before you have set foot in the vet, he is going to be picking up the scent of a lot of dog pee from the surrounding pavements, even though you are carrying him in your arms. This dog pee tells your puppy a lot and it will often have been left by a dog that was in an anxious state when it peed (this wee will smell different to the wee of a relaxed happy dog, due to the chemicals it contains)! As soon as you enter the vets, your puppy will again be bombarded by a variety of smells and different energies, including fear and anxiety from other animals and humans in the waiting room. It is vitally important that YOU stay relaxed and confident as you enter the waiting room. Your puppy may be absolutely fine, and if he is, you have nothing to worry about at this point. But if he is unsettled or nervous, the key signs being lip licking, yawning or shaking, DON'T be tempted to smother him in love and feel sorry for him. If you share this state of mind with him at this moment, firstly you are showing him you aren't fit to lead in this moment (so he will have to rely on himself) and secondly if you stroke him and praise him, you are telling him that it is OK to feel frightened and nervous, whereas what you actually want to happen is for him to COPE with these feelings by relying on YOU to take care of him. Think of when you first went to the dentist with your mum or dad. That whirr of the drill, the other scared children, the smell of the antiseptic. All these things probably put you on edge and made you scared. If your parent was calm, supportive and didn't make a big fuss, you would trust them to take care of you and make sure everything was ok. Do the same for your young puppy - give him calm support by holding him firmly but in a relaxed manner close to your body and breathe nice and deeply.

Your vet will give him a thorough check over before he is vaccinated and microchipped and this is a great time to observe how to look at his teeth and check other parts of his body. Watch carefully what the vet does. Doing this regularly in your home without fuss gets him used to being handled by other dog professionals, whether it be the vet or the groomer, so do get into the habit of doing this. Try to check the following each day or every few days from the very moment you bring him home. Before you start handling him, make sure you are CALM AND RELAXED! Drop those shoulders, relax those facial muscles and take a nice relaxing deep breath. Sit with him on the floor and beckon him to you. Don't chase after him. You want him to willingly join you when asked. There is no need to use treats. Now do the following:

Whilst stroking him, lift his ears (if they are floppy) and gently run your finger around the inside of them (obviously, don't poke your finger in his ears, just get him used to having the inside of his ears touched without fuss). As a very young puppy, he really shouldn't mind you doing this. His mum will have licked his ears regularly so having them touched should already feel like a pleasant thing for him.

Now gently wipe your fingers (clean, obviously!) over his eyes so that he isn't alarmed by this happening either. You may want to get a piece of damp cotton wool and gently wipe this over his eyes to remove any tear stains.

Gently open his mouth and run a finger around his gums. Lift his gums to look at his back teeth. You can talk to him all the time you are doing this, but use a calm, soothing voice.

Try opening his mouth a little wider too, so you can have a look deeper into his throat. This isn't something he will have experienced from his mother, so he may be surprised at you doing this, but again, it is important he gets used to it. It is much easier to get a tablet into a dog by popping it down his throat than trying to hide it in his food (they invariably eat everything BUT the tablet!), so having his mouth opened like this will teach him to trust you to do this, should you need to pop a tablet in at a later date. If you do have to give him a tablet at any point, open his mouth wide, drop the tablet to the back of his throat, then gently hold his jaws closed and tickle his throat. This will prompt him to swallow. Immediately release him once he has swallowed and give him calm praise.

Moving down his back, have a good old feel of all of his body for any lumps and bumps. Familiarise yourself with his body, so that you can spot anything unusual further down the line once he has started going outside (like ticks or grass seeds or insect bites).

Lift his tail to have a look at his bottom. If he is long haired, get into the habit of doing this regularly as he may get little bits of poo stuck in his fur and this can be uncomfortable for him. You can snip this out with a pair of safe scissors (get some dog grooming ones) when it dries.

Now on to his legs. Run your hands up and down his legs and lift each one up and gently bend it back and forth. You will know for sure if his joints are sore for any reason, as this action will trigger a squeal or a yelp if he is injured.

Finally, the paws. Dogs have very tickly feet so most don't like having their paws examined, but this is one of the most common places for your puppy to get injured when you are out on a walk. There are likely to be times when you have to pick a thorn out of his pad, or remove some sticky buds from between his paws, so getting him used to having his paws touched is very important. Lift his leg and feel between his pads, spreading his toes as you do this. He may pull back, but just relax and pause for a second if he does, before continuing. He may try to mouth you. Again, if he does this, pause and relax until he stops mouthing, all the time keeping a gentle hold of his paw, and then continue. You are teaching him to trust you to do something he isn't keen on. Acknowledging that he doesn't like it is vital. That is what the pause is for. It's an acknowledgement. BUT it is also vital not to give up if he shows signs he doesn't like it. Why? Because if you stop when he shows signs he is uncomfortable, such as squirming or mouthing, you will simply teach him to do these things each time you try to examine him, and this could escalate to him actually nipping you or even growling as you approach, which you really don't want.

Let's get back to the vet now. Once the vet has given him the once over, it will be time for the dreaded needle. Some puppies don't even notice the needle being inserted, but if yours does and squeals, remember it is YOUR reaction to his pain which is going to set the bar for how he behaves next time he is in the consulting room. So, stay calm and matter-of-fact and DON'T smother him with love and pity after his vaccination! He will have forgotten about it in a matter of seconds, so you should too. The microchip needle has to be fairly large and can be quite an unpleasant experience for your puppy, so be prepared for him to be a little distressed by this, but remember to be calm, relaxed and supportive in this moment and afterwards. Some puppies don't notice the needles at all, so don't assume it is going to be a nightmare and go in there in a fearful/anxious state of mind, as you will put your puppy on edge before the vet has even touched him!

All staff at the vets love a new puppy, so encourage as many as possible to give him a pat and a cuddle after the vet has finished with him. If they offer him a treat, let him have it. Finish your vets trip on a positive note and leave in a calm, relaxed frame of mind. Do this and keep doing this each time you come and your puppy will hopefully avoid developing vet fear!

Case Study: Terrified of Touch

Bailey's owners called me because she had a terrible fear of the vet. She could cope with being in the waiting room, but when the vet came to touch her, she would go ballistic and have to be muzzled. Naturally, this was very distressing for all concerned and the vet found it difficult to examine her fully as she was so traumatised by the whole experience. Her owners reported that she had been fine as a very young puppy when she had her vaccinations, but it was after the microchipping that the problems first started. She didn't react well to the big needle and naturally, her owners had given her lots of comfort and love when they saw her so distressed. The next time they took her to the vet, for another ailment, she started shaking the minute they opened the car boot and continued to shake the whole time they sat in the waiting room. She wasn't interested in taking treats at this point, she was too scared, so they were unable to distract her. When the vet tried to examine her, she growled at him, hence the muzzle being deployed.

In order to help Bailey, it wasn't just a case of helping her cope whilst in the room with the vet, she needed help before she had even got out of the car. She needed to be in a following state of mind at all points of the visit, so I showed her owners how to spot when her anxiety kicked in (indicators being lip licking, yawning, widening eyes and tension in her body), to acknowledge to her that they were aware of how she felt (by relaxing and focussing their attention on her but NOT petting or consoling her), and then for them to intervene with a gentle noise and share relaxation with her until she returned to a calm state (through using deep breathing and the zen technique). I encouraged them to drive to their vet regularly and do this, without even getting her out of the car. Next step was to have her come out of the car and sniff around the area outside the vets, again without actually going in and again, intervening whenever her body language showed her brain activity was escalating and the nervousness was kicking in. I suggested that they carry something tasty with them and share it with her when she was in a calm state of mind. This was NOT to distract her; we were teaching her to accept the vets surroundings and smells. The use of food was to cement her trust in us at that moment. It was also to help her owners feel more confident - she was unable to eat when stressed, so her taking food gently was a sign that her mind was in a better state and so THEY felt that they were helping her and making a difference. It was important to help them not feel guilty about vet visits, and their delight in her eating was helping with this.

I suggested that, going forward, they arrange with the receptionist that Bailey wait outside the vet's premises, rather than being in the waiting room, to minimise the influence of other waiting animal's fear on her state of mind. When she was called, her owners were to take her straight in with no fuss, adopting a calm and confident demeanour as they did so. She was fearful when she first went into the room, but her owners remembered to do their breathing exercises and focus on being calm and confident in the presence of the vet. I can report that, whilst still not happy about being examined, she looked to her owners for support and lent into their bodies during the examination, rather than focussing on the vet. She endured his touch for their sake, as she was now trusting them to take care of her, rather than feeling the need to take care of herself by warning the vet off with growling.

It is sometimes hard to know when a visit to the vet is needed, outside of these routine vaccination visits. It is inevitable that your puppy will have things happen to him at some point which might be a cause for concern and require a visit to the vet. Having owned four dogs so far throughout my life, along with numerous other types of pets, and also been a professional dog walker for a number of years, I am going to share with you my views on when a visit to the vet is necessary, and when, perhaps you can trying dealing with your dog at home yourself. Do remember, these are MY views based on my own experience with my own and my clients dogs and if you are in any doubt at all, ALWAYS phone the vet.

Tummy Upsets

These are quite common in puppies and aren't normally a major cause for alarm. It is inevitable that your puppy will swallow something at some point that doesn't agree with him. You'd be hard pushed to find any dog owner whose dog has never had a tummy upset. A tummy upset will either make your puppy vomit or have diarrhoea or both. I could write a whole chapter on this, but you will probably just want to know when you should be concerned. There is a big difference between your puppy throwing up once and repeatedly throwing up, or having a soft poo once versus having constant diarrhoea. The biggest red flag is when vomiting and diarrhoea occur at the same time, as puppies get dehydrated very quickly and dehydration should be taken very seriously. On the subject of diarrhoea (lovely!), how exactly is this defined? According to the kennel club, diarrhoea is unformed or loose stools, usually occurring in large amounts and/or more often than usual. My personal view is that a "good poo" can be picked up in its entirety with a poo bag without leaving any mess behind. The more mess left behind the looser the poo, until you get to full-blown diarrhoea, which is pure liquid. Charming. But essential to be aware of. Losing fluids from either end for a sustained amount of time is a reason to call the vet. However, if your puppy has one dodgy poo and then nothing else happens, he has probably just eaten something that mildly disagrees with him. Keep a close eye on him and if there is no vomiting, he will most likely recover on his own. If things are coming out both ends repeatedly you MUST call your vet.

If you find your puppy's stools are persistently soft, it may be that he has some sensitivity to an ingredient in his regular food. How you deal with this is up to you. You could experiment by changing the brand, choosing a brand with one key ingredient absent (e.g. chicken) and see if this makes a difference, but do make sure you do this gradually over a couple of days, phasing in the new brand. You could see if a particular type of puppy treat is causing the loose stool, so again switch to some that are free of one key ingredient for a while. Or you could take him to the vet and have him screened for allergies. Normal poo helps empty your puppy's anal glands each time he goes to the toilet. If his poo is repeatedly too soft, this could result in impaction in these glands.

Anyone who owns a dog will tell you that they do vomit from time to time. Sometimes inexplicably! And then they are absolutely fine! Again, with your puppy, just keep an eye on him if he vomits. If it continues over a number of hours, again this is a red flag, due to potential dehydration. If it has blood in it, this is a big red flag. Red flag = call the vet! Every owner will find their own method of dealing with tummy upsets. My preferred one is to offer my poorly dog tiny meals, say five times, over the course of the day and see if he or she tolerates this. I don't follow the route of chicken/fish and rice, as is often commonly advised, but prefer to keep my dog on the food it normally eats, but just offer it in much smaller portions. I have found that this works with both of my dogs. If they don't want to eat, that is fine, so long as they are still drinking water. Dogs can go days in the wild without eating, so don't assume that your puppy will starve if he misses a few meals, just ensure that he has ready access to fresh water at all times and that he is drinking it.

Cuts and Grazes

Hopefully you won't ever have to deal with a major injury either in the home or when out with your puppy. You are likely, however, to have to deal with a minor cut or sore patch. You will know if something is hurting your puppy because he will be nibbling or licking a particular spot more frantically than he would during normal grooming. He may stop dead and refuse to walk, particularly if the injury is to one of his pads. You should have taught him from Day 1 to allow you to inspect his body all over without fuss, so if he does appear injured, just do a thorough check of the area and remove any small things that might be hurting him, like thorns or grass seeds. If you can see glass, only remove it if the shard is very tiny, as if it is large and deeply embedded, removal may trigger more significant bleeding. In this instance, if you are in your house, get your first aid box, cover the injury with a wound dressing, kept in place by pet-friendly bandage, and take him straight to a vet. If you are on a walk, the same applies. If you are in the habit of carrying a bag for your poo bags, water bottle, car keys etc, pop some vet bandage and a pack of wound dressing in there so that you always have something to hand in emergencies. If he starts limping when out on a walk, check his paws to see if he has anything stuck in them and if he doesn't, it may be that he has simply landed awkwardly whilst running around. Pause for a minute, give the sore leg a gentle rub and then encourage him to move on. Nine times out of ten, this will do the trick and he will running around normally again.

Sore Eyes

Your puppy may get sore eyes from time to time. It may be that something has got in there (such as dust) and irritated them a little. If his eyes are just a little bit red, applying a cold, used teabag a couple of times a day can provide some relief. If his eyes have discharge in the corner, you can initially try cleaning them gently with a cotton wool pad soaked in cooled, boiled water. If this doesn't help after a day or so, however, you should talk to your vet. If you spot something obvious in your puppy's eye, don't be tempted to remove it yourself if it looks solid as there is a danger you may scratch his cornea. Again, speak to your vet if his tears don't flush it out on their own.

Pupology

Chapter 12 – First Trip in the Car

The outside world is both fascinating and somewhat intimidating to a young puppy. Up until now, the only experience he has had of the outside world is his trip from the breeders to your home and to the vet for his inoculations and his microchip. There is absolutely no need for your puppy to develop any fear outside your home, provided you approach things sensibly from the start. Most young puppies are fearless and take everything in their stride, but there are those who might be born a little more highly strung, so no matter what your puppy's nature, take the same approach to avoid future issues. Let's look at the different experiences your puppy is going to have outside of your house, the first being trips in your car if you have one.

Before your puppy is allowed to walk on the ground, you should be taking him out and about to experience all the smells and sights of the outside world, carrying him safely in your arms. This is the perfect time to get him used to travelling in the car before you start taking him for proper walks in the park. Car travel should not be stressful for your dog at any age. The Highway Code (Rule 57) states that *"dogs are to be suitably restrained so they cannot distract you while you are driving or injure you, or themselves, if you stop quickly. A seat belt harness, pet carrier, dog cage or dog guard are ways of restraining animals in cars."* While breaking the Highway Code is not an offence in itself, allowing dogs to distract you whilst driving could be taken into account in the event of an accident. You want your dog and your passengers to be safe when driving, so take sensible precautions to secure your dog.

If he is on the seats, whether front or back, he will need to be secured with an appropriate harness and seatbelt attachment. If he is travelling in the boot, you will need to either have him in a crate or have a dog guard separating the boot from the back seat of the car. It is entirely up to you where you put him in your car and you may have to experiment to see where he is happiest. The key to teaching a puppy to enjoy car travel is NOT to make a big deal about it. Remember, your goal always is to have your puppy in a calm, relaxed state of mind throughout the day. The same applies to car journeys. Make a massive fuss and your puppy will associate the car with excitement, which is something we definitely DON'T want! There is nothing more tortuous (and dangerous) than being in a car with a perpetually barking/whining dog, whether the noise is being caused by excitement or fear. The message you should be giving your puppy at the outset is that the car equals calm relaxation. This means that whether you are going on a quick trip to the park or a 5-hour journey to a holiday destination, your puppy will behave the same way – he will settle down and chill until you reach your destination.

Some dogs feel sick in the car. This is something you can't predict easily; you will just find out when you make those first few journeys. Minimise the chances of your puppy feeling sick by avoiding feeding him just before a journey. If he is due a meal when you are about to leave, either bring that meal forwards by an hour, or delay it until you get to your destination. You may find that WHERE he is in the car, determines how sick he gets, so do try different positions.

So, how do you get your puppy to enjoy car travel? There are several approaches you can take, depending upon how many of you are travelling in the car. If you are on your own and would like your puppy nearby, turn off your passenger airbag and place a small dog bed on the passenger seat next to you (or a dedicated doggy car seat). Secure your puppy with a harness and seatbelt attachment, making sure that the attachment is sufficiently short to stop him climbing over the handbrake area onto your lap. It is very important from the outset that he learns to lie down in his bed whilst you are driving and NOT move around. To teach him this, I would advise doing a few short journeys up and down your street initially. Pop him in his seat and start the engine. If he immediately tries to move out of his bed, gently nudge him back in with your forearm (not your hand), saying "Ah, Ah" and then immediately relax. I can't stress enough how important it is for you to be calm and matter-of-fact when you are doing this. If you are tense, worried or annoyed, your puppy will pick up on this and you will unsettle him and cause an increase in his brain activity. If his brain is excited, he is even more likely to want to come on to you. Remember, we want him calm and relaxed in the car, but also want him to learn what the boundaries of car travel are i.e. he must stay in his space! If you keep calmly returning him to his bed by blocking his access to you with your forearm, he will soon learn that he is NOT allowed to climb onto your lap whilst you are in the driving seat. You can now try moving the car. If the movement triggers an attempt by him to climb onto your lap, block him with your forearm and gently, but firmly, move him back into his bed. Keep your eyes on the road, obviously, whilst you are doing this. There is absolutely no need to look at him. Be calm, confident and, most importantly, CONSISTENT, with this rule. Do NOT USE FOOD to get him to stay in his bed. If you do this and he is excited by food, you will simply teach him that the car equals food and excitement, and we definitely don't want that either.

If you are driving with another person in the car, I would encourage you to have the bed/blanket and seatbelt set up on the back seat, with your passenger sitting next to your puppy. They can do the same exercise as above, teaching your puppy that when in the car, he is expected to settle in his bed. Having him on the passenger's lap is, obviously, an option, but you will still have to teach him to settle nicely in a bed for times when a passenger isn't travelling with you, so it will speed things up if you just teach him this from the start. Your other option for car travel is to teach him to be in your boot from the outset. A crate is the simplest way to do this, as he is both safe and secure. It may be he doesn't like being so far away from you, but again, if you start with very short journeys and remain calm and confident, offering him calm, vocal praise if he is quiet on the journey, he will soon get used to the crate. I wouldn't advise putting a very tiny puppy loose in a big boot without providing him with a nice deep bed to settle in. Otherwise, he may be flung around a bit too much when you go around corners. Better to have him strapped in initially, and then once he is used to the movement and sound of the car, you can then try him in the boot. The transition should be fairly straightforward if you have already taught him that the car equals calm relaxation.

One last thing to mention about the car. There will be times when you might need to leave him in the car for a few minutes on his own.

Perhaps you forgot something and need to pop back into the house or perhaps you need to pop in to a shop and need to leave him alone in the car for a few minutes (obviously only do this in cool weather). You leaving him should, again, mean nothing at all to him. Don't make a fuss, just go. If you are in a calm state when you leave, he should remain in a calm state too.

Case Study 1: Crazy Car Barker

Misty's owner contacted me because they were finding car journeys with her to be absolute hell. She would get into the car seemingly happily, but the moment the car started moving she would pace around, pant and whine and seemed unable to relax and settle. Furthermore, whenever she spotted a person on the pavement as they drove along, she would start barking frantically. If they stopped at traffic lights and a bike stopped next to their car, she would go bonkers! The family had tried everything, but she wasn't interested in taking treats when she was in the car and no amount of reassurance from them stopped Misty being agitated and vocal.

Having assessed Misty and watched her carefully once she had jumped into the boot, it became obvious that she was very nervous of being in the car, even before the boot was shut. She was wide eyes, panting and yawning. She was most definitely NOT RELAXED and enjoying the experience. Constant reassurance and soothing by her owners WHILST she was in this agitated state had reinforced the behaviour. Unwittingly, her owners had been telling her that it was OK to be in this state of mind in the car, when actually it really wasn't OK. Being in a heightened state of mind (whether excited and happy or worried and nervous) is precisely the opposite of what Misty needed to be. She needed positive reinforcement to happen when she was calm and relaxed, not when she was worried or triggered by the sight of a person on the pavement. She wouldn't take treats because she was so pumped full of adrenaline. Can you eat when you are scared? Of course, you can't - your body goes into fight or flight mode and your digestive system shuts down.

In order to help Misty, she needed to be taught that the car equalled calm relaxation, so I encouraged the family to first of all teach her NOT to be anxious when just sitting in the car with the boot open. The simplest way to achieve this is by sitting on the edge of the boot whilst your puppy is in the boot and focussing on getting yourself calm and relaxed. Drop your shoulders, relax your face, and take some slow deep breaths. Gently hold your puppy's lead whilst you are doing this (do NOT have tense hands!). Just sitting quietly whilst sharing the boot space with your puppy should result in his mind calming. It may take a while but be patient. Helping an anxious dog takes time and dedication because it is about trust. Now, you can't stay in the boot when it is time to drive, obviously, but this was only part of the approach with Misty. The family needed to drive every day, so I suggested that for their daily drives, they should have Misty inside the main body of the car and not in the boot, until they had taught her that the car equalled relaxation. Giving her calm support by having her lie down next to them, or on their lap, would show her what state of mind they wanted her to be in whilst in the car. They needed to keep a close eye out for any signs that her brain activity was increasing (widening of the eyes, ears up, panting, lip licking) and intervene at this moment with an "Ah, Ah" sound followed by relaxation on their part. They were saying to Misty in her own language "don't get excited/nervous, relax with me", just like she was taught by her mother from a young age.

An interesting footnote to add to this case study is that when Misty travelled in my car during her training she was as quiet as a mouse and perfectly calm. Why the difference? Because the first time I put her in my car I took the time to make sure she was calm and relaxed before I shut the boot and stayed calm and relaxed when I switched on the engine. She did start to get a little excited when the car started moving, but a quick verbal intervention followed by calm praise showed her that this was unwanted behaviour. She didn't have a prior equation for travelling in my car with me (unlike with her family), so this first journey was the perfect opportunity to set up that equation. Getting it right from the start is so important.

Case Study 2: Fear of Getting into the Car

Jazz's owners contacted me because they were having trouble getting her to jump into the boot. She was a large breed so, whilst this hadn't been a problem when she was tiny and easy to lift in, she had grown rapidly and was now too heavy to lift. They also didn't want to be lifting her up when she was muddy either. She seemed perfectly happy once in the boot of the car and was no trouble on journeys, but despite trying everything, from chicken to climbing in the boot first, nothing could get her to jump in on her own. Again, the owners had felt that reassurance when she was scared was what she needed, but as you will probably have learnt by now (at least I hope so!), this is NOT what she needed. What she needed was calm, confident support and to be shown that there was nothing scary about jumping in the boot.

My first step was to work out exactly when Jazz's fear kicked in. Was it right next to the car or was it further away from the car? When you are inexperienced at reading dog body language, it is easy to assume that the fear is happening at the precise moment that the dog is refusing to do something, but a lot of the time that isn't the case. The fear has actually started much sooner and spotting that moment when a dog changes from happy and content to fearful is crucial in helping them overcome the problem that has arisen. Stepping in the **second** the brain activity changes from calm to more agitated is the key.

On watching Jazz approach the car, it became apparent that her state of mind changed from relaxed to fearful at the moment she reached the pavement at the top of the drive. The walk up the drive had been fine, but as soon as she reached the pavement and spotted the car, her fear kicked in and her brain shut down. She simply wouldn't budge after this. In order to help her, it was important for me to let her stop at the exact location that she became fearful. I then ensured I was in a calm, confident state of mind, knelt down and put a small amount of pressure on her lead, and I am talking TINY PRESSURE! I wasn't pulling the lead or trying to make her move, I was simply taking up the slack on the lead and adding a miniscule bit of pressure. My state of mind was telling Jazz that I could be trusted. When she realised she wasn't going to be pulled towards the car, she started to relax a little and at this point I increased the pressure ever so slightly until she voluntarily moved one of her paws slightly forwards. Immediately she did this, I released the pressure to show her that if she moved her paw, nothing bad was going to happen; I wasn't going to force her to keep going. We did this again, and this time she took a whole step forward, and in this moment I offered her calm encouragement, led her towards the car and she jumped in. Once she jumped in once, there was no looking back. Trust was the key here. I didn't force her to do something that frightened her, I simply led her through her worst fear and out the other side with nothing bad happening. All movement came from her. The only thing that I needed to do was to unlock her brain with a tiny movement, facilitated by that very slight pressure on the lead. After teaching her owner to spot even the slightest hesitation in Jazz as they approached the car and to confidently guide her through it, I can happily report that she is now jumping in and out of the car without issue. For whatever reason, the approach to the car had been accompanied by a fearful reaction in Jazz. Maybe at some point there was a loud sound at that moment, who knows? But what matters is that we were able to create a new equation in her brain for approaching the car that didn't involve fear.

First Trip in the Car

Now that you know how to take your puppy in the car, you can drive him to lots of different places to start experiencing the big wide world. Take him to your local high street, the garden centre (if they allow dogs), the train station, the pub, and, of course, the local park (but don't put him on the ground and do keep an eye out for other dogs jumping up at you!). Carry him in your arms or in a puppy carrier when he is tiny and not fully vaccinated but do make sure he is wearing a collar and lead or a collar and harness. This is not just for added security should he be a wriggler, but also because by law he must wear a collar with a name tag when he goes outside your house. Exposing him to all these sights and sounds whilst under your full protective care is a good way to ensure he is bomb-proof going forwards. Lots of people will want to stroke him when you are carrying him. Make sure you ask them to follow my advice about touching any dog – ask them to gently ball their fingers into a relaxed fist, tucking their thumb inside, extend this hand to the puppy and give him the choice whether he is comfortable to be touched or not. If he moves towards their hand to sniff it, he is telling you he is comfortable and they can then give him a tickle under the chin. If he moves away from their hand, he is a bit unsure and you should ask them NOT to touch him yet. Encourage people NOT to reach out and pat him on the head. This can freak out some nervous puppies and make them hand shy. The extended, relaxed, curled fist to sniff is always the best approach. Ignoring whether or not a dog wants to be touched, whether it is a puppy or an adult, is foolhardy, and in the worst-case scenario can lead to a nip. Always ask the owner first if you can say "Hello" and always give the animal the option to NOT say "Hello" if he isn't comfortable. Teaching your children to respect a dog's personal space is good practice and will keep them safe.

Pupology

Chapter 13 – First Pavement Walks

Oh, my, this is such an exciting day! Your puppy is now fully vaccinated, and you can't wait to take him for his first walk. You are keen to introduce him to everyone, humans and dogs alike. Keep the walk short as he is still tiny. There are several things you should keep in mind on this first walk to ensure it all goes smoothly. Let's look at his first pavement walk starting from your house. Everyone wants a dog that doesn't pull on the lead, but what a lot of dog owners don't realise is that the WAY YOU LEAVE YOUR HOUSE determines whether you will raise a lead puller or not. Over the years, one of the most common problems I get asked about is lead pulling, often from owners who have already attended puppy training classes and tried to teach "heel" using food rewards. In fact, when I started my business, teaching dogs not to pull on the lead was the only training I offered! I had worked out how to stop my own dog from pulling horribly on the lead and my intention was purely to teach that skill to clients. However, it soon became apparent that all lead pullers had other issues too, which is how my business expanded into covering all aspects of dog behaviourism!

Plenty of owners manage to train their dogs to walk on a loose lead using the conventional method of teaching "heel" using a tasty treat. If you persevere, the chances are you will get there eventually. But there are some owners for whom this method simply doesn't work and they can't understand why. The answer may be simply that the dog isn't food motivated, so a treat isn't going to cut the mustard when it comes to getting the dog to stay by your side when there are a million different smells pulling his attention to the environment around him. Whatever the reason, don't despair, there is an alternative approach to lead pulling which doesn't involve teaching a close heel command. Let's think again about why the treat method might not be working. The explanation for this is two-fold. Firstly, the dog is usually hugely excited at the prospect of food. Secondly, the owner is usually letting the dog lead the walk from the outset. They aren't asking it to heel until they get to the pavement. Obviously, this isn't always the case, some owners will ask for a heel before they exit the house, but in my experience, most owners are unaware that it is what happens INSIDE the house before you even open your front door that matters!

You may wonder what is wrong with starting to ask for "heel" when you reach the pavement? Well, if you think back to what I said in the beginning about the way dogs interact in the wild, I mentioned that when dogs walk together patrolling a territory they are walking in unison as one entity - a pack who are mentally connected to a pack leader. They are in a "travelling" state of mind when doing this. Whilst this may strike you as irrelevant to having a dog that doesn't pull, rest assured, it can be hugely important. The quickest way, by far, to get a dog to stop pulling on a lead is for the HUMAN to be leading the walk in the role of pack leader. And this means the HUMAN invites the dog to join them on the walk. The dog is mentally connected to the human and taking direction from the human. It is FOLLOWING the human's lead and it will instinctively drop into a "travelling" state of mind. If, in the dog's brain, HE is taking the human on the walk, he will expect the human to follow HIM, so wherever his nose takes him, he will expect the owner to follow! Trust me, his nose is going to take him all over the place! We've all seen it – the zigzagging dog dragging his owner about. Is that the kind of walk you want? Or do you want what I teach – the one-fingered walk, where your dog is trotting happily by your side whilst you drink your takeaway coffee? Impossible? Absolutely not. A dog can be taught to do this at any age, but it is by far the best policy to teach this from the outset with your puppy. A dog who is taught to walk like this is also much easier to train off lead. Recall becomes so much easier too, as you have already trained your dog to walk WITH YOU as part of your gang.

Before we get to the actual walk, let's talk about the equipment you will need. Your puppy should be wearing a collar with a name tag on it that has your telephone number, your surname, and your address. The collar should be tight enough that you can only slip two fingers into it. Any looser, and there is a substantial risk that he will get loose if he suddenly backs up in fright for some reason. A lot of owners choose to use a harness on puppies for this very reason. They don't like the collar being tight because they are worried about the puppy's windpipe and are also aware of the risk of it slipping off if they leave it loose, so they choose a puppy harness instead. Whilst this is absolutely valid, one of the main reasons I get so much work helping people to stop their dogs pulling is that these dogs have been wearing harnesses from the outset and have learnt to walk with their noses on the ground and are pulling their owners here, there and everywhere. Consequently, the owner has absolutely no control over what their dog's head is doing! Once a dog learns how to walk WITH you in the way I have described, he can wear anything, including a harness, but whilst he is learning not to pull and to follow your lead, it is very important to keep that nose off the ground!

So, I would suggest a correctly fitted collar (i.e. tight enough!) and lead, and if you are worried about your puppy slipping the collar, you have two options. My preferred method to teach loose lead walking is a slip lead (sometimes called a gundog lead). When positioned correctly (secured high up on your puppy's neck, behind his ears and under his chin), this gives you excellent control of your puppy's head without placing pressure on his windpipe. If you are not confident about using a slip lead, your next best option is to use a lead on his collar, with another lead attached to a harness for back-up, in case he slips out of his collar. Having two leads is a bit of a faff, so I would suggest a normal collar and lead is the best option with the collar fitted sufficiently tightly. Your puppy will be very small at this point and is not very strong so is unlikely to be pulling so much that his neck gets hurt.

Let's get ready for that first pavement walk. Firstly, it is hugely important for your new puppy to be confident out in the big wide world and have the chance to investigate all the interesting smells and sights in the beginning to help him build his confidence in all the different environments he is going to encounter. So, on that first walk, I would suggest that you teach him to leave the house correctly but don't worry about the lead pulling issue for the first few walks. The chances are that he will follow you out of the door anyway, but if he doesn't, you must make sure that he understands that you will be inviting him to walk with you, not allowing him to charge out the front door as soon as it opens.

Here are the steps I would advise you to take when doing your pavement walk, even that very first one. We have already discussed this technique in Chapter 10. This time we will be using it to exit the house with our puppy:

Most importantly DON'T MAKE A FUSS ABOUT GETTING READY FOR THE WALK! Just calmly pick up his lead, your keys, your shoes, your coat (with poo bags in the pocket) and head to the front door. He will follow you there.

Now calmly bend down and clip his lead onto his collar, saying "Lead" as the clip makes the noise (doing this will prove hugely helpful further down the line in the park). If you are using a harness, this is the time to put his harness on. Take your time doing this. The last thing you want is a puppy who constantly mouths and bites you whilst having a harness put on. Kneel on the floor, take a nice deep breath and relax and then place your puppy into the harness. If he puts his teeth on you, PAUSE AND RELAX, stopping what you are doing. He should relax too and take his teeth off you.

Once he has done this, proceed, stopping each time he puts his teeth on you. You are asking him to TRUST you to put something on him that he is unsure about. If you rush things and fight him, he will learn that the harness equals excitement and mouthing (or even worse, a fun game) and you definitely don't want that! You may also accidently pinch him when you do up the clips, which again you don't want as we don't want him to develop an equation that the harness equals pain. Make sure the harness is nice and snug so that he can't slip out of it. Now clip the lead on, saying "lead" in a calm, firm voice as you clip it on.

Now that his lead/harness is on, drop the lead on the floor and sort yourself out. You want your puppy to learn to wait patiently until you are sorted before you make the journey out of the door. Disconnecting from him mentally at this point and concentrating on yourself teaches him to pause and wait until YOU are ready.

Once you are ready, go towards the front door. Your puppy may well rush forward to be at the door first. You are now going to teach him that there is an exclusion zone in front of the front door. Why? Because this teaches him door manners from the outset, and this is hugely important from a safety point of view and for how he views YOU in the relationship. Getting this bit right is fundamental in teaching him NOT to pull on the lead.

If he is pressed against the front door, get in-between him and the door with your body, pick up his lead, using the lead to guide him away from the door with your outstretched arm. Walk towards him until he turns fully and walks away back down the hall. Only move sideways or forwards when you are doing this, NOT BACKWARDS. You are BLOCKING his access to the door and CLAIMING the area by the door as your territory. You are moving him out of the exclusion zone with your body in a CALM AND CONFIDENT manner. This is what dogs do to each other all the time and it is a simple way of telling him that the front door area belongs to you. Don't talk to him at all when you first do this, just use your body as a physical means of blocking his access to the door area.

The second he turns and walks away from the front door, drop the lead and DISENGAGE WITH HIM MENTALLY AND PHYSICALLY and go back to the edge of your chosen exclusion zone (think of this as a large square area in front of the door), keeping one eye on him, just to make sure he doesn't suddenly charge past you. If he tries to move into your exclusion zone, repeat the exercise, until he politely stays back from the area in front of the door. REMEMBER, STAY CALM AND RELAXED THROUGHOUT.

Put your hand on the door and start to open it, turning to block him again with your body if he attempts to push past into your exclusion zone. Remember, NO TALKING! If you continue to 'police' the door area, he will stay back at a respectful distance. You can now pick up the lead again. But do remember, this is NOT a signal for him to move forward towards the door! If he does, you must repeat the exercise whilst still holding the lead. Do make sure you are holding the lead the correct way (see below for tips!).

Once you are sure he is mentally connected to you (you will know this because he will be calmly looking into your eyes!), test to make sure he isn't going to make a rash decision and try to move forward into the space by the door. Do this by standing to one side and giving him a full view of the door. If you have total control of him, he will stay put. If he does move forward, repeat the above blocking and claiming. If he *stays put, slowly (but calmly – no tension, remember!) open the door, keeping a close eye on him. Your goal is to be able to have the door open wide and him stay back at a respectful distance whilst maintaining eye contact with you WITHOUT YOU SAYING A WORD.*

If you are struggling at this point, you have probably inadvertently tensed up or are holding your breath. Relax and breathe!

Put one foot over the threshold, again keeping an eye on him and swinging round to block him again, should he make the wrong decision and move forwards. If he stays put, move your other foot over the threshold. If he is still looking at you, you can now take a step backwards onto your doorstep and CALMLY invite him through the doorway to join you with a wave of your hand, or by patting your leg. DO NOT CALL HIM IN AN EXCITED VOICE!

Once you have mastered doing this without talking, you can replace the physical actions (blocking him and moving towards him) with a noise, such as "Ah, Ah" or "Hey", delivered in a calm, confident voice. He needs to learn the physical actions first before you put in these noises, but once he understands the invisible boundary lines he must not cross, you can start to influence him with just noises alone. These noises are his signal that he is doing something unwanted (remember how his Mum taught him in the very beginning?).

Your ultimate goal is to be able to get ready for a walk, open the front and walk through it with your puppy calmly following behind you.

Whilst this might seem like a lot of faff, believe me, it is worth doing and doing right, because what will happen is that your puppy will learn to respect door thresholds and not charge through them, which can be very dangerous, particularly when it comes to the front door. You will have taught him that door thresholds belong to you, and they are only to be crossed with permission and in a calm state of mind. HE WILL AUTOMATICALLY RESPECT THEM WITHOUT NEEDING TO BE TOLD. This is incredibly helpful because, as you are aware, your front door gets opened and closed a lot, whether it be because family members are coming and going, or because you are often answering the door to delivery drivers. Having a dog that stays back and doesn't rush out makes life so much easier and safer. Similarly, having a dog you can stop dead with a simple noise is also hugely important and this technique, with the accompanying noise interventions, allows you to do this.

As you will see in further chapters, being able to influence your dog in this way using the simple blocking & claiming technique, is hugely important in so many day-to-day situations that you will encounter with your growing puppy. Learning how to do this in your own home from the outset will give you the confidence to take the method outdoors to more complex situations.

If you find the front door is too much of a temptation for him initially, practice doing the technique on INTERNAL doors in the house before you try the front (and indeed the back) door. The front and back door are very high value doors to your puppy because they lead to the outside world – the front door means a walk or a car journey is in the offing and the back door is the gateway to that wonderfully exciting garden/backyard of yours! Many owners ask me if they should be using this technique EVERY time their puppy goes through a doorway, even internal doors in the house. The answer is "No!". You only need to use the technique if your puppy is charging through a door in an excited state of mind when he shouldn't be. If he is playing in the house and running from room to room that is absolutely fine, but if you are moving through a doorway with him and he is trying to barge past you rudely, you should be reminding him that this is unwanted behaviour using the above technique. When he is calmly walking through doorways he is doing nothing wrong, so there is no need to intervene. What we are doing is teaching him a default **calm state of mind** around doorways, particularly the ones that really matter!

Let's get back to that first walk. You have made it out onto the doorstep and by now, your little puppy will be eagerly sniffing at all those lovely smells on the ground. He has an incredibly sensitive nose, which will be drawn here, there, and everywhere. It is absolutely fine on those first few walks to let your puppy zig zag about exploring all these smells. He is very tiny and you want him to learn to be confident outside of your house, so at this point we aren't going to focus too much on HOW he is walking on the lead. Let him get to know the streets immediately around your home, let him gain confidence at the sound of passing cars, let him look at the neighbour's cat from a distance and any other pets you come across (from a distance), so that he learns to view all these sights and smells as normal. I would strongly encourage you to allow him to wee all around your neighbourhood at this point, because once we start to teach him to walk on a loose lead we will NOT be allowing him to do this all the time, for good reason. However, allowing him to place his scent on your local streets in the early days is a good idea because, should he accidently get outside the front of your house on his own, he will be easily able to find his way home by following the scent trail he has left previously. Hopefully you will never find yourself in this position, but it does sometimes happen and many escapees do actually find their own way home because they have peed around their local streets.

On these first exploratory walks, your puppy will sniff anything he comes across, including rubbish. Get into the habit from the outset of teaching him that he is NOT allowed to pick up rubbish or, even worse, eat it. So many items are dangerous for puppies to swallow. They have tiny bowels and foreign objects can easily get stuck in there, so make sure you keep your eyes peeled as to what he is sniffing and if he moves towards a piece of rubbish, give the lead a tiny flick and <u>immediate</u> release, say a firm "Leave", and guide him away. If he is insistent and won't move away from an item, put yourself in between the puppy and the item (just like in the front door scenario) and BLOCK & CLAIM it, moving your puppy away from it with your body, whilst using the lead to guide him backwards. Do not PULL your puppy away from the item. Pulling on the lead will trigger him to pull forwards TOWARDS the item and cause his brain to become more excited. Dogs don't pull each other off objects that they believe they own, they CLAIM them, so that is what you should be doing with your puppy and rubbish on the streets. You are telling him that EVERYTHING on the ground belongs to you and is not for him to touch without your permission. Do this from the very start and your dog will learn to ignore stuff he finds. Yes, he may take a little sniff, but if you have taught him correctly, he won't pick the item up. Yellow-box that rubbish!

In the event that you don't notice in time (and we all know this happens!) and your puppy manages to get some rubbish into his mouth, don't overreact and get cross with him. You are a calm, stable leader. You want him to be calm in these situations and not do what some dogs do, which is swallow the item as quickly as possible to stop the human getting it! I once saw a dog swallow half a squirrel whole rather than give it up to some humans. One massive gulp and the squirrel was gone. What made things worse was that it was the head end the dog swallowed! If your puppy picks something up in its mouth, calmly and confidently put your hand right into his mouth and take the object out. If his jaws are clamped shut, which is unlikely with a young pup, but can happen, you need to employ a method that dogs use on each other when having a dispute over an item in their mouths. Have you ever seen one dog calmly walk up to another and take a toy out of the dog's mouth with no resistance? That is what you are doing when you calmly take the rubbish from your puppy. But let's imagine BOTH dogs want to have the item. How does this get resolved? Well, the more dominant and persistent dog will hold the item calmly with its teeth until the other dog eventually submits to its authority and lets go. It doesn't tug or pull, it simply calmly holds the object in a confident way, giving the other dog the mental message "this is mine and I am having it". Us humans can replicate this behaviour by calmly holding whatever part of the object is protruding from the puppy's mouth in a calm, confident way, whilst slipping a couple of fingers of the other hand into the puppy's collar. We need to do this to keep the puppy's head still, as his natural instinct will be to pull back away from our hand and we don't want that. If we allow him to pull backwards, a tug of war ensues. Keeping his head stationary, taking a nice deep breath and relaxing, then calmly, but firmly, holding the object whilst mentally saying to yourself "this is mine, I am having it" will eventually result in the puppy loosening his hold on the object. As soon as you feel his grip loosen, move more of the object into your hand. He may just release it fully in one go, but if he doesn't, you will gradually gather more of the object into your hand as his jaw loosens until you are holding the majority of it. At this point he will let go.

It is VERY important to master this technique whilst your puppy is very young. If you wait too long and he learns to steal things and refuses to give them up by growling at you and clamping his jaws shut, you will find it much harder to take back possession of objects. It is still possible but shouldn't be done without the help of a professional because you absolutely DO NOT want your puppy to learn to control you with the fear of a bite. Very young puppies automatically capitulate to more senior pack members, so get this installed in his brain right from the outset that any object he takes that you don't want him to have is going to be calmly taken off him without any fuss. I can't stress enough that you SHOULD NOT USE TREATS TO BARGAIN FOR OBJECTS THAT YOUR PUPPY PICKS UP. If you do this, you will simply teach him to steal in order to get a food reward!

On this first street walk with your puppy, you may bump into other dog owners out walking their dogs. It is very important that you get these first meetings right with your new puppy. You absolutely do not want him jumped on or squashed by an older dog! So, I would advise at this point that you skip ahead to Chapter 18 on reading dog body language so you can spot in advance who looks like a good candidate for an introduction. It is down to you to decide which dogs you let your puppy say "Hello" to when out walking. Many owners will say their dog is friendly, but that doesn't mean it isn't a bit excitable and even a friendly dog can give your new puppy a fright if it is too boisterous. We want to avoid from the very start your puppy developing any nervousness around other dogs. Don't be paranoid, obviously, as you will pass this feeling on to your puppy. Just be sensible! If you see a nice, calm looking dog approaching, shorten your puppy's lead and place yourself in between the puppy and the other dog but remember NOT to grip his lead tightly with tension! Now ask the owner if they can have a sniff of each other. If the owner is happy, gently tell your puppy to go to say "Hello" whilst letting his lead loose. You want him to happily allow the other dog to sniff his bottom and to have his bottom sniffed (more of this in Chapter 14!).

Let's now move on to teaching your puppy how to walk on a loose lead on the pavement. As I said before, on the first few walks with him you want to allow him to explore and gain in confidence and needn't worry about him pulling on the lead at this point. However, it is important for him to learn to walk on a loose lead without pulling, so I would start this training fairly sharpish after he is allowed on public ground before he starts developing bad habits. Lead pulling is an incredibly annoying behaviour and a very common one. What most new puppy owners don't realise is that when a dog is pulling it is LEADING the walk. YOU should be the one leading the walk, not your puppy, because if he is leading he is making his own decisions about where to go and what to do and his little nose is going to take you in the direction of anything that smells interesting. Those smells are all over the place, so he is going to be veering about, criss-crossing in front of you and not paying the blindest bit of attention to what you are doing or what you want. You may think this doesn't matter if your puppy is small or if he is a small breed, so will remain small, but, believe me, it does. If he is leading your walks on lead, he is also likely to be leading your walks when off-lead and that is going to make recall training so much harder. Teach him to walk WITH you, both on and off lead as part of your team, and everything will fall into place much easier.

It is possible to fix the issue of lead pulling by teaching your puppy to heel, but on the whole, this type of training relies on holding a food reward in your hand whilst you walk and has nothing to do with your RELATIONSHIP with your puppy. If you have established that you are inviting your puppy to join you on YOUR walk and you replicate how he would walk in the wild with a more senior dog, he will instinctively drop into a "following" state of mind and trot along quite happily beside you without pulling. Now you probably don't believe me on this point, but I can assure you that I have taught hundreds of dogs to loose-lead walk in this way. My aim is for my clients to be able to drink a cup of coffee whilst walking their dog on lead, without fear of being burnt by a spillage! They shouldn't even notice that they have a dog with them if their dog is fully mentally connected!

You can tell dogs that are walking in a "following" state of mind by their ear, head, and tail position and what they are doing with their eyes. A dog in following mode will have its ears back, its tail in neutral, its head fairly low and will be looking straight ahead. It won't have its nose on the ground, and it won't be sniffing. This is KEY! There is no time to stop and sniff when a dog is on a pack walk with its pack. The dogs are simply moving forwards in formation with one ear on the leader. They are TRAVELLING from A to B. That is what you can teach your puppy to do if you want him to not pull on the lead. Remember that homeless person's dog? Trotting along on the streets, with no lead? He was travelling and that is what you need to teach your puppy if you want him to walk on lead on one finger whilst you drink your Costa or Starbucks! Other good examples of dogs travelling in a "following" state of mind are dogs walking with prams or mobility scooters.

There are two key things that need to happen for you to successfully teach your puppy how to walk like this. Firstly, you need to leave the house in the correct way and secondly you need to keep your puppy's nose off the ground initially until he understands that you want him in "following" mode. You will be letting him stop and sniff occasionally, but it will be when YOU decide, not him. Leaving the house correctly has already been covered earlier.

In order to keep your puppy's nose off the ground whilst you teach him loose lead walking, I advise using a collar and lead, or a slip lead (provided it is placed correctly on your dog, high up on his head, behind his ears and under his chin). His collar should NOT be sitting on his windpipe. Move it up a little when you start the walk if it is, so that it is sitting high up behind his ears, and initially keep the lead short so that it doesn't slip down again.

Leave the house in the way that I advised and pause on your doorstep. You are now going to put your puppy in the position you want him to adopt whenever you ask him to walk WITH you (i.e. go on a journey from A to B with you leading). He won't always be in this position. There will be times when you send him onto a patch of grass to have a wee or a poo, for example, or just a nice sniff. The key is that YOU will be deciding when he does this, not him. We want him to be in two states of mind. Firstly a "following" state of mind, when he is walking by your side, calm and relaxed, and then secondly an "exploring" state of mind, when you have given him permission to have a sniff around. Once he learns these two states, when you pop him in the position for a "following" state, he will automatically drop into following you! Funnily enough, I like to call this position "Position" for the puppy, rather than heel. This is because once he adopts a following state of mind on a lead walk, I am no longer going to insist he stays by my heel. He can be anywhere on one side of me, so long as he isn't pulling and he is mentally connected to me. He can even be in front of me eventually when he has truly got the hang of this. I stop, he stops (without being told!), I go, he goes. You get the picture. We are one unit, a team, moving together.

Let's get back to teaching him that we want him to walk nicely on the lead without pulling. You are now on your doorstep and ready to set off. Before you do that, I want you to run through a mental checklist of yourself. Are you standing up tall with your shoulders back and down? Is your body relaxed? Are you feeling confident and happy? Are your arms hanging loosely by your side and completely straight? Is your face relaxed and your eyes soft? I want NO tension in your body, just calm confidence! Which brings me to how to hold your puppy's lead on a walk.

A lot of owners make the mistake of wrapping the lead around their wrist and holding it tight. What is this telling the puppy?! You are tense before you have even set off! Remember, tension is our enemy in dog communication. He won't listen to you or trust you if you are tense. Yes, when he is tiny you might get away with it, but I can guarantee that it will work against you when he hits puberty! What you need to be doing is holding that lead with as little tension as possible. Either bunch it up in a nice, relaxed hand or, if you are worried about safety, put the loop over the wrist of the hand furthest from your puppy and then rest part of the lead nearest your pup in the other hand, which is hanging down above his head. If you are prone to tension in your hand, try holding that part of the lead between just two fingers. Or perhaps have part of it resting on your ring finger. Or even better, if he is a small puppy, have it balanced on one finger! Which way your hand is facing when you are holding the lead can also have an impact. If, when your arm is hanging loosely by your side, your palm is facing FORWARDS, your arm is already twisted and there will be tension in your muscles. I have noticed that a lot of owners hold the lead this way! When your arm is hanging loosely, you want your palm to be facing inwards toward your body. The lead can then sit between your thumb and your index finger and, if you find it comfortable, reappear between your ring finger and pinkie. This allows you to use your ring finger alone to flick the lead and communicate with your puppy. DO NOT BEND YOUR ELBOW – you are not communicating with your arm!

Whatever position you choose, you will be doing a TINY flick and release of the finger to communicate with your puppy down the lead if he moves out of position by your leg. We want him to stay next to you by your side. If he moves out of this position, a tiny flick sideways or upwards on the lead for a NANOSECOND will communicate with him that he is doing something unwanted (i.e. moved out of position). And I do mean a FLICK. You must not pull or yank your puppy. You must RELEASE the tension as soon as you have flicked. You are talking to him down the lead, not physically restraining him. The lead is simply an extension of your body - it is a tool for communication, not control. He is more likely to be aware of this signal if the lead is on a collar, than a harness. As I said, harnesses were designed for pulling. They were designed to "harness" the strongest part of an animal's body, the shoulders, and your puppy is less likely to notice a little flick on the harness than he is on his neck. He MAY notice, so give it a try if you really aren't keen on the collar and lead, but remember, we need his head up and his nose off the ground!

Now, most young puppies follow naturally anyway so you may think there isn't any need for all the above palaver. But remember, if you want to get him moving with you in a following state (think of those dog owners you see who DON'T need a lead when walking their dogs), you must get this message across at this early age. There are lots of things you don't want him doing on walks, such as picking up rubbish, zigzagging and tripping you up, peeing every few seconds on the walk or charging over to people and other dogs. A puppy who has learnt to follow from the start won't do these things. If your puppy is particularly excitable, you may manage to exit the house calmly but then he immediately starts pulling the moment you head down the path before you get a chance to intervene with the lead. Owners are often bewildered as to what to do if this happens. Why has it happened, they ask? The simple answer is that you have failed to maintain calmness in your puppy. You invited him out of the house and over the threshold but then you let him pass you and get excited again. If this is happening you will have to put in an extra step to your journey to the pavement, which may seem like a load more work but I can promise you it will pay off. You will need to mentally divide that journey down your path to the pavement into tiny sections and ensure that your puppy remains calm in each section by using the blocking & claiming technique to move him back towards the house WHENEVER he gets excited again, beckoning him a little bit further forward each time if he maintains a calm state of mind, until you finally reach the pavement.

Repeat this until he gets the message, then try leaving the house all in one go without stopping until you get to the pavement. If you have repeated enough times, he should just happily trot along beside or behind you. He may need a verbal reminder or a tiny flick and release of the lead if he forgets himself, but do try to sense when this happens, rather than watching him closely all the time. A quick glance should be enough. You want to be focussing on your destination (the pavement), rather than him.

Back to teaching how to walk this way. You are in position now on the pavement and your puppy is in position by your side in a calm state of mind. You have started walking and are giving him a tiny signal each time he tries to move ahead of you. You must relax the lead IMMEDIATELY after each of these little signals. Try very hard not to overthink this. Overthinking leads to tension in humans and we absolutely don't want that! Try not to look down at your puppy all the time. This is hard to do when they are tiny, I know, as you want to see where he is, but if you can, pick an object further down the road from you and fix your gaze on that and head for it at a nice, brisk pace. Your puppy should fall in beside you and match that pace if you keep his head up off the ground. He should automatically go into a following state and trot along beside you with his ears flat, his tail neutral and his eyes fixed forwards. If you feel him trying to pull his head towards the ground, give him that tiny signal that this behaviour is unwanted and keep moving. If he is really persistent, make things a little easier for him by placing him on the side AWAY from the strongest smells. It may be the pavement has a verge and trees that all the other dogs wee on. Or it may be there is a wall on one side of the pavement but no verge. Whichever is the case, place him as far away from those tempting smells as possible to set him up for success. He will quickly learn that when you put him into position by your side and set off at a brisk pace you are "Doing the Walk" as I like to call it. You are travelling from A to B. You aren't doing a leisure walk, which is all about stopping, sniffing, and marking with pee. You are on a journey. Take a look at people walking dogs with prams, or people in mobility scooters with dogs or on bikes. Those dogs are in "travelling" or "following" mode, they are "Doing the Walk" in the way I mention.

If he stops dead in the middle of this exercise to do a wee or a poo, let him. But only once. He can answer the call of nature because that is only fair. But he should only need to do it once when we are teaching him this method of loose lead walking. Once he has got the hang of it, you are going to start letting him have a break from being in "position" and send him to have a sniff around a patch of grass or a tree for a few seconds by saying "On you go, have a sniff" when you reach such a destination. Once you feel he has had enough time sniffing, guide him back to your side into "position" again, then set off on another part of the journey. Remember, we are in the teaching phase at the moment. Once he happily trots out of the house behind you, walks on a loose lead by your side and is clearly paying attention to you all the time (test by stopping and starting at will and he should mirror you), you can be a bit more relaxed on the walks as he now knows how to "Do the Walk" in a well-mannered way. You will still need to keep an eye out for potential triggers, such as cats, dogs and people, but so long as you are calm and confident and he is in a following mode, you shouldn't have any trouble when you see any of these. He is already in a calm, following state of mind so, whilst he might become mildly curious at the sight of these things, he is less likely to react much. If he was in an excited, pulling state of mind and in charge of the walk, rather than you, that would be a different matter.

Case Study 1: Totally In Charge but Nervous

I met Cleo when she was a year old. She was a miniature dachshund, and her problem was she barked incessantly when out on walks. Like many daxies, her owners used a harness and flexi-lead to walk her. She was used to having the freedom to walk in whatever position she fancied and have a good sniff of everything into the bargain. Whilst this wouldn't have been an issue, had she been quiet on the walks, her barking was taking the enjoyment out of walking for her owners. It was clear when I met Cleo that nerves were behind her barking issue. She was afraid of everything that moved! She wasn't just nervous outside the home, she was also nervous in the home. By leading the walk on a flexi-lead, her anxiety was hitting the roof by the time she was outside of her home and every little thing was setting her off, whether it be the sight of a person, a dog, a child, a bicycle, or a cat. Her owners reported that she had been jumped on by a much bigger dog as a young puppy whilst out on a walk and they believed this to be behind her anxiety.

In order to help Cleo, it was important to re-set what the walk was all about and who was leading it. We started work in the house, focussing on getting her ready for a walk in a calm state of mind. She got very excited when her harness was brought out so I switched to a collar and lead to take this excitement out of the equation. She was a bit perturbed about having the lead around her neck, so staying calm and relaxed was absolutely essential at this point. Cleo's owners lived in a flat and it was important that all parts of the journey to the outside world involved a calm, following state of mind, so we started with exiting the flat into the corridor in the correct way. Once we had repeated this a few times, Cleo stopped trying to rush past and happily trotted along behind us. This exercise was repeated at the first internal door to the foyer and then again at the last door, the one that led to the car park. We worked on each section of the walk to the outside several times until it was clear to Cleo what we wanted of her. On getting outside, we paused again on the doorstep. She had smelt the air and all the lovely neighbourhood scents by then so had become a little more excited again, so it was important to do a reset here and ask for calmness again. Think of dividing that journey to the pavement into bite-size chunks. You have to teach your puppy how to behave in each "chunk" and not allow them to switch into a leadership role at any point. Trying to keep a puppy from pulling ahead using the lead is much harder than claiming the space from them with your body using the blocking & claiming technique. It may take a few goes, but your puppy will soon understand that this outside space belongs to you and that you are leading them through it to the pavement. Cleo quickly got the message and had a whole new equation for going out on a walk. She was no longer anxious and could leave the flat happily and quietly.

Case Study 2: Attacking the Lead

Maggie, a young Samoyed puppy, had developed a bad habit of attacking her lead and nipping her owners whenever they tried to put the lead on her to take her for a walk. She was only three months old when I met her and it was unclear as to what had prompted this behaviour. Being a Samoyed, she was very fluffy and it may be that at some point, unbeknownst to her owners, her fur had got caught in the clip. This would be enough to cause her to not trust the lead. Or perhaps some fur got caught when her collar was being put on. No matter what the reason, it had become hard to get her ready for a walk as she would nip and squirm whenever someone tried to attach the lead to her collar. This is often the case with puppies who have been accidentally nipped by their harness or collar clips. They learn to mistrust the equipment and the process and can become squirming, bitey devils when the harness or lead comes near.

The first step with Maggie was to re-introduce her to the lead from scratch. I needed to work out the exact moment that she was triggered into reactivity. Was it the sight of the lead? The hand approaching carrying the lead? I got the lead out and started clicking the catch at a distance. She noticed but wasn't unduly bothered. However, when I approached her with it in my hand and reached out to her, her state of mind escalated. She was not happy. Trust had been lost at that point and had to be re-established. Getting myself into a nice, calm state of mind was the first step. Regaining trust was the next step. To do this I used some smelly treats to get her nose to kick in. I needed her to be using her senses in the right order, namely nose before eyes. Curiosity got the better of her and she came to investigate. At this point, I had a new lead nearby but not in my hand. This lead was a slip lead that could be easily dropped over her head with no need to touch her fur with my hands or touch her collar. It was very important for her to come to me and for me NOT to pursue *her with the lead. I wanted her to willingly approach me when I had the lead in my hand, so the first step was to have her come near of her own free will with the lead in sight and show her that I was not about to grab her when she got close. As she ate the treat, I calmly picked the lead up and moved it around in my hand. Next, whilst she ate another treat, I gently stroked her body with a tiny portion of the lead. She began to trust me that nothing bad was about to happen. We worked up to me dropping a large loop of the lead over her head and letting it hang loosely. Again, nothing bad happened, so there was no negative reaction from her. I then got up and walked away with the slip lead in my hand. By nature of its design, it gradually tightened as I moved away but I stopped before it made full contact with her fur. I then beckoned her towards me and she came. My message was, this thing around your neck isn't going to hurt you, you can trust me, you can follow me with this on you.*

Maintaining a calm, relaxed state of mind throughout allowed Maggie to listen to what I was telling her with my body and mind. At no point was there any fear or force involved. I repeated this process again and again, each time making the dropping of the lead over her head more obvious to her, until I was able to put it on and calmly tighten it enough to be safe. A lot of effort, yes, but well worth it. This was a young puppy who had clearly developed lead fear and was using aggression to keep humans away from her neck. Learning to trust her humans again, AND the equipment were the key.

Pupology

Chapter 14 - First Walks in the Park

The first time you take your puppy to the park is a very exciting day. This is what it is all about, after all! People get dogs for all different sorts of reasons - companionship, exercise, social interaction with other dog-minded people. Whatever your reasons for getting your puppy, if you want your puppy to grow up balanced, taking him to the local park to meet other people and dogs is a must in the early months. Even if you have absolutely no intention of doing this going forwards when he is older and envisage yourself instead taking long solo hikes across the countryside without bumping into a soul, please bear in mind that, for your dog to be well-behaved even in these solo situations, you need to get him off to a good start with other animals and other humans. If you don't, you may find that when you DO come across the path of another dog or human, he may not behave the way you envisaged. Likewise, if your solo walks end with a nice pint in a country pub, if you don't socialise with him from the start, he may struggle to cope in this sort of environment and may struggle to lie quietly at your feet.

Let's imagine that you are going to a typical park for your first walk. We will focus on this very first walk and talk in more detail in Chapter 15 about problems you may encounter in the park as your puppy gets older. Your first walk in the park is likely to be at a place where dog owners and non-dog owners share a green space. There may be a playpark for children, or even a café. There may be football pitches or a woodland walk. It doesn't really matter what environment you take your puppy to initially. What matters is that you teach him from the outset how you expect him to behave in this environment, and any other environment. As always, teaching him from a young age will set you up for success further down the line, PARTICULARLY when he hits puberty and all your hard work gets challenged for a while.

I'm going to tell you how I would advise you to tackle this first walk, but your puppy is very young at this point, so it may be you just do a tiny bit of exposure first of all, rather than follow everything I am about to suggest. By all means, do it this way, but do read on and try to do the following at some point in those early weeks and then follow this routine going forwards.

Let's imagine that you have arrived at the park in your car. The first thing your puppy needs to learn is that when the car stops, he should not be whipping himself up into a frenzy of excitement at the prospect of getting out of the car. Let him do this and there is a greater likelihood that he will end up being the kind of dog who starts whining, or worse barking, the second you put your handbrake on. He may also develop a habit of jumping out of the boot right away without waiting for permission, which could be potentially dangerous. What we want him to learn is that the car stopping means NOTHING. The car door/boot opening means NOTHING. The car door/boot opening means WAIT PATIENTLY UNTIL YOU ARE INVITED OUT! We want him to remain calm and relaxed when we arrive at the park. We want him to wait politely whilst we open the car door or the boot and unstrap him/pick up his lead. When he is small you will be lifting him out of the car and placing him on the pavement. As he gets bigger, he will be jumping out (and back in), and we want him to wait until he is invited before this happens, so teaching him to be calm and relaxed on arrival at the park when he is tiny sets you up nicely for doing this further down the line as he grows.

Teach him calm relaxation on arrival by being calm and relaxed yourself (take a nice breath, drop those shoulders, relax those facial muscles and hands). Remember, he takes direction from you and if you are in a frenzy of excitement squealing "Are you ready for walkies!!!?" or some such phrase, you can guarantee he will get excited too. You may think this doesn't matter, but don't forget that dogs develop one equation for each situation they find themselves in, depending on what has happened the first time they were in that situation. So, with arrival at the park, we want that equation to be "wait calmly until my owner invites me out". If your puppy is naturally excited, despite you being calm, simply take another nice deep breath and block his exit from the car with your body (don't push against him with your hands!) and

WAIT until he calms down. How can you tell he is calmer? He will relax and sit down and look at you without being told. If he has a tense body, wide eyes and pricked up ears, or is staring or peeking past you, he isn't relaxed and he isn't focussed on you, he is focussed on the environment outside the car. Have patience on these first few walks and he will quickly learn exactly what you want in terms of his behaviour when you arrive at the park. Rush things and let HIM decide what state of mind he is in on arrival and, rest assured, the next time you arrive he will replicate this behaviour, and it may well get worse. You may be thinking what a mean person I am by now! You LOVE to see your puppy excited when you arrive at the park, it makes you happy! Well, yes, it does, but it won't be so nice to see or easy to manage when he is fully grown! Having him exit the car safely is very important from a safety point of view too, remember, and you have a duty to keep him and other people safe. Rushing, pulling, barking and shoving are all bad manners in my opinion, and are often the precursor to other unwanted behaviours.

You may wonder why I don't simply advise you to teach a "Wait" command here (or perhaps "Stay"). I do use words like "Wait" once the dog has learnt physically and mentally what I want using dog techniques. I don't use them initially because I like to layer commands on top of a default behaviour. I want the default behaviour when the boot opens to be "don't do anything except remain calm". I don't want the dog to be poised in an excited state waiting to jump out and be waiting for a verbal release. I want the energy to be low from the outset, not have to keep asking the dog for calmness at each stage of the walk. The simplest way for the dog to learn this is the dog way, in my opinion.

Case Study 1: Walks Have Become a Nightmare!

I was called to help Jerry when he was around 9 months old. He was a popular breed, a golden retriever and a lovely dog, but his owners were finding him to be a complete handful when it came to walking him. Amongst other issues, he was very excitable in the car, both on the way to the park and also when he arrived. The minute they opened the boot he would barrel out and start pulling on his lead, or worse jumping up at his owner in a frenzy of excitement. He was just SO excited about going on a walk! This had been cute and funny when he was tiny, as his owners loved seeing him so happy, but as time went on, Jerry grew bigger and stronger and by 9 months was a sizeable, strong dog. On one occasion he jumped out of the car when they opened the boot and chased after some children he had spotted on the street before they had a chance to grab him. He just wanted to play, but it was scary for the children and very dangerous for the dog and other road users. It had become an annoying and dangerous behaviour.

I spent some time teaching Jerry that the car was NOT a place for excitement. I took him out several times on my own and on the very first occasion I put him in my car I blocked him from jumping in without permission. Why? Because he needed to know that the car was MY territory, not his and that I was only going to invite him into it when he was in a calm state of mind. He quickly became respectful when I opened the boot and jumped in nicely and sat down. I had ensured, by the way, that he was tethered on a long lead to a safety point in my car boot. When we arrived at the park, he immediately stood up and was ready to leap out as soon as I opened the boot. I needed him to learn that this was NOT what I wanted to happen. I needed him to move back away from the boot door as I opened it. He clearly didn't know this so had to be taught from scratch, as in his brain, the opening of the boot meant rush forwards and jump out. Training a new behaviour takes patience and repetition, and it is important to break each stage down until the dog fully understands what you want it to do.

The first step was to deal with the opening of the boot. I opened it slowly and, naturally, he tried to shove his way out (he was tethered for safety, remember, so I had no concerns about him succeeding). I blocked his exit calmly with my body but was careful not to push him with my hands. If I had pushed him back in, his automatic reaction would have been to push against me and a pushing battle would have ensued. I needed to BLOCK him, not battle him, and remain very calm and confident throughout. He was a bit baffled at first. Why wasn't I letting him jump out? He was SO up for a walk! But he quickly realised that I was going to stand firm and backed away. He sat down and gave me full eye contact. At that point, I moved to the side and stopped blocking his exit. I needed to test if I had his full attention. He started to stand up, so I swung round and blocked his exit again, giving him an "Ah, Ah" intervention as I did so. He sat again. He was now getting the message: "Ah, she doesn't want me to move!" Quite right, Jerry! I want you to sit calmly and wait until I give you a signal, but I am not going to command you to

"Sit" and "Wait" because I know you will still be an excited state, waiting to be released from the command. And excitement is what I don't want, because you are a big strong dog and are going to leap out and then drag me about if I let you out in this state! I tested Jerry again by stepping to the side and this time he remained sitting and calm, giving me full eye contact.

Next step was to pick up his lead and unclip it from the tethering lead that had been keeping him safe. Again, this was NOT a signal that he could jump out. And he didn't. If he had moved at that point, I would have blocked again or made a verbal intervention, as I needed to signal to him that, no matter what I was doing, he needed to wait calmly and patiently. He very quickly picked this up and once I was ready, I calmly invited him out of the boot. Note that I invited him out CALMLY, not in an excited way! The end result? He stood calmly next to me whilst I sorted myself out and locked the car. Now, being young and being used to getting excited in the boot, he did stand up again when I took him home after the walk when the car stopped, and did move towards the boot door as I stood there, but I just held up my hand and as I slowly opened the boot, gave him my verbal "Ah, Ah" intervention and he backed up and sat down calmly. He now knew what I wanted and waited calmly until I invited him out. I taught his owners how to replicate this routine for getting in and out of the car and I can happily report that Jerry is now a much calmer boy and is behaving well when they arrive at a park.

Back to your puppy and his first walk. You have now got him out of the car and it's time to go into the park. You might be tempted to have him on an extendable lead for this walk but I would advise against it, simply because if you encounter other dogs on your walk and either they or him get super excited, they can all get tangled up and, in the worst-case scenario, get injured. I would recommend you have him on a normal lead on his collar. This first walk is about exploring sights and sounds and learning to meet other dogs and humans who will want to pet him. Whilst most puppy owners use a harness (for reasons we have already discussed), my view is that you need to have control of your puppy's head on these first walks when he meets other dogs, so if you are determined to use a harness, please do take another lead with you that you can clip on to his collar for any dog encounters. You are going to be teaching your puppy that bottom sniffing is an important part of meeting another dog and it is much easier to teach him this if you have more control of where his head goes!

Your puppy is very small when you first take him out. Even if he is a larger breed, he is still likely to be smaller than a lot of the dogs he meets on these early outings. Furthermore, he is inexperienced and, unless he is born with a nervous disposition, totally trusting. He will likely want to say hello to every human he meets and every dog he meets. This is wonderful, naturally, and we should tap into this natural curiosity from the outset but do remember that you have NO control over how other people and their dogs will behave in the park. Yes, you might be able to ask them to keep their big bouncy dog from squashing your new puppy, but you can't guarantee that they will respond in a friendly way, or even do something about a situation like this. And that is the key here. Situations WILL arise with your new puppy and you won't necessarily be equipped, as a new dog owner, to deal with them. I am not scaremongering here, but a lot of the work I get as a behaviourist is the result of puppies having a bad experience early on in their young life, particularly with regards to other dogs. It may well be that your first visits to the park with your puppy go without incident and that is wonderful. I really hope that happens. But forewarned is forearmed and it is surely better to be aware that things can go a bit awry and have the knowledge of what to do if that happens.

In this chapter, we are going to focus on those very early encounters when your puppy is very young. In a dedicated chapter later, we will look at other scenarios that can arise as your puppy gets bigger and more confident, and also as he enters puberty, which comes with its own set of issues! As you enter the park, let your puppy sniff around and explore everything (remembering, of course, NOT to let him pick up anything with his mouth by keeping your beady eyes on him and moving him away from anything tempting). Let him wee and poo at will and just generally have a lovely time. If you bump into some people and they spot your cute little pup, politely tell them that this is his first walk and you are training him to be polite when he meets people, whilst keeping him back from them. Hopefully they will listen to you and not rush forward and start stroking your puppy without permission. Ask them to crouch down and offer a curled-up hand to your puppy to sniff. This will help him learn to keep ALL four paws on the ground when he meets people. He is so young at this point that he is very likely to WANT to sniff their hand, but again, if he seems a little nervous, let HIM make the decision and don't allow people to force themselves upon him. If random people invade his space when he isn't comfortable, he is going to learn to be wary of strangers and you absolutely don't want that. Your job as his owner is to let him know that YOU will control who touches him, you will advocate for him in all situations. This may seem a little over the top with a new puppy and in the majority of cases, as I said, your puppy will WANT to meet everyone you come across, but don't forget that there will always be the occasional puppy who is born a little highly strung and may be overwhelmed in this situation.

The biggest complaint people make about dogs in parks is that they often jump up at people and get their clothes all muddy. Jumping up is common thing I get called about as a behaviourist and I can't stress how important it is to teach your puppy NOT to do this from a very early age. If your puppy starts jumping up at a person you meet in the park, DON'T tell that person to turn their back on the puppy. This is advice I hear people give time and time again for dogs that jump up, but I happen to disagree with doing this. It deals with the issue AFTER it has happened, and yes, the dog may give up jumping up eventually, but it won't teach them not to jump up in the first place. What you should ask people to do when your puppy jumps up at them is to MOVE TOWARDS THE PUPPY WITH THEIR BODY. Why? Because this is telling the puppy, in "dog speak" that they aren't welcome in the person's personal space. This is what dogs do to each other – they CLAIM territory. You want your puppy to learn that the territory around a new person belongs to the person, not to the puppy. In effect, there is an exclusion zone around a person that the puppy must not enter unless invited. Your puppy needs to learn that he will only be invited into this space if all four paws are on the ground. If your puppy is tempted to jump up, you should also mark the unwanted behaviour with a verbal intervention, such as "Ah, Ah" whilst he is jumping up. I encourage my dog owners to teach their puppy to either stand for a tickle under the chin or come in sideways to the human and lean against them for a nice stroke on the side of their body. This works particularly well with big dogs who love to lean!

To recap, when you want your puppy to meet a new person in the park:

Use the lead to keep him near you.

Ask the person to crouch down and offer him a relaxed, balled fist to sniff, saying to your puppy at the same time "Do you want to say hello?"

If he sniffs their hand, ask them to tickle him UNDER HIS CHIN *or stroke him on his side but to* NOT STROKE HIM ON HIS HEAD.

If he backs away from their hand, tell the person he is a little shy and it's probably best not to touch him at the moment. If he is tiny, you can always pick him up and try it that way, as you are giving him calm support in your arms. But again, if he doesn't want to sniff their hand, ask them not to touch him. Make sure when you are holding him that YOU *are calm, relaxed and confident.*

If you do feel the need to pick him up, make sure you do it correctly. The safest way to pick him up is to use one hand to scoop him under his belly, holding his front leg between your thumb and your index finger. Now use the other hand to scoop up his back legs. Holding him likes this prevents him squirming out of your arms and being accidentally dropped.

If he is tempted to jump up whilst on the ground, ask the person to calmly move towards the puppy with their body to move him OUT *of their personal space. At the same time, you will be giving a verbal intervention, such as "Ah, Ah" or "Hey" to indicate his behaviour is unwanted.*

Once he has had his little fuss with the person, thank them and call him back to you, giving a tiny flick and release on his lead if he ignores you. He needs to learn that you decide when the meeting is over and follows you as you walk away.

Now let's talk about your new puppy meeting other dogs in the park. It is very important to get this right for several reasons. If you are a new

First Walks in the Park

dog owner, you may not be well versed in the way dogs interact with each other when on and off lead. Understanding this sort of dog behaviour is essential if you are going to raise a well-balanced dog from puppy, because you are going to find yourself in all sorts of different situations when you are out and about with your puppy that involve other dogs and if you DON'T understand why your puppy and another dog are behaving a certain way, it can be very stressful for you. You absolutely DON'T want that because that will impact on the way your puppy learns to behave around other dogs.

So, let's start with the easy situations. You are in the park, with your puppy on a lead and you meet another dog on a lead. Your puppy is on lead when meeting other dogs initially so that you have more control of what he is doing. I will be advising you to have him off-lead after you have done a couple of initial walks with him, but at an appropriate time. But first, he needs to learn how to greet other dogs. The approaching dog appears friendly, as does the owner. Before you let your puppy close to this dog, ask the owner "Is your dog OK with young puppies?". If the answer is a resounding yes, then say to your puppy "Do you want to say Hello?" and let him go up to the other dog. He will more than likely put his face right up to the other dog's face, and this is fine, but you also want to encourage him to sniff the other dog's behind. Why? Because this is how WELL-BALANCED DOGS meet! Think of it as the equivalent to telling someone your name and shaking their hand when you first meet them. You wouldn't go up to a total stranger on the street and give them a big hug without warning, would you? You'd get an earful if you did! No, you would tell them your name and perhaps offer your hand, because this is the polite way to meet a new person.

Young puppies have a habit of not being polite initially because they are young, excited and inexperienced. Consequently, they tend to barrel up to other dogs and stick their nose in their faces whilst frantically dancing around. They don't tend to stand still long enough for the other dog to get a sniff of their bottom. Why does this matter? Well, it matters because your puppy's scent tells the other dog all about his personality and his demeanour and also whether he is neutered or not (which of course, he won't be!). It is your puppy's own personal blueprint. Another dog won't necessarily fully trust until it has had a good sniff of the other dog's butt and decided that he feels ok about this dog. This is particularly the case with unbalanced dogs who have had a bad experience previously. A handy way of getting older dogs to accept your young puppy is for you to encourage bottom sniffing from the outset. If another owner is in agreement, ask them if they mind letting your puppy sniff their dog and vice versa. Here are some tips for doing this if the two dogs don't automatically butt sniff:

Let the older dog sniff first. Pop your fingers in your puppy's collar and turn his rear end towards the other dog. Make sure you are nice and relaxed! No tension, please, as we want your puppy to learn this is a good thing to do and not something they should be worried about.

Place your other hand gently under your puppy's belly so that he can't wiggle his bottom too much.

Now invite the other owner to let his dog sniff your puppy's bottom, ensuring that you stop your puppy turning his head backwards whilst this is going on.

Now swap around and ask the owner to do what you have just done and encourage your puppy to sniff their dog's bottom!

Now that the introductions are over, the two dogs should happily interact with each other. If the other dog gives any signs of tension after this butt sniff, I would move on with your walk and not let your puppy interact with this dog. There will be the occasional dog who does the butt sniff and then decides it doesn't like your puppy's energy!

Let's imagine you are in the park, and you meet an off-lead friendly looking dog. Before we go any further, let me ask you something. Do you know what a friendly dog looks like?! Many people will say a dog that is wagging its tail. Not necessarily! This is a massive misconception. Just because a dog is wagging its tail doesn't mean it is friendly! What this indicates is that its brain is excited/highly stimulated. But excitement isn't necessarily a positive thing. Think of a lion hunting. It may be a positive thing for the lion, but it certainly isn't a positive thing for its prey! The tail position and action tells us lots of things about what state of mind a dog is in at any given moment. In the case of a wagging tail, yes, it can mean that the dog is social and happy, but if it is more of a thrashing action, particularly to the left, this indicates a more dominant, challenging/combative state of mind. You would do well to familiarise yourself with the different body, head, and tail positions that dogs adopt and what they mean (see Chapter 18) BEFORE taking your puppy to the park so that you can make a decent judgement about which dogs to allow near your young puppy.

You have decided the approaching dog looks friendly and have called out to the owner to check. This is a good time to check out the owner's demeanour, because this too can be a clue as to whether their dog is actually friendly or not to young puppies. If the owner looks a bit tense or is trying to call the dog back, err on the side of caution. If the owner puts their dog on a lead the minute they spot you, again, err on the side of the caution. It may be that they are simply being polite and there is absolutely nothing to worry about, but you won't know for sure until you get closer. It could be that they have a specific reason for putting their dog on lead, possibly because it is a bit over-friendly with puppies, or maybe snappy with them. If an owner spots you and immediately turns in the other direction, that again is a good sign that your puppy shouldn't be meeting their dog!

Let's assume the approaching dog is fine. As with the on-lead dog, as the dog approaches, ask your puppy "Do you want to say Hello?" This will make your puppy look up at you. We want your puppy to do this each time he sees a dog, so doing this right from the very beginning is a really good way to instil this behaviour. There are going to be times when you will NOT be letting your puppy go up to say hello to other dogs, but more of that later. You will be teaching your puppy that whenever he sees a dog one of two things will happen, either you will be giving him permission to say hello, or you will be asking him to ignore the dog: either way it is YOU who will be making the decision, not him.

You have now shown your puppy on his first walk how you expect him to behave when he meets either dogs or people. Let's now look at getting him off lead from an early age, something a lot of new dog owners worry about a fair bit. I come across a lot of dog owners who didn't let their puppy off lead until it was maybe five or six months old because they were under the impression that they needed perfect recall before they could let the pup off lead. This is absolutely true, your puppy should have excellent recall if he is to be off lead, but there is an intermittent step that you can take from Day 1 which taps into a young puppy's in-built instinct to stay near you when it is still tiny. By the time you get to around five or six months your puppy's hormones will be starting to ramp up as he enters puberty and he will no longer be viewing you the way he did when he was 12 weeks or so old. At this young age, you are his protector and his leader and he does not question that. He will stick close to you and run back to you for reassurance and security whenever he is a little unsure. Yes, there is still a risk at this age that he could bolt if a situation overwhelms him, such as a large group of dogs suddenly running towards him, but these situations are rare and, as a dog owner, you should be on the lookout for any potential trouble whenever you are walking your dog.

A very handy command to teach him at this young age is the "Middle" command. Teaching him that the space between your open legs is a safe haven for him at all times, gives him a place to seek out when he is worried, and also a place you can call him back to if YOU are worried about his safety. Puppies are naturally drawn to the security of their owners legs when they are very young, so tap into this instinct by turning it into a direction you give your puppy. This is very easy to do. You can teach it in your home first, before you even go on your first park walk:

Open your legs so that your feet are slightly further apart, allowing space for your puppy to fit underneath you as you stand.

If your puppy naturally enters this space without being told, say "Middle" as he arrives and give him gentle praise. You can also give him a treat if you want, to reinforce the command and get him to learn it faster. Encourage him to come through your legs from behind so that when you look down, you are looking at his head, not his bottom!

DO NOT say it in advance until you have repeated the above numerous times when he does it by accident or of his own accord. Then, and only then, should you say it in advance to see if he has learnt what "Middle" means.

If he has successfully learnt what the command means, do it repeatedly when you are out and about in the park with him, particularly if there is a lot of activity from other dogs going on. This is a safe space for him to watch other dogs play and to return to if he becomes overwhelmed. It is far preferable to him bolting if something worries him, as that could result in him getting lost.

Tapping into your puppy's natural instinct to stay near you gives you a golden opportunity to teach him to "pack walk" with you from the outset and to build in good recall from the very start. Why pack walk? Well, this is what your puppy would be doing naturally if he was born into a wild dog pack, so it really is the most natural thing in the world for him to do and if he learns to replicate this behaviour when he is with humans, he will naturally stick close to you and be mentally connected to you at all times. There is no need to spend all your time controlling him with commands!

The best place to start replicating the pack walk with your puppy is in a location which has a natural walking route. Woodland walks are particularly good, as they will have a natural path to follow but only limited open spaces where your puppy might spot things further away that pique his interest. That's not to say you can't start this exercise in an ordinary, open grassy park! You can do it pretty much anywhere, but I would strongly advise that you DON'T do it in an area close to roads. Choose somewhere where the roads are quite some distance away, to be on the safe side. The first few times you do this, I would suggest that you choose somewhere fairly quiet, with few people and dogs around to distract your puppy.

Now to the nitty gritty. When you have chosen your place to "pack walk", swap your puppy from the lead on his collar to a puppy line on his harness (a puppy line is a light-weight thin line without a hand loop). As you unclip the lead on his collar, get into the habit of saying "Lead", as this will come in very handy as you progress with your walks. At the end of this exercise, when you clip his lead back onto his collar and take the puppy line off, again say "Lead" as you clip the lead on. What your puppy will quickly learn is that the command "Lead" means the lead is coming on or off, so you won't need to recall him when you want him back on lead. He should just come to you to have his lead clipped on when he hears the command "Lead"! There is no need to give him a treat whilst doing this. We want this to be a default behaviour accompanied by a calm, "following" demeanour. We do not want him excited when the lead is clipped on. Obviously, if by now your puppy isn't excited by food treats, by all means, give him one, but there really is no need.

Back to the puppy line training. The line should be about 1 metre long with a couple of knots tied at the end to stop it slipping beneath your boot should you stand on it. If you can't find one of these, I suggest you use an old lightweight lead of a similar length, with the loop handle unpicked and a couple of knots tied at the end. This line is going to be your safety net should you (or someone else) need to stop your puppy suddenly. It is clipped to his harness, rather than his collar, to prevent you pulling on his neck, should it need to be stood on. Now that the line is attached, drop it on the ground and let it trail behind your puppy. He is effectively now "off lead". You are ready to go.

Start walking away and your puppy should naturally follow you and stick close whilst you walk along. This is particularly the case in the early weeks, but he will get a little more confident with each walk and start to explore a little further away from you. Get into the habit of calling him back with his name when he does this. Praise him calmly when he reaches you and give him a little puppy treat every so often. There is no need to treat him each time as this is very much a "casual" recall. We will get to a more formal recall ("Barney, Come") in a minute. Teach him to keep one eye and ear on you by changing direction frequently on your walk and saying "This Way", to encourage him to follow you. Again, no treat needed. You are simply instilling the habit of him

First Walks in the Park

following you when you change direction. To check if he is really paying attention to where you are, stop dead when he is in front of you and see if he notices. If he doesn't notice, call him informally with his name and do a 180 degree turn and start walking the other way. He should follow you. Do this "Stop" check repeatedly on the walk. You will know when your puppy is fully mentally connected to you when he automatically stops when you do. It may take him a little time to tune in to pack walking but don't worry, every puppy is different, and he will get there. As I said, puppies naturally stick close to you when they are tiny, so this is the perfect time to instil this kind of behaviour. You may well need to repeat this exercise again for a week or so at puberty, but because you have already taught it, any rebelliousness at puberty should be short-lived.

Once you have done this type of walk in a quiet area of your walk on a pathway, try doing it in a more open area of grass. This time, zigzag your way across the grass, saying "This Way" whenever you change direction. Your young pup should follow you. Once you have done this for five minutes or so, try zig zagging WITHOUT saying anything at all. If your puppy is fully connected and pack walking, he should follow you without being told. Well done! Now, obviously your puppy is going to get distracted by sights and smells and particularly by other dogs and humans. This is where the puppy line comes in. If you see a dog or human approaching, pick up the line and use it like a normal lead (remember what we did above to teach your puppy nice manners around people and dogs). If your puppy starts to rush off before you get the chance to pick it up, DON'T SHOUT, just trot after him and step on the line to stop him dead. This won't hurt him as it is attached to his harness. He MUST learn that when he is off lead, he can't just charge up to anyone and anything. Instil this behaviour from the very beginning, rather than leaving it until he is much older. Stop him dead, decide whether you want him to meet the dog or human and then follow the on-lead protocol mentioned earlier.

In time, as he grows and demonstrates calm behaviour when meeting dogs and humans, you are going to start to trust him to meet nicely and not have to pick up his puppy line, but in the beginning you must control who he meets and how he meets them if you want him to grow up well-mannered. Now that he knows how to follow you and keep his eyes/ears on you whilst walking "off-lead", you can build in some more formal recall. I teach my clients two kinds of formal recall - "Come" and the dog whistle. The "Come" command is preceded by the puppy's name e.g. "Barney, Come". If the informal recall, where you are just saying the puppy's name, doesn't result in him turning and coming back to you, you will then need to go up a gear and use the formal "Barney, Come".

It is very easy to teach a formal "Come" if you remember to stick to some basic rules. Be calm, confident, and consistent! Don't keep changing what you say verbally - choose your phrase and stick to it and make sure all the family knows what it is. Don't change what you do when your puppy arrives - I teach a particular protocol when the puppy successfully comes back, which I will detail below, but you can choose your own, just stick to it to avoid confusing your puppy. Don't be hesitant, be commanding - this is going to be very important at puberty, so get into the habit now of always delivering the command the same way, in the same tone, with the same confidence. There will be times when things go pear-shaped and you are unable to deliver the command verbally with confidence (e.g. when your puppy has started running towards something dangerous or particularly tempting, like a squirrel) and that is where the whistle will come in, but more of that in a minute. You may wonder if you have to stick to doing "Come" this way forever? The answer is no, you don't! Once you have reliable recall with your dog, you can phase out the final stage where he has to sit, take a treat and look up at you before you release him again. He will eventually just stay close once you call him back, so you can drop this phase, and drop the treat! A well-balanced, well-connected dog shouldn't need treats by the time he has reached adulthood.

This is how I teach a puppy the formal "Come" command:

Get a super tasty treat especially reserved for teaching the formal "Come" and have it ready in one hand. Do have it ready in advance, rather than start scrabbling around for it when your puppy arrives! A treat pouch is really helpful for this training.

Whilst holding your puppy's training line, say his name and "COME" in a calm, firm voice and is he doesn't respond instantly, give the line a tiny flick and release to get his attention. This should make him turn towards you.

Use lots of encouragement as he moves towards you. You can be excited at this point, but you must return to a calm, commanding state when he arrives.

When he arrives at your feet, bend the elbow of the treat hand up towards your shoulder. Most puppies will automatically sit when you do this, but if he doesn't, tell your puppy to "Sit".

As he sits, say "Good Boy" or "Nice" in a calm voice and give him the treat.

Once he has taken the treat, immediately open the treat hand up and hold it above him in a "wait" gesture (with your hand face-down and fingers spread) but **don't** *say anything!*

Once he has finished eating, he will naturally look up towards your hand, as this is where treats come from. If he looks you directly in the eye, say "Ok, on you go" or a similar phrase to indicate he can resume walking.

If he doesn't look you in the eye but gets up and tries to walk away, bring him back to your feet with the puppy line, tell him to sit again and put your hand up again in that "wait" position. This should make him look up at you and make eye contact. Once he has made eye contact, you can release him verbally with your chosen phrase and resume your walk.

Why is it important to teach the release? Because he needs to GET PERMISSION to leave you and leave you CALMY, and he only gets that permission when he makes full eye contact and is calm. That is why you need to switch from excited encouragement as he approaches you, to a calm state of mind when he arrives. Too many owners teach their puppies to come but then immediately let them run off again in an excited state once they have eaten their treat. They don't learn to stay and wait for permission to leave again. This is precisely WHY we teach a formal come, because it gives the owner an extra level of control and the time to clip a lead on if necessary. The informal calling of your dog by his name doesn't require him to wait for a release, and this is what you will use to first call your puppy back to you whilst walking. But the formal "Come" does because, as I said, there will be times when you need him back and don't want him rushing off again (we will look at problem situations a little later on). So DO teach a formal "Come" command in this way because I can guarantee that you are going to need it at some point.

Set yourself up for success with recall training by starting off in a very quiet environment and not moving up to a busier environment with more people and dogs until you completely trust your puppy to recall to you in the quiet environment. Far better to incrementally increase the stimuli that are likely to grab your puppy's attention than to throw yourself in at the deep end and become disheartened when your puppy doesn't listen to you. Many owners inadvertently train their puppy NOT to come when called, by repeatedly saying the "Come" command without success, getting annoyed and then going to drag the puppy away from whatever has gotten its attention. If you do this, you are doomed for failure. It is NOT your puppy's fault that it hasn't learnt to recall, it is YOUR fault for not having the patience or the knowledge to teach him properly. Another thing to point out here is that you will see I am not advising you to find an enclosed safe area to teach recall. In an ideal world, this would be a great place to train, but a large number of new puppy owners DON'T have access to this type of space. The above method gets around this problem and also helps teach your puppy in a more realistic environment, whilst keeping him safe by having him on a long line. I actually prefer to teach out in the open amongst other dogs and other humans as it replicates real life. Having perfect recall in an enclosed space like a tennis court does not mean your puppy is going to have perfect recall whilst walking through a park full of dogs or people having picnics!

Once your puppy has learnt on a short line to come back when formally called and to wait for the release, you can pop him on a longer line and call him back from a greater distance. Many owners buy a ten-metre line to teach recall, but I personally would advise against this for several reasons. Firstly, you don't want your puppy to get into the habit of being ten metres away from you. This is too far for training purposes, in my opinion, and too far from a "pack walk" perspective. Dogs pack walk <u>together</u>. We want this to be your puppy's default. Secondly, a ten-metre line can prove pretty dangerous if there are lots of other dogs around. You NEED other dogs around if you are going to successfully teach your puppy to ignore them. You need to be very careful when using training lines in company and a very long one is much harder to utilise. So, stick to something about five metres maximum. If your puppy is a very small breed, make sure the line is lightweight as he will find this hard to pull along on the ground, particularly when it is wet and muddy. You will need to incorporate the trailing lead stage into your training before you can fully let him off lead.

You have moved up to a longer line and are now calling your puppy back from a greater distance. Build this recall training into your pack walk around the woods. Let your puppy trail this long line behind him whilst you walk him, and every so often practise a formal recall with him. If you see someone approaching, either on their own or with a dog, pick up the long line and shorten it so that your puppy is walking closer to you as the person/dog approaches. Make a habit of allowing your puppy to meet some people or dogs but not others. You want to remind him that YOU make that decision, not him. Once that dog/person has passed, drop the line on the ground again and carry on. With these four or five metre length lines, you can now also deeply instil the need for your puppy to stay within this range of you. We started with your puppy "off lead" on a metre long puppy line, but you will find as each day goes by that he gets a little braver and starts running a little further ahead of you each time. Now is the perfect time to instil in him that the MAXIMUM distance you want him ahead of you is the length of this longer training line. Why? Because, if you let him get used to going much further ahead of you, you are going to have less influence on him and are more likely to get into issues with recall and may have to rely on the whistle. It makes for a much more pleasant walk all round if he learns to pack walk WITH you, rather than rushing away out of sight all the time and having to be called back. Remember, YOU are leading this walk, not him!

To ensure he learns the distance parameter, simply keep your eye on his trailing line and if it starts to move past your feet, step on it. He should immediately turn and look back (if he doesn't, simply wait until he does!). He will do one of two things. He will either stand and wait, looking at you, in which case you can give him a thumbs up (to let him know this is wanted behaviour) and then tell him to carry on with a chosen phrase (e.g. "Ok" or "On you go"). Alternatively, he will drop back and rejoin you, in which case you simply start walking again. What I don't want you to do is recall him in any way, either informally or formally. DO NOT SPEAK! We want his brain to automatically tell him to turn and look for you when he reaches this distance and, trust me, if you do this right he will! Repeating this stopping and starting exercise will result in him learning a default distance that he is supposed to stay at when he is in a calm state of mind. If his state of mind escalates due to a trigger, such as a squirrel or another dog, THEN you can recall him. What we are creating is a natural comfortable way of walking that doesn't involve you constantly having to recall him to control where he is. He will naturally stay in your orbit and keep an eye on where you are if you train this way and you will only have to use recall occasionally when he is stimulated into excitement by a sight, sound or a smell.

Let's bring the whistle in at this point. I recommend whistle training to all my clients because it gives you an extra tool to use on those occasions when your puppy/dog makes the wrong decision i.e. doesn't come when formally called because the thing that has got his attention is just way too interesting. Puppies make mistakes. They are young and immature and need guidance, so don't be surprised if from time to time you find your formal recall isn't working. This is when your whistle gets deployed! All you have to do to whistle train your puppy is to build it into the formal recall training above. After you say "Barney, Come", simply peep your chosen whistle signal and when your puppy arrives give him a massive BONANZA of treats! You have to make this treat-fest super-duper because you want him to learn that when he comes back to the whistle he has really hit the jackpot. What whistle training does is it allows you a means of communicating with him when your voice has changed due to stress. When you do a formal come in a non-stressful situation, your voice should sound the same. We all know what happens when we are super stressed. Our mouths dry up, our voice goes up and we sound different. This will impact on the effect you have on your dog as your "Barney, Come" won't sound the same as it normally does. If you have trained your puppy to a calm, confident "Barney, Come", you can't expect him to respond to a significantly altered version of this! The whistle provides you with an alternative recall tool that ALWAYS sounds the same! Furthermore, it is more likely to get through to the brain of an excited dog than a human voice! You will use a bonanza of treats whilst initially training with the whistle, but once you have reliable whistle recall (and indeed formal recall), you can start to phase out the treats then dispense with them altogether. You will simply be rewarding with vocal praise and a pat when he comes back to you.

Many puppy owners ask what type of whistle they should use? I strongly recommend that you don't buy a cheap one from a pet shop. These aren't calibrated, so if you buy one, lose it and then replace it, your new whistle won't have exactly the same pitch as the old one and you will have to retrain from scratch. Far better to invest in a slightly more expensive, calibrated professional dog whistle (you will know if it is calibrated, because the whistle will come in a choice of pitches which are likely to be assigned numbers, such as 210.5). If you lose this whistle and replace it with the same size, it will have exactly the same pitch and there will be no need to retrain your puppy. Similarly, if you need several whistles for your family, these will all have exactly the same pitch. These whistles usually come with a lanyard, which is essential for whistle training. You need that whistle on hand at all times and having it around your neck is the perfect place - you won't have time to go digging around in your pockets or your bag in situations where you need to use the whistle for recall!

One last thing to build into your walks in the park with your young puppy is a fun game called "Find Me!" This is a game of hide and seek that you can play with your puppy, either when walking on your own or, even better, if you have a family member with you. In a safe location, far away from any roads with your puppy on his long line, let your puppy wander a little bit ahead and when he turns back to look at you, duck behind a tree or bush. Crouch down and yell "Find Me!" in a high-pitched, excited voice. Because your puppy saw where you went, he will come barrelling back to you. Greet him with open arms and loads of love and cuddles, and lots of high pitched "Good Boy" praise. This is one of the few times I am going to say it is good to use high excitement with your puppy when he arrives! Do this a couple of times when he has seen where you were hiding and then do it BEFORE he turns back to look at you. We want him to be sniffing around ahead of you, not paying attention, when you choose your hiding place. When you yell "Find Me" he is going to have to follow the sound of your voice to find you, so keep yelling! If several family members are on the walk, take it in turns to hide so that he ends up running in between you. I can guarantee he will LOVE this game. It is a good one to teach because if all else has failed when your puppy has become distracted, you dropping to the ground and yelling "Find Me" should do the trick! Obviously, we don't want to be using this for recall all the time, this is just a last-ditch thing to try!

Case Study 2: A Pesky Fox!

I was chatting to a client who had done my puppy classes and had learnt the "Find Me" game. She was out walking with her husband when their puppy spotted a fox and took off after it. They tried their regular recall, but it didn't work. They didn't have a whistle on them, as they had forgotten it. The husband was yelling and shouting at the puppy to come back, but the wife remembered the game they had taught him. She threw herself to the ground and screamed "Find Me!" at the top of her voice. The puppy stopped dead, turned around and came charging back to her, the fox all forgotten! Phew! She was so impressed that he came back that she just HAD to tell me!

Chapter 15 – Problems When Out Walking

If you have got your puppy off to a good start by making it clear to him who is leading the walk, you shouldn't encounter many problems when out and about, either on lead or off lead. Why? Because your puppy will have already learnt to look to you for direction in any situation, rather than follow his instincts, which might include warning off an over-excited dog or barking at a scary looking human. If you DO encounter any problems, they are more likely to be down to someone else not having control of THEIR dog, so let's look at some of the situations that may arise and what impact they can have on your puppy, particularly if you don't know how to deal with them from the outset.

One of the main things I get called to help with is dogs who have developed reactivity to other dogs because of a bad experience they had as a puppy. What has normally happened is that the puppy has been pounced on, or even worse, attacked by an older dog whilst out on a walk when it was quite young. This has been a horrible experience for the owner and led to them worrying about their puppy being "attacked" again. I will just add at this point that most altercations between dogs in the park are NOT full-blown attacks, but more of that later. Back to puppies being alarmed by another dog at a young age. This first incident triggers a pattern of behaviour which is repeated over and over across the country with so many dog owners; the owner has a bad experience with another dog whilst walking their puppy, they then become nervous about it happening again and their puppy picks up on this change in their demeanour and becomes more distrustful of other dogs. Whilst not always the case, a puppy may learn that, to keep a dog away, the best thing for it to do is to growl, bark or lunge. This situation can easily be avoided if you know how to act as an owner the very FIRST time anything untoward happens in the park with your puppy (or on the street, for that matter). Understanding WHY another dog might have a go at your puppy and how you should behave during and immediately after a bad event will have a massive impact on whether or not your puppy becomes fearful/distrustful of other dogs, and indeed grows into a reactive dog itself.

Firstly, let's look at why unwanted things happen and then how you should approach an "incident". The most common reason young puppies get told off by older dogs is because they are annoying! Young pups lack self-restraint, are generally very sociable and usually super excited to be in the park. They usually (but not always!) love every person and every dog they meet and want to play with them, particularly the dogs. But not every dog is enamoured with puppies. Teenagers usually have no interest in hanging out with toddlers, do they? You will encounter plenty of dogs who will happily play with your young puppy, but you will also encounter plenty, particularly older ones, who simply aren't interested and will be quick to let your puppy know, with a growl or a quick air snap. DO NOT TAKE THIS PERSONALLY! They are not ATTACKING your puppy when they do this, they are warning your puppy off and are perfectly entitled to do so. This is totally natural behaviour, and it will only occur if the puppy INVADES the older dog's space. This is why it is so important for your puppy to learn from a very young age how to politely approach other dogs. It is also important for you to learn that it is ok for an older dog to give your puppy a quick reprimand when his attention is unwanted.

It is a whole different ball game if an older dog charges at your puppy or pursues it, without the puppy provoking at all. That is NOT natural "warning off" behaviour. It may be that the offending dog has been attacked itself at some point and so is pre-empting an unwanted approach from your puppy by chasing it off. It is the owner of this dog who has the responsibility for putting a stop to this behaviour, but you will come across plenty of owners who do nothing in this situation. If your puppy is the subject of unwanted advances from an over-excited/potentially aggressive dog, what can you do? Firstly, I would strongly advise you to teach your puppy the "Middle" command from a very young age, as mentioned in the previous chapter.

Secondly, I would advise you to learn how to send an approaching dog AWAY if its advances are unwelcome. You have several options when a dog is heading towards you and you don't want it to interact with your puppy. What you do depends on how far away the approaching dog is and also your assessment of how much risk the dog poses. This includes risk to you, so do familiarise yourself with dog body language as you don't want to be putting yourself at risk at any point from an attack from a dog that could do you serious harm. If in doubt, confidently but briskly walk the other way and put some distance between yourself and the dog.

If the approaching dog is some distance away and just appears excitable or curious, your first course of action should be to try to stop it in its tracks before it gets any closer. To do this, get your puppy back on its lead (if it is currently off-lead) and place him behind your legs, holding the lead very short but with a relaxed hand. Now FORGET ABOUT YOUR PUPPY and concentrate on the oncoming dog. Swing your right hip slightly forwards towards the oncoming dog and adopt a "warrior stance". You will now use your right hand to firmly instruct the incoming dog to "Go", by extending your arm in a "halt" position and flicking your wrist to indicate you want the dog to move away from you. This is telling the approaching dog two things 1) the puppy belongs to you and is not for touching 2) the oncoming dog is NOT welcome in YOUR personal space. This method is your best defence against approaching dogs, but you must BELIEVE that you have the power to send the dog away and you must do it before the dog is in close proximity to you. Your body language and energy will convey this, so even if you are feeling like a jelly inside, ACT as if you are a warrior in charge of yourself and your puppy.

You could pick your puppy up, but this is not advisable - only do this if you believe your puppy is in danger of serious injury. It is NOT a good idea to repeatedly pick your puppy up every time a dog approaches. Why? Because most people when they pick a dog up place it in front of them on their chest, with its vulnerable underbelly exposed to the dog at your feet. If the offending dog jumps up to nip, it is your puppy's belly which is going to get bitten and that is not a good thing. Familiarise yourself with the safest way to hold a puppy in your arms. Scoop your puppy up with your left hand, placing your thumb and fingers around its front paws to hold it securely, then rest it on your left hip, tucked under your arm. When you turn sideways towards the oncoming dog, your puppy will be behind you on your hip in a safe place.

Hopefully, this situation won't ever arise, but forewarned is forearmed. I once had three huskies approach an outdoor puppy training class I was teaching during the Pandemic and got rid of them with this method. They were simply curious as to what was going on in their local park, and fancied seeing who all these tiny dogs were, but they stopped dead and turned tail when I took up the warrior stance and ordered them to go away from the group of puppies I was teaching! Had I panicked and started yelling at them, this would simply have drawn them in closer and would have made myself even more interesting. My weak, nervous energy would have made me appear more like prey than a predator to them. This energy would also have set the puppies on edge and made them nervous. In acting as their protector, the puppies were able to relax and trust me to take care of the situation. Be your dog's protector and get rid of unwanted advances.

It is always a good idea when sending an unwanted dog away to call over to the owner and make it clear you are not being rude, that you are just training your puppy and he isn't ready yet for interaction with other dogs. They might think you are a bit nuts, but that's better, surely, than letting their dog get too close and ending up with a bad situation if the approaching dog turns out to be unbalanced.

There may be times when you have allowed your puppy to play with another dog, but then the play gets too boisterous and you want it to stop because you are worried your puppy is going to get hurt, or your puppy might hurt the other dog (if he is bigger!). I encourage owners to teach their puppies the "Enough" command, which indicates they should stop playing and take a breather. This is easy to do if your puppy is on a puppy line. Let him play and when things get a little too elevated, simply pick the line up and gently pull your puppy towards you, saying "Enough" as you do so. You WON'T be treating him for this. Why? Because you don't want him to learn to play too rough in order to get a treat! This is a case of him learning basic manners with other dogs and following your lead when told. As always with teaching commands, repeat a number of times WHILST you are moving him away and then see if he has learnt the command by saying it without a gentle tug on the training lead. If the other dog comes back for more whilst you are removing your puppy, simply block access to your puppy with your body and send the other dog away with a firm "Go". There may be times that your puppy simply doesn't listen to you when you tell him "Enough" and if that happens you will need to step in and physically remove him from play. Take hold of his collar gently with ONE finger, kneel down placing yourself between him and the other dog, take a nice deep breath and RELAX (particularly the hand that is holding him!). This action alone should bring his brain activity down and calm him. When you feel he is calm, simply release him and walk away. Don't ever be tempted to pull your dog backwards away from another dog by his collar or harness. He will instinctively pull FORWARDS if you do this and get more excited. Placing yourself between him and the other dog is far more effective. If another dog is pinning your puppy down and you want him to stop, ask the owner to remove him as your puppy needs a break. If you know the dog well and know it is balanced, you can remove it yourself, but don't do this unless you are confident it is a friendly dog (your puppy shouldn't be playing with an unfriendly/unbalanced dog anyway!). Again, don't try to pull the other dog off as he will simply pull forwards. To remove him off your puppy put a couple of fingers in his collar and pull him FORWARDS AND UPWARDS, then flip him over to the side. Again, only do this in a calm, confident state of mind and do tell the owner you are about to remove the dog off your puppy.

Case Study 1: Lack of Self-Control Equals Trouble

Ruby was a rescue and had missed out on socialisation as a puppy. As a result, she had not learnt how to play nicely with other dogs. Whilst she enjoyed playing, she would get over-excited and too rough and this sometimes tipped over into aggression, landing her in all sorts of trouble. Her owner became fearful of letting her off lead, because she couldn't be sure that she would be able to call Ruby back if she spotted another dog she wanted to play with. Several bad incidents had led to Ruby's owner being told off by other owners and she no longer enjoyed taking her dog out for walks.

With Ruby on a short-training line I carefully chose some well-balanced dogs to introduce her to, one at a time, and to teach her to come away from play when I asked her to. We did this over a number of sessions, allowing Ruby to have a short, nice play, then calling her away before she was able to get too excited. If she did get too excited, I picked up the training line and removed her from play whilst saying a firm "Enough" command to indicate that this word meant disengage and stop playing. As in most of my training, I did NOT give her a treat for stopping play. I didn't want her to learn to play roughly in order to get a food reward. I wanted her to learn that she would be allowed to play with another dog if she kept control of her energy levels and played in a social way, but if she exhibited any signs of her brain escalating too much (too much snarling or being over-dominant with the other dog), I would be intervening and stopping play. She picked this up very quickly and I am glad to say, despite not being shown the ropes as a young puppy, she was able to enjoy life as an adult dog once she learnt that there were rules and boundaries to the way she interacted with other dogs.

Case Study 2: Terrified of the Outside World

Nala was a family-bred border collie puppy who had developed an intense fear of going outside the house due to an attack at a young age by a large off-lead dog. Her fear had been exacerbated when she was subsequently chased by a group of other dogs. Her owner had tried everything to get her out of the house for a walk, but she simply froze with fear and started to shake all over as soon as they came out of the front door, or even the back garden. Nothing could persuade her to move. Consequently, she was no longer being walked and the only exercise she was getting was ball play in the back garden. Nala was an extreme case and quite a challenge to help. She was incredibly loving and lived quite happily with an older German shepherd. Naturally, her owner found it very distressing to see Nala so terrified, and yet understood that she needed exercise and stimulation outside of the house for her own well-being and health, which is why she got in touch.

The first step was to gain Nala's trust. She wasn't just terrified of the outside world; she was also scared of humans visiting her house. Once I had got her to trust me and allow me to put a lead on her, it was time to take her outside. Predictably she froze as soon as she realised where we were going. She tried very hard to pull me back towards the house, but I remained calm and stationary, until she worked out that I wasn't going to move. For that first session, we just stayed where we were, with me ensuring I was remaining very calm, but confident. I needed Nala to trust that I wouldn't let anything bad happen to her and for her to experience this nerve-wracking environment for herself, without incident. Working at her pace, I gradually managed to get her a little further from the house each time I led her out on the lead. She did panic if a person walked by, but again I stood firm and calm and allowed her to experience the trigger with calm support, but importantly without any retreat, until the adrenaline drained away and her brain calmed. With time and patience, we got Nala walking again on the lead. She is still wary of other dogs due to her experience as a puppy but can at least enjoy a proper walk with her owner, knowing that her owner will take care of her, no matter what.

We have looked at the more serious problems above, but let's also look at some less serious issues you might have whilst you are out and about. I am going to call them the **common why's**. These are things I get asked a lot by owners during a puppy's first year. They aren't necessarily problems, they are just questions I often get asked. There will undoubtedly be more queries you would like answered, but here are the most common ones I have come across!

Why does my puppy stop and wee so often?

The most likely reason, once he has emptied his bladder initially, is because he is marking territory. He is leaving his calling card to let other dogs know that he has passed by. Both male and female puppies do this. They tend to mark where another dog has marked, so you will often see a line of boy dogs queuing up to mark one after another on the same spot!

Why does my puppy drag his bottom along the grass?

If he has just pooed, it's because he may still feel something there, either inside or stuck on his fur near his bottom. Have a quick look in that area before calling the vet. If you can't see anything obvious it may be that his anal glands are a little full, or indeed compacted. When this happens, they can feel uncomfortable so your puppy may "scooch". Don't worry about this, unless it is happening all the time, in which case, get your vet to check your puppy's glands. If they are blocked, he will be a little smellier than normal and may keep licking his bottom area!

Why is my puppy wary of some dogs/humans and not others?

Your puppy will be reading the body language and energy of every dog he meets (likewise humans) and will respond accordingly, depending on what that dog is telling him about his character and his demeanour. It has nothing to do with the dogs' breed, size, or colour. This may only become a factor AFTER your puppy has had a bad experience with a dog of a particular size/breed/colour, but hopefully you will have dealt with that in the correct way and prevented any bad association from happening.

Why does my puppy keep eating other dogs' poo?

This is a tricky one to answer, as I don't claim to be an expert in the content of dog poo (or any animal poo) and why it is so appealing! There are various reasons why this may be happening, ranging from the simple fact that it tastes nice to them, to them having some dietary deficiency which is causing them to supplement their regular food intake. Once thing we can all agree on is that, from a human point of view, this is a pretty disgusting habit, so make it clear to your puppy if you catch him doing this that you don't want him to, by saying a clear "Leave" every time you see him heading for poo/eating poo. DO NOT REWARD HIM WITH A TREAT! Remember, you don't want him to seek out poo, in order to be rewarded with his favourite biscuit for leaving it!

Why does my puppy run after a ball, but not bring it all the way back to me?

At some point you have inadvertently taught him to NOT bring it all the way back and that you will fetch it for him! You won't even know that you have done this. You will, for example, have thrown the ball.

He will have gone after it and picked it up and started heading back to you. Then he will have dropped it for some reason (maybe he got distracted by a noise or a scent), and you will have shouted "Fetch" at around this time, to try to get him to bring it to you again. But if he doesn't and you move forwards to pick it up, you will have inadvertently changed the meaning of "Fetch"! Fetch now means, go after it, bring it halfway back, drop it and then my human will get it and throw it again! To fix this, simply start from scratch and if he drops it halfway, finish the game by walking off in the other direction. Surreptitiously pick the ball back up next time you walk past it! Once you have done this a few times, your dog will soon learn that the only way you are going to play is if he brings it ALL the way back to you each time!

Why does my puppy steal other dog balls in the park and run off with them?

Chances are that you inadvertently taught your puppy to steal! It's only natural when he is little that he is interested in any toys being thrown around in the park. It is important to teach him from an early age that he is not allowed to play with other dog's balls unless he is given permission. As with any objects you don't want him to touch, say a firm "Leave" if he moves towards a ball that isn't his. If he looks up at you when he hears this, say a calm "Well done" or "Nice" but DON'T reward him with a treat. You want him to learn to ignore other dog's balls, not seek them out in order to be given a treat for not touching them! I personally have taught my dogs "Not Yours!" and this has worked really well – my collie plays with her own ball but no longer picks up other dogs balls. Even if your puppy steals a ball and gives it back to you, don't treat him, or you will simply teach him to deliberately steal balls in order to get a food reward.

Why does my puppy keep obsessively sticking its nose up other dog's bottoms or try to hump them?

Sniffing bottoms is a natural behaviour, but if it isn't just a quick sniff whilst your puppy is first greeting another dog and is a more obsessive type of sniff, with your puppy relentlessly following a particular dog around with his nose up its bottom, it is most likely because your puppy is entering puberty. The same applies to the humping behaviour. Humping is a natural behaviour and it will happen from time to time with some puppies. Some are more driven to hump than others and it isn't a problem unless, again, it becomes obsessive. No-one wants their puppy to be a sex-pest in the park. It can be very annoying for other dogs and also isn't good for them physically if the humper is bigger and heavier than them. Neutering should help hugely with a puppy that pesters other dogs in this way.

Do I always need to take water with me for my puppy?

Puppies can become dehydrated very quickly, particularly in warm weather, so it is a good idea to carry water on you when walking a young puppy. Whilst not strictly necessary in the colder months, your puppy may still work up quite a thirst when he is playing with other dogs, so having fresh water handy is useful and a good habit to get into. Drinking fresh rainwater won't harm him, but you don't want him drinking any stagnant water that has been sitting around for a while. The base of trees is a common place for this water to gather, so do be aware that if your puppy is a big drinker, he may head for these places for a quick drink, even in the winter. Stagnant water may give him a tummy upset, so having fresh to hand is definitely preferable. It is absolutely essential for you to carry fresh water on you when the weather warms up. Dehydration is a serious issue, as is heat stroke. Use your common sense. Don't let him charge about in the sun for too long, particularly if he has a thick coat, and offer him regular drinks.

Is it fine for my puppy to play in the sea at the beach or in streams?

Be careful at the beach with a puppy, or any dog for that matter. It is not good for any animal to swallow lots of salty water or, indeed, sand. It can quickly result in salt poisoning, which is hugely dangerous. Drinking even a tiny bit of sea water is likely to upset your puppy's tummy, so if you do take him to the beach, let him paddle in the shallows, but don't let him drink the sea water or gulp down lots of it whilst retrieving a ball. Keeping him on lead will give you more control of what he is doing whilst in the sea. Do NOT throw balls out for him to bring back to you. Just like humans, he could find himself out of his depth, or caught in an undertow. Again, common sense should prevail here. Using common sense around freshwater bodies is also essential. Algae can be a problem in the warmer months, or pollution and, again, a puppy (or dog) who ingests a lot of contaminated water is going to get sick.

Pupology

Chapter 16 – Take Your Puppy Everywhere

We all want a dog we can take anywhere with us, whether it be on a local trip to the café or the pub, or perhaps on holiday with us. If you want your dog to be able to go anywhere with you, with no stress or worry, start taking him everywhere as a puppy! Think of him as an extension of yourself, rather than an animal who needs to be controlled! If you are calm and relaxed about all environments, he will learn to be too, so don't tense up and anticipate trouble, just relax and enjoy taking him to new places. All you need to be able to do is step in if he gets too excited about something and return him to a calm state of mind.

You should know how to do this by now. A quick verbal intervention (such as "Ah, Ah") should be sufficient if he is only mildly excited by the new environment. If he isn't listening to your verbal intervention, you can use a physical one, such as a quick flick on his lead (don't forget, this is a quick flick <u>and</u> RELEASE and NOT A PULL) or if he is super excited, the blocking & claiming technique (stand facing him, with yourself between him and the thing exciting him, and move him backwards with your body until he turns to walk away and reconnects mentally with you by looking you in the eye). The other thing you can do to ensure he doesn't get excited about things is use the "Leave" command which we talked about earlier.

If you dream of taking him to cafes and pubs, make sure you teach him how to "settle" from an early age. I mentioned the "Settle" command in an earlier Case Study, but let's just recap in a bit more detail and use the pub environment as an example. Wherever the location, do make sure you enter it with your puppy walking calmly beside or behind you and NOT in front of you. If he drags you through the door in an excited state, you are already off on the wrong foot! He should be accompanying you into the space calmly, just like everywhere else he goes. To teach him to settle, do the following:

Go to your chosen table, sit down and tell him to lie down on the floor either next to you or under the table, depending on how much room there is. Under the table is better as there is less chance of him getting trodden on or something being dropped on him from above. If he has a favourite blanket, take that with you and pop the blanket in this spot.

If he won't lie down, at least get him to sit. If he won't sit on command, gently push his bottom so that he does sit. Now RELAX! *Do not hold his lead tight or hold him by his collar to get him to stay there. You want him to learn that when you ask him to sit under or next to a table, you expect him to do just that and not move - his self-control will be keeping him there, not you.*

If he only went into a sit, but then voluntarily lay down with sleepy eyes, say "Settle" in a calm voice at this precise moment. If he laid down right away and looked relaxed, say "Settle" then. What we are NOT *doing is using treats to get him to sit or lie down. Why? Because the food may excite him and we want him calm and relaxed in this situation.*

If he gets up and tries to move around, calmly return him to his spot and ask him to sit or lie down again. DON'T *tell him off. If he is calmly sitting, this is absolutely fine as a starting point. He will lie down eventually of his own free will because he will get sleepy or bored. But if he isn't calmly sitting, putting him into a down position will help, as a lying down dog is calmer than a sitting dog, and a sitting dog is calmer than a standing dog!*

Each time he tries to move, return him to his spot and repeat the above, remembering at all times to remain relaxed yourself and not to hold the lead tight. Don't forget to say "Settle" if he lies down and relaxes. You can start to interrupt any signs of movement from him with a verbal intervention (like we have talked about before). The second you spot that he may be thinking of moving (key signs being wider eyes, ears forward, head up), use your verbal intervention (such as "Ah, Ah") and remember, IMMEDIATELY RELAX *afterwards. Tension is your enemy. Calm, confidence is your friend.*

Once he has got used to relaxing under your table or beside you, you can sit back and start to enjoy yourself. Don't be tempted to keep petting him or talking to him and please, please DON'T *feed him treats! There is no need. The message to him is that whilst you are sat at a table, you expect him to snooze quietly. If you bring food into the equation, you are in danger of teaching him to lie down for a bit, receive a treat for lying down, then get up again, be told to lie down again, receive a treat and so on.*

He may well be stimulated to get up if another dog or human walks past your table. If he does break his position when this happens, just repeat the initial actions WITHOUT FUSS. Don't get angry or annoyed with him. He is young and learning, remember. Other dogs and humans are interesting to him, particularly humans carrying plate loads of tasty, smelly food. Just keep one eye on him and if you see those signs that his brain activity is elevating because of a trigger, step in verbally, or if necessary, physically (by returning him to a sit with a gentle nudge on his bottom) and he will soon get the message.

Once you have repeated the "Settle" command a number of times when he has actually been lying down calmly under the table, ask him to get up and come to you for a pat and then say "Settle" and see if he lies down and relaxes for you. If he does, he has successfully learnt the command. If he doesn't, you need to keep repeating the training for a little while longer.

You should repeat this process whenever you take him out with you in public, whether it be to a pub, a café, sitting on a park bench, on a train or visiting a friend's house. Your aim is to get him to settle wherever you take him, regardless of the stimuli around him. What you will find is that in time he will automatically settle whenever you sit down and won't need to be asked.

Case Study: He Just Won't Calm Down!

Harry was a big, bouncy puppy of around 8 months old. His owners contacted me because they were struggling with his over-excitement. They longed to be able to have lazy Sunday lunches in pubs after a nice long dog walk or be able to grab a coffee at their local café in the sunshine, but whenever they tried to do this, they ended up cutting their visit short as Harry was just too excitable and refused to lie down quietly anywhere. Even if they did manage to get him to sit or lie down for a bit, he would be up on his feet again the moment anyone walked past. They tried to bribe him with treats, but this just wasn't working. In the end, they stopped taking him out with them.

It quickly became apparent on meeting Harry that all his issues were down to pure over-excitement. On meeting people, his knee jerk reaction was to jump up and plant his front paws on them and, if they tried to push him off, he would grab their hands with his mouth. In fact, any attempt to touch him was met with mouthing, which wasn't a nice experience for the human as by now he had his big adult teeth! His equation for humans was excitement, pure and simple! Hardly surprising, then, that he found it impossible to relax in a pub or a café. These places were full of humans of all shapes and sizes, not to mention FOOD!!!! And Harry was very excited by the food. He was in such a state of frenzy when exposed to these triggers that he was deaf to anything his owners said to him. Imagine being deprived of sweets as a kid for a week and then being let loose in a sweet shop? Would you hear anything that was said to you? Would you pay attention? Of course you wouldn't!

Harry had been given huge amounts of love and attention as a younger puppy, but very little in the way of direction when it came to rules and boundaries. He did conventional puppy training with food rewards and was very good at basic commands, but he wasn't holding those commands for very long. He was excited by food so when he followed a command, such as "Sit", he did it in a heightened state of mind, rather than a calm one, which made it even harder for him to stay sitting. A bit like when your mum and dad told you as a child that you had ants in your pants! Because his owners hadn't insisted on him waiting for a signal to break the command, he had gotten used to following the command and then breaking it. So, he would sit for a few seconds, then get up and wander off. Even if they had taught him to wait for a release from the command, they would still have had a problem, because he would still have been in an excited state of mind AFTER the release, as he had never been taught to be calm and have self-control.

I spent some time with Harry working on getting him to pay attention to me. Not by offering him food. Food treats were strictly forbidden whilst we worked with Harry. No, I used my dog communication methods to show him that a) my personal space was not for invading and b) when I asked him to calm down by interrupting his excitement and sharing calm energy with him, I expected him to join me. He did continue to challenge me for ownership of space for a bit, particularly in his house, but by not getting frustrated and maintaining a calm demeanour throughout, he soon got the message that I was not up for a battle over space and I was simply going to own it for myself. He was particularly bad at flying onto the sofa whenever any human sat on it, which made it impossible to drink a cup of tea safely. I taught him, using blocking & claiming, that he was only allowed to join humans on the sofa if they invited him up. In order to be invited up, he had to be in a calm state of mind. If he wasn't invited, he was expected to "Settle" on the floor at their feet. He quickly *picked this up and became much more respectful around the house. I was able to have a cup of tea safely without getting burnt! Teaching him manners in his own home was the first step to getting him well-behaved in public. Being confident in your ability to communicate with your dog in your home and influence his behaviour, gives you a real boost when it comes to tackling behaviour outside the home. All Harry's owners needed to do was replicate the techniques in the pub or café environment and instruct Harry to settle when asked.*

Let's think now about taking your puppy on holiday with you. One of the great pleasures of having a well-behaved dog is that you can take it anywhere with you and enjoy holidays all over the country, whether it be in a tent, a caravan, a hotel or a holiday cottage. Many new puppy owners worry that they can't have this sort of break with their puppy, but I would encourage you to do this from a young age (once your puppy is fully toilet-trained), so that it becomes a natural thing for your dog to do as he grows older. Having him be able to sleep anywhere and behave in any environment also makes it much easier if you need to ask a friend or relative to look after him for any reason. If you have followed the advice I gave at the start about crate-training your puppy and about teaching him manners around the house, you need not worry about taking him elsewhere. Just replicate the same rules wherever you go: no going on the furniture unless invited, sleep quietly in your crate when we switch the lights off, no digging in the flowerbeds, have your paws wiped every time you come in from the garden, no charging out the front door when it is opened, quietly settle at our feet when we are having a pub lunch or are in a cafe. You get the drift. Life shouldn't be any different just because you are in a different environment. If your puppy looks to you for direction at all times on how to behave, he will do the same no matter where he is! Dogs are creatures of habit. Keep the routines the same and the behaviour will stay the same. Change the goalposts and the behaviour may well change. And most importantly, change how YOU are behaving, and I can guarantee your dog's behaviour will change too. So don't stress about being on a campsite or in a pristine holiday cottage or hotel. Just act the same, follow the same routines (as much as is practical) and you will be fine!

Now, you may have found that the crate didn't suit your puppy. Whilst that will make things a little different when you take him elsewhere, you should still be able to manage fine if you have taught him to sleep in a particular bed at night or on a particular blanket. Simply take that bed/blanket with you and put it on the floor next to your bed, or the room he would normally sleep in, such as the kitchen. Make sure he knows that he isn't allowed to jump on the furniture in the new room, particularly if he usually sleeps on your bed at home. Use the blocking and claiming technique to make it clear that the bed in the hotel/cottage is out-of-bounds for him. Be very clear about this with him, and also over the sofas and chairs. Your hotel/cottage may welcome dogs to stay, but they won't thank you for ruining the bed clothes or the sofa!

Taking your puppy on public transport is another thing I strongly advise clients to do, whether or not they intend to use it in the future with their dog. Public transport is a much noisier environment for a dog than an owner's car, obviously. Buses in particular, with their noisy air brakes, noisy doors and their rattling interiors can be a real challenge for some dogs. Even if you never plan on taking the bus, getting your puppy used to these noises will help him cope when out on walks. If he learns to ignore loud, strange noises from an early age, he is more likely to grow into a well-balanced dog who can be taken anywhere. Just sitting at a bus stop or near a train line and you acting calm when the bus or train goes past will put an equation into his brain that this sound isn't something to worry about. Same with busy roads or locations busy with lots of people. Regular exposure throughout his first year to these different environments will set him up for a trouble-free adulthood. Again, there is no need to feed him treats whilst you are exposing him to these triggers, particularly if he is excited by food.

Chapter 17 – The Challenges of Puberty

As I mentioned at the start, as a dog behaviourist, the most common time I get called in to help owners is when a puppy is between the ages of 6 months and 2 years old. Most dog owners know that puppies go through a teenage phase when they get a bit rebellious and stop listening, but many don't understand what is behind this change in behaviour. As I explained earlier, it is all to do with the changes that occur in the puppy's body once puberty starts. This can be any time from around five months onwards, but obviously varies by breed and by individual. They are changing from being of non-breeding to breeding age, from a "puppy" to an "adult". It is not just the physical changes that are important at this time, but also the psychological changes and this brings us back to what a puppy in the wild is genetically programmed to do at this stage in its life. This chapter is by far and above the most important one for dog owners when it comes to understanding their puppy's behaviour. If I had to pick one word to describe an owner's reaction to their puppy's altered behaviour at this age it would be "bewilderment". Even the sweetest natured puppy can show unexpected and often alarming new behaviours at this age, such as growling or lip curling. Invariably owners have a light-bulb moment once I have given them a very simplistic explanation of why this altered behaviour may have occurred. Again, I must stress that this explanation is my personal take on things based on my own experiences and research into the topic.

Adolescent dogs, both male and female, are programmed to challenge for leadership at this crucial age. This in-built behaviour goes back to the dynamics of the wild dog pack and nature's way of ensuring that the pack survives, should the established leader pass away or be severely injured. In my teaching, I don't go into this in any great detail as I am no expert on wild dogs, but I do tap into the theory to explain to owners why their puppy might be proving challenging as adolescents - most owners think that their dogs are being naughty at this stage and deliberately not listening to instructions that they would previously follow without question.

Being "naughty" is a human concept. It clearly means not behaving properly or disobeying, but what a human thinks of as "naughty" behaviour is most likely to be simply a dog responding to instinct. And this is where the changes that happen to a puppy in adolescence come in. If, in any given situation, your adolescent puppy detects a lack of leadership in his 'pack' (basically a vacancy!), his instinct once he is an adolescent, is to step up and take over as "leader". Why? Because if YOU aren't showing calm, confident leadership in the moment, in the puppy's brain his survival instinct tells him that someone has to! If you aren't fit to lead, he will! This is why is it so important for you to master the art of calm, confident leadership no matter what is happening at any given moment! Knowing how to deal with any situation where your puppy is in a state of mind that is no longer calm and relaxed is ESSENTIAL to a smooth journey through puberty, because we don't want him to be forced to take over and take charge of things himself.

A puppy who is born to lead is going to be more of a challenge at puberty than a puppy that is born to follow. I learnt that the hard way with my second puppy! Just like humans come with all sorts of different personality traits, so do dogs, and puppies, like humans, have different natures from birth. I noticed early on with my work as a professional behaviourist that some dogs were clearly born to lead and others to follow and I ended up developing a quick simplistic test to give me an idea as to what sort of nature a dog leaned towards. This simple test involved a dog treat and some blocking and claiming of said treat. The way the dog responded to this test on the first meeting gave me a helpful insight into whether it was likely to relinquish leadership easily or be more challenging. I might add that I only did this test if I felt it was safe to do so. There were obvious occasions when it clearly wasn't an appropriate thing to do, based on the dogs' behaviour when I entered its' home. Safety always has to be paramount when working with animals.

Hopefully you will already have understood what is needed of you from previous chapters when it comes to approaching the "teenage" phase of your puppy's life. But it is worth recapping and sharing some common scenarios where your puppy might previously have coped fine, but now, at puberty, is behaving very differently. Some of the most common areas for things to go awry at puberty are recall and interaction with other dogs. Let's look at recall first. Hopefully, you will have trained your puppy to pack walk with you from the beginning. That doesn't mean he isn't going to prove a bit challenging at this stage, but it does mean that getting through any kick-back from him will be a lot quicker and easier. So why might he no longer come back when you call him at puberty? Complacency on your part is the most common answer. You worked hard on recall in the beginning, but then maybe became a bit less stringent as he got older, perhaps not insisting each time you recalled him that he come all the way back to you. You may have enjoyed good recall from him up until this point, but as he enters adulthood, his brain is telling him that his role in the pack is now changing. As an adult he will be expected to take part in the hunt for food, a role which as a young puppy he didn't have before. So, it is important to make it clear to him that it is NOT his job to go after prey. The walk you are doing is not a hunt, it is simply a territorial patrol (as described in my earlier chapter). He can't help but be triggered by prey on the ground, such as squirrels, foxes, birds or heaven forbid, deer! You need, at this stage, to be especially vigilant and watch him closely for signs that he has either picked up a scent or spotted something worth hunting. Make sure he is still responding well to the "Leave" command so that he knows to disconnect from any prey that he spots, rather than chase it. YOU decide, remember, what he can and can't chase.

Putting him back on a training line for a while and going back over the basic recall training is often necessary at puberty. Do this as SOON as he starts not recalling when you tell him. Don't wait a little while in the hope it is just a phase, and he will get over it. I can promise you, he won't! Dogs grow INTO behaviour, not out of it! The more they do something, the more it becomes the default equation, so nip it in the bud right away if he starts to challenge you on walks and stops listening. Reboot him and stay on his case whilst he goes through this particular phase. You will be glad you did, as he will settle down again into following your lead if you make it clear to him that you are not about to give up the job of being in charge of your walks.

It's time to talk about what might happen at puberty in terms of his reaction to other dogs. What you will find, whether your puppy is male or female, is that other dogs will behave differently towards them. If you have a bitch, they will become VERY interesting to male dogs, both intact and castrated, as they approach their first season. This can be quite a nuisance, not just for you, but also for the owners of these male dogs, as they will simply lose their minds when a bitch is about to be/or is in heat in the park. They can't help it, they are just following their instinct to mate, even if they no longer have the equipment! So, the kindest thing you can do for your bitch puppy and other dog owners is to street walk your puppy as soon as you notice other dogs taking a very keen interest in her backside! Do this until her season is completely over.

If your puppy is male, you are going to face a whole different set of issues when he reaches puberty, the most likely one being that other male dogs (again, whether neutered or not) are going to take exception to your puppy being in the park. You will notice when your male dog is entering puberty because he will be taking more interest in the ladies and may start cocking his leg. As I keep saying, every dog is different, so it isn't a given that EVERY male dog will be disgruntled by the arrival of your puppy, some may not be bothered at all but there is no doubt that you will encounter some male dogs who will make it clear to your adolescent pup that they are aware he is intact and that his testosterone levels are increasing. These dogs may be a bit bossy around him. Why? Because in most cases, he has something they don't! The ability to mate! If there are female dogs present, they are even more likely to give him a hard time, even if these females are spayed. This will most likely just consist of them rushing up to him and being a bit dominant. They are letting him know that they are aware he is bringing something extra to the party. There may be the odd dog who gets a little feistier, and it is these dogs that you need to watch out for.

I have worked with many a dog who has developed dog anxiety or reactivity because it has been pounced on as an un-neutered adolescent.

The Challenges of Puberty

Again, you can avoid this happening to your male puppy if you are aware that other dogs will treat him differently until he is neutered and, indeed, for several months after he is neutered whilst his hormone levels are decreasing. You need to be prepared to advocate for him calmly, by asking these dogs to move away. What you MUST NOT do at this stage in your puppy's development is get stressed and agitated if he attracts negative attention from other dogs. Just accept that they are behaving in a way that is totally natural to them and take charge of the situation so that your dog learns not to be freaked out by this reaction or react in a negative way himself. I can't stress enough that, in my opinion, neutering is the solution here. There is no need to leave your male dog (or female dog) intact unless you specifically intend to breed from them. There will be many that disagree with me, and that is absolutely their right, but as a behaviourist I speak from my personal experience with the hundreds of dogs that I have worked with. Time and time again I have found that the problems owners were experiencing improved markedly after their dog was neutered, whether male or female. Furthermore, you will find that dog boarders and dog walkers will often not look after an unneutered dog, whether male or female, because it upsets the dynamic in their home or walking group.

Let me try to show you an example of when this might happen. Imagine you are out in the park with your adolescent puppy, who at this point still isn't neutered and another older dog comes over and starts giving your puppy a hard time. It may be that this dog is being a bit bossy, or perhaps a little snappy, but either way, your puppy isn't happy about the negative attention he is getting. You at this point are getting annoyed, because not only is your puppy getting hassled, but also the other owner appears to not be able to call his/her dog away or get it to stop. You are no longer in a calm, confident state of mind, are you? You may THINK you are providing your puppy with back-up by yelling at the other dog and dragging him off your pup. You may THINK you are dealing with the situation properly by shouting at the owner to control their dog, but what you are actually doing is showing your puppy that in that very moment when he needs you, you are UNBALANCED. He can't follow an unbalanced pack member - he is programmed to only follow calm, commanding leadership. So, you give him no choice but to step up and take care of himself. Which gives him two options 1) totally submit to the other dog, by making himself as small as possible/lying on his side 2) fight back and see the other dog off. We as owners don't want either of these behaviours. When our puppy was pre-adolescent, he would have run back to you for safety, because there was no question in his brain at that point as to who was in charge. You were. But now he is an adolescent, his brain is telling him to take the lead in situations where you don't. This can have serious consequences going forwards, because the NEXT time he meets a dog with this sort of energy and YOU, based on your previous experience, show the same behaviour (and possibly are even more anxious/annoyed), he may default to the fight back option. Indeed, he may do this even before the other dog has got near, by showing his teeth or growling. This is where dog reactivity problems start, which is why it is so important for new owners to understand the need to be prepared for puberty and the challenges it brings.

One of the most important things a puppy owner should be doing when their puppy reaches puberty is NOT getting annoyed or angry. You may feel like this if you believe your puppy is being naughty. Just remember, your puppy isn't being naughty, he is just following his natural instincts. If you stay calm, confident and consistent in your approach to him and, if necessary, go back to basics for a while in the areas where he is proving a bit challenging, he will soon go back to following your lead. Lose your rag, blame him for his perceived waywardness and you will set yourself up for failure at this stage. If he perceives you as unfit to lead in any given situation, he will take charge himself. Quite simply, he will develop a new equation for a situation and it's highly likely that it won't be the one YOU want him to have!

I keep referring to the puppy as a 'he' in all these scenarios. That is simply to avoid having to say he/she all the time. If you have a bitch, as I said, she is going to attract attention too as she enters puberty. Again, the way YOU deal with this is of supreme importance. You should be following the same guidance above – get rid of unwanted dogs calmly and confidently. Don't get agitated, don't start finger pointing at other owners. Take charge, advocate for your dog and do your utmost to ensure that you don't inadvertently cause behavioural problems in YOUR dog because you deal with the situation in a human way, rather than the dog way!

Case Study: Banging His Own Drum!

Rex was a pug cross and by all accounts, a lovely little dog. I was called in to help him as his owner was concerned about the deterioration in his recall. When she first got him as a puppy, his recall was excellent. He would stay close when off lead and always come when called. However, as he gained in confidence out and about, she noticed that he had started to run off further into the woods. He had become over-excited in the woods and barked a lot. He did come back eventually, but only once he decided to.

Rex had not been neutered. He was a small dog and fully grown, so he was old enough to be neutered at this point. I explained to the owner how being intact meant that she had to work even harder at influencing his behaviour, particularly when he was off lead. If there were bitches in the park or the woods, whether neutered or not, his hormones were going to be playing an even bigger part in his behaviour if he wasn't neutered. I also questioned his owner about his lead walking and she told me that he liked to be out in front on pavement walks and that she used a harness. It was clear that as Rex had entered puberty his instinct to be in charge when off-lead had kicked in. When he was little he had stuck next to his owner off-lead, as most puppies do, but as his hormones ramped up, his instinct to hunt and to sniff out the ladies had kicked in, and his owner's influence had weakened.

This behaviour would have been gradual, but in that very first instance when he hesitated about coming back to her call, the die would have been cast for his future behaviour. It is highly likely that in the crucial seconds when Rex hesitated, his owner had become frustrated and annoyed that he wasn't doing as he was told. She was no longer in a calm, confident state of mind. Rex would have picked up on this and his instinct to take over leadership of the walk would have kicked in. If she wasn't leading, he had to! This is an incredibly common scenario. Rex was not being deliberately naughty. From his point of view, what he was doing was completely natural. But from the human point of view, he appeared to be being naughty!

In order to help Rex and his owner, it was necessary to tackle both his on-lead and off-lead walking. I did advise neutering as soon as possible for starters. Even if she decided not to neuter Rex, it was important to make it clear to Rex that he was being invited to join his owner on her walks, whether it be on the pavement or off-

lead in the woods, and that she was in charge of the walk throughout, not him. I taught him how to leave the house calmly and crucially BEHIND me and how to pavement walk in a "following" state of mind. Once he had got the hang of this, it was time to show him how to pack walk off-lead, which meant putting him back on a long-line until he got to grips with being mentally connected to me on the walk and following my direction at all times. We worked on entering the park and woods correctly, being let off lead calmly and in a following state, and also on three levels of recall (casual, formal and whistle). It did take a lot of work on the owner's part, but Rex did eventually get the message and his walks became pleasurable again.

Case Study 2: A Case of a Nervous Disposition Leading to Dog Reactivity

China had always been nervy, right from the outset when she was a tiny puppy. Her nervousness wasn't an issue when she was tiny. She made friends with other dogs and played happily in the park. She could be a bit nippy, but that was a known characteristic of her particular breed. It was around 6 months of age that her owners noticed her behaviour changing - she became increasingly wary of other dogs, particularly ones she didn't know, but she also showed reactivity to the dogs she did know too. Nothing major, but it was clear that she wasn't fully relaxed in the company of any dogs. It was my view that as her hormones ramped up, she had become increasingly distrustful of other dogs. She was particularly unhappy about any dogs around her rear quarters. Her nervous disposition and changing hormones led her to be in an unbalanced state of mind when out in the park. Any dog that approached was warned away with a curled lip initially, but soon a full-blown bark and lunge. Letting her off lead was no longer an option, as she couldn't be trusted not to turn on a dog which entered her personal space. So where did her owners fit into this scenario? They were confused and bewildered as to why their lovely puppy has become so anti-social. They simply didn't know what to do. They also tried to reassure her whenever she was agitated, giving her love and affection when she was in an unbalanced state of mind. Naturally, they kept her on-lead and also avoided walking her anywhere where they were likely to bump into other dogs, particularly those off the lead. They were nervous and she was nervous. Not a good combination. Avoiding confrontations with other dogs was not going to solve the problem.

The first thing I needed to do with China was to get her to trust me. She had become wary of strangers as well, particularly in her own home, so I worked on building a relationship with her by taking her out for walks on my own. The quickest way to bond with a dog is to walk it. Walking her in the correct way was also essential, if

I was to tackle her dog reactivity. I had to show her that I was inviting her to join me on MY walk and that I would take care of any issues that arose; it simply wasn't her job to protect either herself or me. You might wonder why I didn't take her owners on these initial walks? I needed them out of the equation as their nervousness was adding to China's nervousness. She couldn't rely on them to take care of any perceived threat because they weren't in a calm, confident state of mind when they were walking her. When working with a reactive dog it is absolutely essential to stay in this calm, confident state no matter what is happening. My job was to spot the initial signs of her brain activity escalating, then step in with a verbal cue to let her know that I wanted her to return to a calm state. I needed to teach her to pass by humans and dogs on-lead without reacting at all. I would be the one taking care of any threats, not her. She was confused at first. Humans didn't normally behave this way! But she soon got the hang of things and I was able to progress from walking her on my own on lead, to carefully introducing her to off-lead balanced dogs, firstly on lead and subsequently on a trailing line attached to her harness. It was wonderful to see her relax and enjoy herself on a walk in the company of other dogs. She started to get playful again. The other dogs helped her hugely. There is no better rehabilitator for an unbalanced dog than a group of balanced dogs!

After teaching her owners how to replicate what I had taught her and show them that she COULD be trusted if they stepped up and took charge of the walk, I can happily report that she is now back walking in parks with her owners and their confidence is growing by the day. She is off lead again. She can still get a bit overexcited during play, but I have shown them how to tell her to disengage when told and also shown them how to send away any dog that they feel she shouldn't be playing with. Understanding what China needed from them as owners was the key to everything. It's hard to let go of our default human behaviour. We are humans after all! But thinking with our hearts rather than our heads because we love our dogs so much does them no favours when they need our help. Learning to be a calm, confident leader and take charge when required has been a game-changer for China's owners.

Pupology

Chapter 18 – Reading Your Puppy

Most of us lack a basic understanding of how dogs' brains work. We are led to believe that all we need to do as a dog owner is teach a puppy commands in order to raise a well-behaved dog. Conventional reward-based dog training concentrates on teaching dogs an action in return for a reward. A dog can be trained to do a plethora of actions, but it is the quality of the training that will determine whether or not the dog follows the command rather than its instinct in a given situation. It is too easy as a dog owner to give up on training when the dog starts to ignore our commands. We talked about that in the Puberty chapter, as this is the age when your puppy is most likely to stop following your requests but might instead start to follow his instincts. Often by the time a command is given, it is already too late, you have already lost your puppy's attention and he is no longer listening to you. Your influence has basically disappeared!

You can help yourself massively in this regard by understanding how important it is to be able to **read** your puppy and to spot when the mental connection between you and him has broken. Many owners don't realise that there are subtle signals that come WAY before a dog actually shows a particular behaviour. Knowing what these signals are allows an owner to step in to prevent a situation occurring with just a noise or a signal, or indeed a particular command. What an owner is doing is stopping their dog's brain from escalating into an excited state. Remember, dogs don't do anything unwanted when they are calm! This is also the perfect state of mind to teach a dog to ignore triggers, because the dog is able to "listen" to its owner and learn what it should and shouldn't be reacting to.

So, back to your young puppy. You should become familiar with the signals he is giving you with his body from a very early age. Let's start with the tail. Familiarise yourself with what we call the "neutral tail". What is your puppy's tail position when he is in a calm, relaxed state? With a lot of dogs this will look a bit like a smile shape if the tail is long (if you are looking at him side on). The tail will be hanging down from his rump and will likely have a slight uptick at the end. It won't be wagging. Wagging is the first sign of an escalation in activity in the brain. It's a bit harder to assess with curly tails or no tail. If your puppy falls into this category, you are going to look a bit more closely at what happens at the tail end when he is excited and then see if you can spot the difference in his rump end when he is calm. This may be quite hard, so in his case, you are going to rely more on his ears, eyes and head position to tell you what is happening in his brain!

Back to the tail. You now know what his neutral tail looks like. His tail directly reflects the amount of excitement in his brain, but it isn't simply a case that when his tail is wagging, he is happy. This is one of the most common mistakes dog owners make. I have heard many times "There was no sign he was going to lunge; he was wagging his tail happily!". The problem here is that a wagging tail doesn't necessarily mean a happy brain. It simply means an excited brain. HOW the tail is wagging is what is important. Now, with a young puppy, the chances are it will be a happy wag. Puppies are social and trusting by nature when they are young. Before your puppy hits puberty, he is unlikely to be showing you anything but a happy tail, thankfully! The only other tail position you might see at this age is the totally tucked tail, where your puppy has gone into a submissive or fearful state. This means he is completely submitting to the other dog in terms of the social hierarchy. He is basically surrendering to that other dog's will. As I mentioned at the start, puppies are born with individual personalities - some will be more dominant than others and some more submissive than others. If your puppy hits the decks with its tail fully tucked every time it meets another dog, it falls into the submissive category. This pup may need a little help gaining confidence around other dogs, but it isn't an issue per se. Just make sure other dogs don't bully your puppy if it is super submissive.

Whilst most puppy's default will be the happy tail, it is important to look out for when this starts to change. Trust me, it will change when different situations arise, particularly when your puppy enters puberty. If you have dealt with any problem situations as advised in earlier chapters, you shouldn't see problem tail positions very often, but it is best to be aware of what these are and is also very useful to know when assessing other dogs. So, let's start with what happens when the brain starts to escalate and how it affects your puppy's tail. Your puppy's tail will go up and down vertically depending on how he is feeling about a situation. A tail going upwards from the neutral position is showing he is getting excited. Now this could be positive, happy excitement, but it could also be territorial/dominant excitement. Either way, its excitement. And you should have learnt by now, that excitement is your enemy when it comes to unwanted behaviour. But don't panic, there is no need to worry yet, because obviously your puppy is going to be excited each day at some point and not all excitement leads to problems! Which brings us to the wagging bit. It is believed that with tail wagging, contralateral control occurs i.e. activity in the left side of the brain, results in wagging to the right and vice versa. The left side of a dog's brain is associated with positive emotions, so if the tail is thrashing to the right, this is a social wag. Your puppy is happy, nothing to worry about. However, if the tail is thrashing to the left, this is a more territorial, combative state of mind. So, a left thrashing tail should be viewed as a red flag - it may be your puppy has gone into hunting mode, for example (he's just spotted a squirrel or a pigeon). Or is feeling defensive because he is feeling threatened by another dog or a person.

Another thing to look out for is a STIFF tail as opposed to a relaxed one. Remember, your puppy's tail is an extension of his spine, and we all know ourselves that when we go stiff, we are tense. So, stiffness equals tension. This doesn't mean something bad is going to happen, but you should be aware that this is another sign your puppy's brain has escalated. As I said before, just become familiar with these different tail states. Nothing to worry about in the early months of puppyhood, but good to know what they mean. Get into the habit of looking at what <u>other</u> people's dogs' tails are doing when you are out and about, particularly any that are showing unwanted behaviours!

Staying with the tail, let's look at what it means when your puppy's tail is down. You are much more likely to know what this means, because a down tail is usually accompanied by sad looking eyes, and we all know how those sad puppy eyes pull on our heart strings! Once you know your puppy's neutral tail position, you will easily be able to spot when his tail is lower than this, which indicates he is feeling unsure. It doesn't have to be fully tucked. A tail pointing straight down but not tucked still indicates that your dog isn't mentally comfortable with a situation. Full tuck is when he is really scared (but remember, this can also mean he is being submissive so look for other signs, like wide-open eyes, lip licking and panting). You are your dog's advocate, remember. You are the one who speaks for him, takes care of him, protects him. So, knowing when he is feeling uncertain or scared is very important, as you need to provide him with **calm support** in these situations and take charge, particularly if it is another dog who is causing this uncertain state in your puppy. Giving calm support is not the same as giving love, by the way. Remember, we don't want to be giving our puppy love when his mind is unbalanced and that includes when he is frightened or unsure. If you pet him and stroke him whilst he is in this state of mind, you are telling him it is ok to be fearful. We do not want our puppy to grow up being fearful, we want him to grow up being balanced and able to cope in stressful situations. Calm support means sharing calm, confident energy with him when he is worried. Holding him close and firm, but without stroking, whilst you relax and breathe.

You now know how to read your puppy's tail. Next up is his ears. They are another great barometer of what is happening in his brain. Contrary to popular opinion, flat ears are not necessarily a sign that your puppy is stressed. Take a look at some videos of a mother dog interacting with her puppies and watch how the puppies will put their ears flat and roll onto their backs in a submissive pose when their Mum interacts with them. They aren't scared or worried, they are going into submission and acknowledging her superior position in the hierarchy. They are being **respectful** to their elders. This is TOTALLY natural behaviour! Flat ears are actually good ears – this is a sign that the puppy has gone into a "following" state of mind. Now let's talk about what happens to the ears when your puppy's brain gets excited. As activity in the brain escalates, the ears will prick up more and point forwards more. Obviously, different breeds have different ears, so you should be looking for change in relation to your puppy's "neutral" position, just like with the tail. Pointy-up ears will swivel forwards, flat ears will elevate a little. Either way, your puppy's brain activity is on the up and you should pay attention!

Reading Your Puppy

Your puppy's eyes are another part of his body that tell you how he is feeling. Have you ever looked at them closely? Have you noticed that sometimes they are big and staring, with maybe even the whites showing. Other times they are soft and sleepy looking. It sounds obvious, but I have found that many dog owners don't really notice the change in their dog's eyes. The more active his brain is, the wider your puppy's eyes are going to be. He won't be in a calm, following state if he is showing the white of his eyes, that I can guarantee!

By now you should be getting the picture that your puppy's body language is crucial to understanding the level of excitement in his brain. If his trunk is stiff and tense, his ears are up, his tail up and his eyes wide, he is in an excited state of mind. This may be momentary, when he first spots something of interest and then his body language might change to being a bit softer once he has assessed what he is looking at. For example, he has spotted a dog and immediately tenses up, but then realises it is a friend of his, so his trunk will relax a bit, his tail will lower and start swooshing from side to side, his eyes will soften, and his ears will relax. In a matter of seconds, he has told you he is in a sociable state of mind. If, however, he spots something, does the first behaviour with his body and then his tail curls right over his back or starts thrashing, his head goes higher, his eyes widen further and he leans forward onto his front legs, what you are seeing is a totally different state of mind. He is now on high alert. A lot of this sounds pretty obvious, but reading the EARLY signs of changes in your puppy's body language rather than just noticing the end product is what is important. Spot when these early changes start to occur and you can step in if they are going the way of elevation, rather than relaxing into calmness. Your puppy is more likely to do something unwanted if his brain is excited and his mind is in a territorial/combative state, than if he is calm and relaxed. It is **your job** to return him to calm and relaxed as quickly as possible once you spot these early warning signs. You are READING him and responding accordingly. You will respond the way his mother would; a verbal intervention initially and, if this is ignored, a physical intervention. Either way you are replicating <u>dog</u> behaviour.

Another indicator you should familiarise yourself with is his head and its position relative to his trunk. Again, get used to spotting his "neutral" head position when he is calm and relaxed. The position of his head in relation to neutral should be taken within the context of what is happening with his tail, eyes, and his ears. An elevated head with a stiff tail, pricked up, forward-facing ears and wide staring eyes is telling you a very different story to an up but relaxed tail, softer eyes, and swivelling ears. The first is a more alert and potentially defensive/territorial state of mind. The second is a more social state. Similarly, if the head is down, there can be a different story, depending on what the other key parts of his body are doing. If his ears are flat, his tail lower, or even tucked and he is looking upwards from beneath his eyelashes, he has entered a submissive state. If his tail is fully tucked and his body much tenser and his eyes are wide, he is likely to be in a more nervous, fearful state.

Your puppy's body (or trunk) is, as we have mentioned, another indicator of the state of his mind. The fur on his trunk is an extra indicator. Most people know about dog's hackles being up. It is when the hair on its trunk along its back and neck is standing up on end. It is a common misconception that this means the dog is feeling aggressive. This isn't necessarily the case. It DOES mean the dog's brain is excited, but it could be a social form of excitement, where the dog is simply highly stimulated by the presence of other dogs, but in a social way, or it could indeed be a warning sign that the dog is in a heightened, aggressive state. Again, it shouldn't be looked at in isolation. You should be looking at what the other parts of your puppy's body are doing if his hackles are up, before you decide if it is a red flag or not.

Let's finish with one last thing that you would be wise to familiarise yourself with when it comes to your puppy, but also other dogs. This is the question of movement and sound and is particularly relevant when it comes to your puppy being in danger. Stillness is a red flag when it comes to body language. If you see a dog that goes very still, what you are likely looking at is a dog in a predator state, if the stillness is accompanied by all the things I have pointed out above which indicate an excited brain – stiff upright tail, a direct intense stare, ears up and fixed forwards (not swivelling), and head held high. This will precede a stalking phase, where the head will drop low, and the dog will start to creep forwards. Not all stalking dogs are in predator mode, some do this when they are about to play, but they will tend to hit the ground first before they stalk, rather than stand and stare in a menacing way. Likewise with sound, a barking dog is actually less of a threat than a totally silent one. Silence is a red flag before, and during, an attack. If two dogs are making a lot of noise and spinning around a lot, this is much more likely to be a "handbags at dawn" situation, where it is all noise and no substance. A silent attack, in contrast, is a very deadly attack.

Case Study 1: Aggression Driven by Fear

Once again, I am going to share the story of one of my own dogs, my little, long-coat chihuahua Boston. Boston came to me as a foster at the age of seven, with the agreement that I would work on his severe aggression issues in order to give him a chance of a successful rehome. I had been warned that if I tried to touch him he would bite me, so I set up a pen in my utility room, with a covered area for him to hide under. I also bought a tiny muzzle. I led him into this pen and left him to settle in. His eyes were very wide, his ears up but his tail right down. His little body was shaking. He wouldn't eat the food I offered him. It was clear to me that this poor little chap was simply terrified. Of everything. He was not an aggressive dog or dangerous. He just couldn't trust at all. It took me two hours on that first day of sitting quietly next to his pen before he allowed me to touch him with my finger. He very quickly learnt that I wasn't a threat and wasn't going to hurt him and we soon bonded. I never used the muzzle!

However, that was inside the house. The outside world was a very different story. From what I could gather, Boston had been attacked as a young puppy and, not only didn't trust humans, but also didn't trust any dogs either. Initially, I had to carry him around the park as if I put him on the ground he simply froze with fear and wouldn't move. God forbid, a human approached to say hello. I had to warn people not to reach out to him with their hands or he would bite them. Initially, I just carried him around and let him observe the world from his safe space in my arms. But crucially, I DIDN'T spend my time reassuring him that everything was ok or stroke him. I simply held him firmly and confidently and let him observe. He learnt to relax and trust me, and we soon progressed to him walking on a lead on the ground. However, I was very careful not to replicate what his previous owners had done, which was allow him to walk ahead of me on a flexi-lead. I taught him to walk by my side in a following state. If he spotted another dog coming, I watched his body language carefully and the minute his ears swivelled forwards, I gave him a verbal warning not to escalate. If he ignored that, I followed up with a physical intervention (a tiny flick and release of the lead with my finger) and if that had no effect, a full-blown block & claim, where I would face towards him, with my back to the oncoming dog and move him backwards with my body until he turned away and reconnected with me mentally. He was soon walking happily on the lead by my side and ignoring other dogs when asked.

We then did the same thing in the park, with him initially on a training line and eventually graduating to no line at all. When I first got him he had never been off the lead, but he was soon off lead and enjoying his walks. He is now 14 years old and an absolute gem of a dog. He doesn't need a lead as he follows me everywhere and has great recall. I adopted him myself in the end, as I fell in love with him. Does he still have issues with people and dogs? Barely. Yes, he can still get annoyed if an excitable dog bothers him. He finds puppies very irritating, but the worst he will do is a little growl and an air snap to tell them to leave him alone. He isn't fond of intact males, but again, provided I read his body language cues and intervene, he will not react. If I miss the cues, the worst he will do is a little dance around and a yap. He will not attack. He will happily let people touch him if they approach him the right way and offer their hand for him to sniff. If they do put their hand out over his head to pat him, he doesn't like it and will back away but he will no longer bite. I should add that he has never bitten me. Ever!

As you can see, being able to "read" body language and energy is a useful and I personally think, essential skill. If you are going to step in and influence your puppy's behaviour in different situations or indeed, influence other dogs behaviour, you need to be able to spot the signals that a dog's brain activity is escalating. Dogs are hugely influenced by other dog's brain energy. If you have a tendency to walk on your own with your puppy and hardly ever come across other dogs, it won't matter so much about understanding all the above. But if you are someone who walks regularly in a park where there are lots of other dogs, it is very useful to know that once one dog escalates, all the others can get sucked in very quickly! Familiarise yourself with what your puppy is likely to do when energy escalates in the park amongst a group of dogs - will he rush to join in or will he watch from afar? If he has a tendency to rush in, pop him on a lead if a tussle happens, so he doesn't get sucked into the melee! It may be that you never witness this, but here is an example of what can happen:

It's a busy day in the park, with lots of dogs and owners about. Two dogs are playing together quite happily but one gets over-excited and starts to dominate the other dog. The other dog isn't particularly happy about this, so shows its displeasure in a growl and maybe even a snap. The owners, meanwhile, are chatting away happily, and haven't noticed the change in the demeanour of their dogs. Suddenly, what was a playful interaction turns into a fight, albeit a "handbags at dawn" one, rather than a vicious attack. Before you know it, many of the other dogs in the park will have been sucked in by the heightened energy and be dancing around the two scrapping dogs. Some will be barking, others darting in and out taking a nip at the fighting dogs, whilst the more cautious ones will be hanging around the edge, watching but still agitated. A bit like a fight in the playground. Hopefully, the owners will understand that this is merely a squabble and calmly step in to separate the two dogs. No harm done. The energy will collectively drop and the spectator dogs will go back to whatever they were doing. If the owners overreact, however, and start yelling and shouting at the dogs and blaming each other's dogs for the problem, the other dogs in the park will remain elevated and take much longer to calm down. Other scuffles may indeed break out. This whole scenario could have been avoided if the owners of the playing dogs had kept one eye on them and recognised when things were becoming a little one-sided and stepped in! Know what your own puppy will do in this situation and take charge and you will be fine. If you are worried about your puppy getting sucked in, the minute you notice any escalation of energy, call him to you and pop him on his lead. Do the same thing if you hear a fracas in the distance whilst out walking, just in case your puppy decides to go to investigate. Stay calm, confident and in charge at all times and you will be fine.

Pupology

Chapter 19 – Other Pets and Small Humans

Integrating your new puppy with other pets in your household needn't be difficult. Dogs can live quite happily alongside other family pets, whether they be an older dog, cats, rabbits, guinea pigs or reptiles. The key to a harmonious household is teaching your puppy from the outset that these other animals are part of YOUR family pack. They are pack members and need to be treated with respect and courtesy, just like the human members of the pack. Being a cat lover myself, I have always had both cats AND dogs living in my household quite happily. Like dogs, each of my cats has had its own personality. Some have been totally uninterested in the dogs, remaining aloof and full of disdain, whilst others have been nervier around them. However, no matter what the cat's personality, they have been able to live quite happily without incident.

We will start with introducing a puppy into a household with an older dog. Again, how your older dog feels about your new puppy will vary, depending on his/her personality. The older dog may be thrilled to have a new companion and playmate! Or they may be suspicious and wary of this new, young lively resident who has invaded their peaceful household. It is your job to advocate for BOTH dogs and to ensure that the transitional period is as peaceful as possible and that the two ultimately become friends. How closely they bond will depend on the dogs themselves. You can't force this. They will find a natural equilibrium in time, but you can't dictate exactly what relationship they will have. Some dogs become besties, whilst others have deep affection for each other but still won't share the same bed!

You may already be an expert at spotting how your older dog is feeling. You know what his body language is telling you, so when you first bring the new puppy home, you should have a good idea of whether he is pleased, or his nose has been put out of joint! Set up the crate and puppy pen a few days in advance of the puppy coming home, so that your older dog is used to the equipment. Having the crate and puppy pen set up will help enormously in introducing your puppy to your existing dog. It allows your older dog to suss out the puppy in a safe way, creating a physical barrier between the two through which scents can be shared. Don't try to force your older dog to interact with the puppy. Just pop the puppy in the pen and let your older dog into the room and let him approach the pen in his own time.

If you are at all worried about this first interaction, you can err on the side of caution and introduce the new puppy to your older dog OUTSIDE the house. Do this on the day you bring your new puppy home. Before you bring him out of the car, get a family member to bring your older dog out of the house on lead and offer him a piece of your puppy's bedding to sniff. This introduces him to your puppy's scent before he meets him in person. Your puppy isn't fully vaccinated, remember, so don't be tempted to put him on the ground for the first introduction. Open your car boot and sit on the edge of it with your new puppy in your arms. Have your family member bring your older dog towards the car and let him pick up the scent of your puppy. You will see him sniffing the air as soon as he clocks that there is another dog present. If he seems calm and relaxed still at this point, invite him towards you to gently have a sniff at the puppy in your arms. Do NOT let him do this if he is excited. If he is excited, simply wait until he calms down, no matter how long this takes. Don't tell him off for being excited. We want him to associate with the puppy with calmness, not excitement. The puppy IS obviously going to be a bundle of excited energy (unless he asleep!), that is a given, but we want your older dog's default to be calm when it comes to the puppy. Obviously, if they get on and play a lot, there is going to be lots of excitement, but you want to be able to influence your older dog's behaviour around the puppy, so it is important that you set the tone with this first introduction. The puppy is YOURS and when you ask for calmness around him, you expect your older dog to listen. What you absolutely don't want is your puppy and your older dog to form their own pack which excludes you! Once your older dog has calmly had a sniff of the puppy, you can take the puppy indoors and pop him in his pen.

Once your new puppy is in the pen, your older dog is going to either spend time near the pen sniffing at the puppy or retreat further away from the pen and watch the puppy from a distance. Either is absolutely fine. Let your older dog decide what he is comfortable with. It is your job to watch calmly and confidently whilst the two dogs get to know each other. If your older dog charges at the puppy pen or barks a lot at the puppy, you need to step in and make it clear to the older dog that this behaviour is unwanted. Use the blocking & claiming technique to move your older dog away from the puppy pen (place yourself in front of the pen and move towards your older dog until he turns and walks away). You are telling him with your body language that the puppy and its pen are YOURS and you don't want this sort of excitement around the puppy. Likewise, do not encourage your puppy to bark at your older dog. He will undoubtedly be excited by the sight of your other dog and may well yip, whine or bark when he spots him, but try to just calmly ignore this behaviour, or distract him with one of the toys in his pen. Don't tell him off for barking at the other dog. Instead, give him lots of gentle praise when he calmly watches the other dog, or calmly interacts between the pen fence with him. If you allow your older dog to be excited or barky around the puppy and vice versa, you are setting yourself up for a noisy future!

Once your older dog is used to the puppy's presence and you are confident that there is no animosity towards the puppy, you can bring the puppy out of the pen and let the two interact with each other. How much your older dog will tolerate from the puppy is, again, down to his personality. Often, the arrival of a new puppy heralds a new lease of life for an older dog, but this isn't always the case, so do watch your older dog carefully and make sure you step in when he shows signs that he has had enough of the puppy playing with him. Remember, your puppy is used to playing with his siblings, who have the same energy levels as him. Your older dog may tire quickly of having a young puppy with needle-sharp teeth hanging off his ears! It is fine for your older dog to warn your puppy off with a low growl, but step in before it becomes any more than this in the early weeks, as your puppy is still tiny. We want your puppy to grow up confident but polite and respectful around other dogs. If you allow your other dog to become too forceful in the correction of the puppy when the puppy is tiny, you could risk the puppy becoming a little nervous of older dogs and we don't want that.

We want him to learn manners but remain confident. As the puppy grows and pushes the boundaries more, yes, you can allow your older dog to follow up the warning growl with a more physical signal that he has had enough. Remember what I said. It is your job to advocate for BOTH dogs. Keep your puppy safe from physical harm by instructing your older dog HOW much he can correct the puppy's behaviour, but also make sure you step in and stop your puppy being annoying and overzealous with your older dog. Think of yourself as a referee at this stage, keeping things nice and friendly!

Teaching your puppy to leave your older dog alone is very important. Your older dog won't necessarily have the stamina to keep up with your puppy and, if your puppy is a large breed, he could actually injure your older dog with his boisterous play as he grows, so do take care to intervene if your puppy is tireless, even if your older dog doesn't warn him off. Let them play for a bit and then step in and tell them both "Game Over". If they ignore you, step in and slip a finger in both of their collars (gently, remember, don't grab them harshly) and step in-between them calmly. When their energy comes down, release them and they should just walk away. You will know if you let them go too soon because one (or both) of them will charge back at the other dog and start playing again! Teaching them both that you are in charge of play will also help your puppy learn to play nicely when he is in the park (see Chapter 14).

Case Study 1: Cheeky Puppy Terrorising her Older "Brother"

Teddy's owners called me to help them because he had bitten a small dog when they had first rescued him. He was an elderly bull breed with an unknown history and they were now concerned at his reactivity towards their 6-month-old puppy, Phoebe, another bull breed. This was particularly the case when it came to food. The two dogs now had to be fed separately, as they could not trust them in each other's company. After watching them carefully, it soon became apparent that poor old Teddy wasn't really the problem in the house, it was his cheeky little "sister"! She was very excitable and playful, as you would expect from a pup her age. Teddy was happy to play with her, but sometimes he would get a bit aggressive with her. This worried the owners, naturally, as he was a sizeable, strong dog. I watched them playing together and it became clear that Phoebe was the one needing work! She was constantly pestering him and wouldn't leave him alone. If he moved away from her, she would follow and start pestering him again. She was leaving Teddy with no choice but to get a bit growly when she refused to get the message. I should add that Teddy had never hurt her. In fact, the owners told me that Phoebe had once gone for him unprovoked because there was a bone near him!

First off, I explained to them that, whilst they were right to be concerned because Teddy could be reactive around food and had been aggressive towards a dog whilst out on a walk, it wasn't just Teddy who needed some work. They needed to look at Phoebe's behaviour too and work with both dogs, firstly teaching Phoebe some boundaries around Teddy, and secondly teaching both dogs that calm, respectful behaviour was required around food. My first advice was to remove ALL food-based toys and all treats from the household. The only food the two dogs should be getting was at mealtimes. Both dogs were taught that all food resources belonged to, and came from, their humans. They were taught to be calm around food – firstly using bits of their kibble and then more smelly treats. I showed their owners how to feed them together but at a respectful distance from each other, with a human in-between them. Should one of them finish first, it was the human's job to ensure that the other dog did not invade the space of the dog who was still eating. They were taught to respect each other's personal space when food was about. They were happily eating in each other's company in no time and Phoebe quickly learnt that the owners would step in and advocate for Teddy if she failed to leave him alone when he had had enough during playtime.

For those cat lovers amongst you, there is absolutely no need for you to rearrange the set-up of your household just because you have brought a puppy into the house. You will need to introduce the puppy to your cat(s) in a controlled manner, that is a given, and you may have to make a few small changes initially, but there is no need for you to banish your cats to just one part of your house. What I would strongly advise against doing is letting your puppy loose amongst your cats without any supervision from the outset. This could prove disastrous. Cats are instinctively wary of dogs. You can hardly blame them; we all know how dogs like to chase cats. Not all dogs, mind, but definitely the majority. Even those dogs that live happily alongside cats are likely to chase an unknown cat that it sees outside its home environment. Why? Because this cat is not part of its pack. If you let your puppy loose from Day 1 and it spots your cat for the first time, there is a very strong possibility it will give chase and that will become your puppy's equation for the cat, despite it being a pack member. Best case scenario is the cat manages to run away and jump up out of reach of the puppy onto some furniture or escape out of the cat flap. In the worst case, your puppy could corner the cat and the cat be forced to defend itself aggressively, hurting your puppy in the process. You do not want either of these scenarios to happen because it will result in a lack of trust between the cat and the puppy. Without trust, the two animals will not be able to live harmoniously together.

To teach mutual trust and respect between your cat and your puppy, I would advise a multi-stepped approach. On the day you bring your puppy home, pop your cat(s) into another room and shut the door. Get your puppy settled in his new dedicated area, whether it be in the kitchen or an allocated room. Hopefully you have followed my earlier advice and have a puppy pen with crate in place. Don't let your cat out of the room for a few hours whilst the puppy settles in. Your puppy will at some point settle down for a nap in his crate or pen. When he does, let the cat out. It will have smelt that there is a dog in the house and likely come to investigate. You absolutely want your cat to do this. He needs to investigate the puppy in his own time, not be forced to interact with it. Let him sniff around the outside of the pen, and if your puppy wakes up and notices, don't do anything, just let the puppy approach the cat. The cat will likely move away if it sees the puppy wake up. This is absolutely fine. The cat may hiss. Again, fine. Introducing them this way allows both of them to suss out the other animal. The puppy will be curious, but the pen will stop him being able to follow the cat if it moves away. This will give the cat confidence that it is safe from being chased. If your puppy gets over-excited by the sight of the cat and starts whining or barking, verbally correct the puppy with a firm "Ah, Ah" and stand in-between him and the cat. You are telling him in dog language that the cat belongs to you and is not for barking at. As soon as he looks at you, give him calm praise (but NO TREATS!!!!).

If you don't have a puppy pen set up, but instead have your puppy in a dedicated room, I would suggest having a stair gate across the door to the room. This effectively replicates the side of a pen. You will initially keep the room door shut and let your cat investigate the smell of the puppy from under the door, and then you can start opening the door a tiny bit so that two animals can see each other. The stair gate will keep your cat safe from being chased.

This early introduction should be repeated every day. If you are bringing the puppy out of his pen (or room) to play or toilet, make sure the cat is nowhere to be seen. Allow the cat freedom of the house when the puppy is safely in his pen (or room). What will happen is that gradually trust will start to develop. The cat knows it is safe. Once the two animals are happily ignoring each other, or even better, calmly interacting with the pen between them, it is time to move on to the next stage, which is having them together with no barriers between them.

The best time to do this in the evenings AFTER your puppy has had the zoomies and you have time to devote to the exercise. Naturally, you can do it at any time of day you choose, just make sure that your puppy is calm and a bit tired before starting. Introducing the two of them with no physical boundary will be easiest to do if you have family members to help, but it isn't essential. If you are on your own, simply concentrate on the puppy and leave the cat to take care of itself. Before you fetch your puppy, put your cat in your living room or similar room where you can relax on a sofa or comfy chair. Shut the door. Now fetch your puppy, making sure he is wearing a collar, carry him into the room and shut the door behind you so that your cat can't exit the room. Sit on the sofa with your puppy, with one finger **loosely** in his collar. Do some nice deep breathing so that he relaxes and lies down on you. If you have another person helping you, get them to pick up the cat (provided the cat likes being picked up!) and sit on the sofa a little distance from you, keeping the cat to the far side of them. You want maximum distance between the puppy and the cat! Both of you should relax now and gently stroke your respective animal. If either animal eyeballs the other one, gently give them a verbal intervention (such as "Ah, Ah") and immediately relax again. The message to both animals is that we are sharing calm relaxation in this situation and it's enjoyable for everyone. If all remains calm, get the person with the cat to shuffle a little closer to you and the puppy, again remaining calm throughout and holding the puppy gently but firm enough so that he can't suddenly lunge at the cat. If the cat remains calm in this situation, let the cat go. He may decide to jump up onto the back of the sofa. That is fine. The puppy may sit up if this happens and stare at the cat. Again, intervene gently. Your puppy needs to learn that a moving cat is nothing to get excited about. If you have done the above correctly, the cat should settle down for a snooze and the puppy too. If for any reason you don't get the above result, this will likely be down to YOU being tense, not the animals being tense. Try using the Zen relaxation technique from Chapter Nine to get you into the right state of mind before entering the room. As with most of my other training, DON'T FEED YOUR PUPPY OR CAT TREATS DURING THIS EXERCISE! Not only is food likely to make both animals excitable, but it could also trigger competition between them for the food resource.

Once everyone is settled, get your family member to get up and call the cat out of the room. You should remain seated on the sofa with the puppy and calmly restrain him from following. Again, he is learning that just because the cat jumps down and leaves the room, doesn't mean he follows. Repeat this exercise and keep a close eye on what your cat is telling you with his body language and energy. The more relaxed your cat becomes around the puppy, the more you can progress with trusting the puppy. Go from holding him on your lap, to letting him lie on the floor with a lead on when the cat is in the room. Initially, have the lead in your hand in case the puppy decides to lunge at the cat, but once you feel you can trust him more, pop the lead under your foot, and eventually dispense with it altogether if the puppy remains relaxed when the cat is moving.

Be very clear to your puppy that the cat is not for chasing. There may be times when he just can't help himself, particularly if the cat has been teasing him (believe me, this happens a lot with cheeky cats!). If he does chase, this is the time to use a sharp verbal intervention to stop him in his tracks. Cats rarely get caught by dogs as they are so agile and can easily jump onto something out of reach of the dog. If your puppy chases the cat and doesn't stop at a verbal intervention, follow him until he stops and then get in front of him and calmly move him back with your body away from the cat, wherever it is. You need to keep reinforcing the message that the cat belongs to YOU and that the cat is higher up the hierarchy in the family pack than the puppy. You may need to pop your puppy back on a puppy line for a while in the house if he does take a liking to chasing the cat. You will need to closely monitor your puppy whenever the cat is around and intervene if he shows any sign of getting excited at the cat, and step on the line if he gives chase. If the cat hisses at the puppy, by all means let it. Your puppy needs to back off when warned, just like if he was warned off by a more senior dog. Obviously, don't let the cat launch a full-scale attack on your puppy. You can use verbal intervention with cats too! Block & claim the puppy from the cat if it looks like it is going to escalate beyond a hiss.

Case Study 2: Banished to the Garden Until Bedtime

I got called to help an 8-month-old labrador cross called Lucky, whose cat chasing had resulted in the family's two elderly cats staying outdoors unless the puppy was asleep in his pen. The cats had kept their distance since Lucky's arrival, but unfortunately Lucky had managed on one occasion to give chase when he found his way into the neighbour's garden through a hole in the fence and caught the cats unaware. The subsequent chase had left the cats deeply fearful of him. The owners naturally felt this was a very unfair situation for the poor cats and were keen to find a solution. In addition to the cat-chasing issue, Lucky also had problems with human aggression, toy and food possessiveness and jumping up. He was also frightened of lots of things, including the hoover, horses and loud noises. Lucky's nervousness, aggressive tendencies and excitement were a massive red flag to the cats, so it wasn't surprising that they now refused to come into the house unless he was safely penned! It was important to deal with these other issues <u>before</u> introducing him to the cats again in a controlled environment.

I had been briefed by the owners that his aggressiveness (which had involved biting and drawing blood on more than one occasion) had been dealt with at doggie daycare with a "tap" on the nose. Whilst this had stopped Lucky biting, he continued to growl at humans when he stole something, had a toy in his mouth or when he was resting and was approached by a human. Hardly surprising, given that he had been physically admonished for growling and biting at daycare. How could he possibly trust humans if they were going to physically punish him when he asked them to stay away? My approach revolved around building up Lucky's trust in humans again, so that he no longer feared their hands. I also showed him that clear boundaries existed within the house in terms of what he was and wasn't allowed to touch and possess. It is very important with a nervous dog to instil trust first, before tackling the issue of boundaries. A frightened dog will lash out when challenged, as will a possessive dog. Having a nervous, possessive puppy is the worst possible situation! Trust is built through calm, slow, controlled interaction with a nervous dog, it is **NOT** built through dominance and punishment. I spent time just sitting with Lucky without touching him. Using food to engage his nose and arouse his curiosity, allowed me to start feeding him titbits, but in a controlled way. No snatching or grabbing! I allowed him to snuffle my hands and then if he politely and calmly backed off, I would open my hand flat and allow him to take the food. Not only was I building his trust, but I was also teaching him that food equalled calmness. Once he was happily taking food from me, it was time to start gentle touching. I was not TREATING him for being touched as that would have been counterproductive – I could easily end up teaching him to tolerate touching in order to get a treat, but he would have been in the WRONG STATE OF MIND if I had done this – he would have been excited in anticipation of a treat! No, what I needed to do was to calmly share food with him in a calm state of mind whilst I calmly touched him. I then showed him how enjoyable a touch from a human was without food. This kind of rehabilitation should ONLY be done by a professional, by the way. Lucky had developed serious issues by the time I met him and although still a puppy, it was no longer safe to use the blocking & claiming techniques as he had already become unbalanced. Had he started off life learning rules and boundaries from a young age, these issues wouldn't have developed and become so extreme.

Once we had reached the point where Lucky was happy to have me touch him all over, with or without food being shared, it was time to teach him some new boundaries in the house. Having tested that he remained in a calm state if I walked towards him (which he did, as he now fully trusted me), I began work with other objects in the house, namely the dishwasher, food treats and his favourite toys. Lucky was polite and respectful in all situations, so it was now time to bring in the cats! As Lucky wasn't a new introduction to the house, there was no need to do the early stages, we simply jumped forwards to the sofa sharing, introducing one cat at a time with Lucky on lead on the floor beside me. Because he already understood that I was now in charge of different territories and objects within his home, he was quick to pick up that I was also in charge of the cats. We introduced the more confident cat first and then, when Lucky was showing calm, respectful behaviour around this cat, we introduced the more nervous cat. I am pleased to report that Lucky accepted the presence of the cats quite happily and even more importantly, the cats, after some *initial nerves, soon realised that Lucky wasn't getting in an excited state of mind when he saw them and wasn't chasing them. They settled on the back of the sofa and Lucky remained on the floor. Their journey towards mutual acceptance had begun and it was down to the family to carry on this work.*

It's not just cats and other dogs that puppies can live happily alongside. Your puppy can learn to live alongside any other animal and also baby humans! The same rules apply - establish a clear protocol for when your puppy is near others, whether it be a rabbit, a guinea pig, a lizard or a human baby. The message to your puppy from the outset is that all these individuals are pack members and, more importantly, higher up the hierarchy than your puppy. So, not only should they be interacted with in a calm state of mind, but they should also be respected by your puppy. They are not siblings or squeaky toys. It is important to make this definition. I have on a number of occasions been asked to help with puppies that are treating human children like siblings, much to the upset of the child and the parents. This has happened because the puppy was not taught that the children held a higher position than them from the outset and that rules and boundaries needed to be observed when interacting with the child. To your puppy, a squealing child who is running around and enjoying being chased by a tiny puppy will still be viewed the same by the puppy (as a playmate and equal) when the puppy has grown much bigger and its adult teeth are coming through. Children quickly become disillusioned about the new family member when the bites get harder and the puppy doesn't understand that the child is no longer enjoying the interaction. This is why it is so important to teach a puppy when play starts and when play stops and teach your children how to deliver this message too.

If you just happen to welcome a new baby into your family at a time when your puppy is still quite young (and this does sometimes happen!), make sure that you are quite clear to the puppy that the baby is YOURS and that certain rules apply. It is much easier to do this from the outset than it is to undo learnt behaviour further down the line. You want your puppy to initially see the baby as an extension of you, not a separate entity. I would strongly recommend from the outset teaching the puppy that there is an exclusion zone around the baby that the puppy can only enter when invited by an adult human. Do this using the blocking &

claiming technique when you are holding your newborn in your arms, but also when your newborn is in a baby carrier, pram, bouncy chair or even lying on the floor on a changing mat or playmat. Make sure you are very calm when you are doing this, even if your baby is screaming its head off. Your baby is going to grow quickly and will soon be on the move, rolling over, crawling and then walking. At all these stages you want your puppy to be calm and respectful.

The same applies to all the baby's paraphernalia – blankets, toys, dummies and, most importantly, food. All of these things should be out of bounds for your puppy. When your baby progresses to sitting in a highchair, the last thing you want is your puppy hanging about below in the hope that some tasty food gets dropped. If you allow this to happen, you are going to find it much harder to stop your puppy taking food out of your toddler's hands as they walk about, because the puppy will have developed the equation in its brain that your baby is a food dispensing machine. Don't get me wrong, you are going to allow the baby and the puppy to bond and form a friendship, but only at times when you feel it is appropriate and when any contact is instigated by you. Invite your puppy to come and sniff the baby when it is asleep in your arms, maintaining a calm, relaxed demeanour throughout. Encourage him to curl up at your feet when you are all having a chill on the sofa. Excluding him is not the answer. Calm, careful control and the teaching of good manners is the way to ensure your puppy grows up with a strong bond with your child but behaves appropriately. Likewise, it is important to teach your toddler to be respectful of your puppy and his personal space. Teach your youngster to leave the puppy alone when he is sleeping and not to grab him or drag him about.

Case Study 3: Nippy with the Grandkids

I first met Ruby when she was only 13 weeks old. In other words, a very young puppy. She was an English Bull Terrier and her owner was very experienced with the breed, having owned a number of them throughout her adult life and never encountered any problems with them. But this puppy was different. She had a lovely nature but was very nippy and this had become quite a serious problem. Her owner was alarmed at seeing this behaviour at such a young age and was concerned for her grandchildren. It was clear on meeting Ruby that the underlying problem was pure excitement. She had all this pent-up energy and didn't have an outlet for it. She was too young to be walked any distance, so wasn't getting tired from her daily exercise. She had learnt quickly that mouthing and nipping people made them squeal (just like her brothers and sisters) and this had become a bad habit very quickly. Being an English Bull Terrier, she was already quite a solid, strong puppy. The adults in the family were able to control her better, but the children couldn't. She needed to learn that children weren't her siblings, even though they acted like they were (by squealing when nipped).

I showed her owner how to take ownership of the children and teach Ruby that they were not for playing with. She could only interact with the children when she was in a calm state of mind. I also taught the adults how to play with her in a more controlled way. I encouraged them to always have a toy to hand to put into her mouth and NOT to allow any contact with human skin. I showed them how to teach Ruby that human skin was for licking not nibbling. If she became over-excited and started nipping, they were to stop play, remain CALM and disengage from Ruby. If she chased after them, they were to block & claim their personal space and make it clear to her that she wasn't welcome in it. She quickly learnt that she could play rough with her toys, but not with humans. Ruby grew up to be the most amazing family dog. She would not have grown out of this unwanted behaviour naturally – dogs grow INTO behaviours, as the more they are repeated the more deeply the default behaviour becomes ingrained. Nipping things in the bud at an early age put Ruby back on the right track to growing into a well-balanced dog.

Pupology

Chapter 20 – Adopting a Rescue Puppy

Many people would love to give a rescue dog a home, rather than buying a puppy from a breeder. Whilst some puppies do become available through UK rescues, they are harder to come by than those from overseas rescues. In both cases, you should be aware that puppies from rescues could potentially come with issues. You may be lucky and be able to adopt a 12-week-old puppy via a rescue that has been fostered in a home environment, but if that isn't the case and the puppy has been raised in kennels, do bear in mind that this could impact on its early social development. Learning social skills at a young age is hugely important for puppies. As you will have realised by now, doing this in a calm, supervised way is absolutely essential if the puppy is to grow up balanced. Kennels are not generally calm environments - stress and noise levels are high and dogs spend much more time alone than they would in a home environment.

Case Study 1: Missing Out on Social Skills Early On

Creed was a 10-month-old German shepherd who came from a UK rescue. Not a young puppy, but still a young dog. He was given up to rescue because his original owners had no experience with dogs and found him too much to handle as he grew and entered puberty. He had been kennelled for a month by the time he was adopted. It was very clear when I met him that his time in kennels had been a traumatic time for Creed. He had developed a deep distrust of people, particularly men, to the point that, if cornered, he would lash out and bite. It was crucial to take things very slow and teach him to trust again, particularly his male owner. The key thing for his male owner was to slow things right down. He needed to work at Creed's pace and the simplest way for him to understand what that pace was, involved teaching him how to read the subtle signs that Creed was giving him that he was uncomfortable. These signs are not immediately obvious to everyone and the owners desire to have Creed love him and trust him as much as Creed trusted his wife was putting too much pressure on the dog.

I showed his owner how to simply sit calmly near Creed and do absolutely nothing. I then introduced something tasty into the equation. Although Creed was some distance from his owner, he picked up the scent very quickly and became interested. Getting him to use his NOSE first was absolutely essential to him learning to trust. I advised his owner to quietly and with no fuss throw some tiny bits of treat to the side of him and not to make eye contact with Creed. Once Creed saw that the owner wasn't showing any interest in him, he got up enough courage to come and take a look and to have a tasty snack. By bringing the little pieces of food closer and closer to the owner whilst he maintained a calm, relaxed state, we were able to show Creed that nothing sudden or alarming was going to happen. Creed needed to come to his owner of his own free will, not have his owner force love on him. Very soon, Creed was taking the food from his male owner's hand, and at this point I advised some gentle touching. Just a tiny touch and, if this was tolerated, a little scratch. We kept away from his head, as this is where most rescues tend to be grabbed by people. Much better to gently touch a leg or his body. I can happily report that Creed soon bonded closely with his male owner, and indeed, became his right-hand man, going everywhere with him. His female owner also benefited from watching the whole process. She had felt a little guilty that Creed seemed happier around her. I advised her to put this emotion aside, as it wasn't helping Creed. What he needed was her to be calmly confident whilst he was adjusting to his new surroundings, rather than feel sorry for him, or feel guilty that he had gravitated towards her.

Overseas puppies not only have the issue of being born in rescue, or taken off the streets when young, they also have to endure travel from a foreign country to the UK, which in itself can be a traumatic experience. The number of organisations bringing dogs to the UK from overseas has increased dramatically in recent years. Anecdotal evidence suggests that it is sometimes easier to adopt an overseas dog than it is to fill the stringent requirements of UK dog rescues. Whilst this is not always the case, obviously, I have been told many times by clients that they had turned to overseas adoption for this reason.

I myself have adopted two rescue dogs, one of whom was born in Ireland, so could be considered an "overseas" rescue! I have also owned two puppies bred by Kennel Club registered breeders, so have experienced both types of dog ownership. Do your research, understand what you are getting yourself into and be prepared for the additional challenges these rescue puppies may bring, particularly those from overseas. I know of many success stories and have met some lovely overseas rescues, but at the same time I have also been kept busy helping owners who were totally unprepared for what a hard journey it can be.

Overseas rescue puppies can come from a variety of circumstances but the most common I have come across in my work as a behaviourist are those born in domestic circumstances and those born to feral street dogs. My own collie had her own unique start, being born in a rescue centre after her pregnant mother was taken into their care. I will discuss her later in my next case study. Overseas rescues born into domestic circumstances are often the result of unplanned pregnancies. Their mothers may be pet dogs or farm dogs, but either way, the puppies end up in a rescue centre and are offered for adoption. These puppies differ from their feral counterparts because they have not been born on the streets. However, they still have to endure time in rescue kennels and then a long journey to the UK, all of which can be traumatic for the pups. Adopters should bear this in mind when they take them on. They come with their own unique set of challenges, and it is very much a lottery as to what sort of dog you will end up with. This journey is unlikely to be the same as the one you would take if you bought a puppy from a domestic breeder. That said, there are plenty of puppies for sale in this country that come from less than reputable breeders and could also be destined to have behavioural issues. The start a puppy has in life and the health and welfare of its parents play a part in that puppy's destiny.

Puppies of dogs living on the streets are the offspring of feral dogs. For these dogs, life is all about survival. These dogs have little or no human interaction, are wary of humans and often other dogs, due to pack rivalries on the streets. A common issue I see with these dogs is a fear of men, particularly men in high-viz jackets. Perhaps these dogs have had run-ins with street cleaners or refuse collectors, the kind of men who would be up early in the morning or late at night when the dogs themselves would be most active? Perhaps they have been regularly chased away from dustbins and had items thrown at them? Who knows, but one thing is certain, high-viz is often associated with fear in street dogs, and as a result I carry my own high-viz vest for desensitisation!

Another problem many of these puppies have is a lack of trust in humans. Again, this is totally understandable if they have had very little human contact, or only negative contact. Thankfully, it is possible to help them build trust, and they will bond quickly with their adoptive family. However, it may take a considerable amount of work for an owner to get their rescue pup to relax around strangers, both in and outside the home. The fight or flight instinct in these puppies is deeply ingrained, and if they have learnt to use aggression to keep humans at a distance, it can be a very challenging issue. Add to this a general feeling of pity that owners feel towards their puppy, particularly if it came from very distressing circumstances, and things become more complicated. Giving affection to a dog who is showing aggression towards anything will NOT help sort the problem. If you find your rescue puppy does have these issues, please consult a professional for additional help and advice.

Case Study 2: Transportation and Car Fear

My rescue collie was born in Ireland. From what I understand, her mother had been rescued whilst pregnant and gave birth in the rescue centre. The pups were kept in kennels until 4.5 months old then shipped over to England to a small, home-based rescue. I adopted one of the pups when she was 5.5 months old. It was clear when we collected her that she was petrified of the car. She was so scared that she wet herself on the first journey, and on subsequent car journeys she would shake and pant, curling herself up into the tiniest ball possible. I believe the journey from Ireland to the UK had been very traumatic for her. I have no idea how she was transported, whether by lorry, van or car, but whatever the mode, she clearly found the journey very scary.

Not only was she scared of travelling in the car, but she was also scared of passing traffic. Being a collie, this juxtapositioned with an obsession to herd moving objects, so she had a double whammy - whenever she saw a car or a motorbike her brain went into overdrive, both wanting to herd it, but also being scared of it. It took a lot of calm, careful exposure to traffic to allow her to cope with the stimuli, likewise time and patience for her to be able to tolerate journeys in the car. Whilst she still doesn't like traffic, she will now tolerate it and not chase, and likewise will curl up and sleep on journeys in the boot of our car, whether it be a 10-minute journey or several hours.

Case Study 3: Food Obsession and Thieving

I met Lila when she was 10 months old. She was a mixed breed rescue from Romania. In addition to helping with general issues of excitement, her owners also needed help with her perpetual thieving. Being of labrador size, she could quite easily reach worktops to help herself to whatever she fancied. Her family had consequently been obliged to rig up a variety of fences to stop her getting into the kitchen area. Lila's mother was a street dog. Thieving is a common issue with street dogs and their offspring. These dogs will be used to scavenging for food and living off food waste discarded by humans. So, it's not surprising Lila had a penchant for raiding the kitchen bin and the kitchen counters. As far as she was concerned, food was for eating, no matter where it was located! What she lacked was an understanding about boundaries when it came to humans and food. Why would she? Things came to a head when Lila stole something containing raisins, which are toxic to dogs, resulting in a hefty vet bill.

I showed her owners how to teach Lila that she could only touch food that had been delivered by a human to her; she could eat treats from their hands or food from her bowl, but that was it. The kitchen counters were out-of-bounds, as was the bin and any food sitting on tables or even the floor. Rebooting Lila's approach to food included changing her default state of mind around it. Food EXCITED her! This excitement had been reinforced when she first arrived by her new owners showering her with lots of tasty dog treats. They felt sorry for her because of her poor start in life and wanted to compensate for that. I showed her owners how to teach her that food equalled calmness and that her owners would only share food with her when she was in a calm state of mind. Understanding that their overseas rescue needed some extra work in the food department helped the family on their journey to rid their kitchen of all the barricades!

Pupology

Chapter 21 - First Year in the Bag!

You did it, you made it through your first year! Well done! It won't necessarily have been an easy journey but hopefully you have remained calm, confident and consistent throughout your interactions with your puppy, at the same time recognising that he is an animal with animal instincts and not a human in a furry suit who understands your every spoken word. By now you should have provided him with clear guidelines as to how you expect him to behave in different situations and also taught him the signals you will give him when he is not behaving within these guidelines, signals that mirror those his Mum used when he was first born. Signals that he understands as a DOG. You should be providing for his needs on a daily basis; feeding him, exercising him and sharing affection with him at appropriate times. And in return he should have grown into a loyal, loving but respectful companion. Your actions should be automatic in key situations and so should his. You should be working in harmony with him, not fighting against his instincts.

If you have got to the end of this first year and you are struggling in any way, think long and hard about the way you are interacting with your young dog and your relationship with him. Think first about what you are sharing with him in any given situation, rather than homing in on his behaviour first. You should have learnt by now that **your state of mind** has a massive influence on his. This is particularly important when he enters puberty and if he remains un-neutered. Is he being forced to follow his instincts in some situations because he isn't able to trust you to take charge in a calm, confident way? He is an animal, remember. He has animal instincts and these will kick in if his human doesn't step up and take charge when his brain is telling him he needs to react in a certain way.

Do recognise that the daily work continues with him going forwards after his first birthday. Consistency is the key. If you repeat the same behaviour on your part every day, he will repeat what you have taught him. If you change the goalposts, however, get a bit slapdash or ease off a bit with the rules you have set, he may learn new unwanted behaviours, so do try to maintain those rules and boundaries you set at the very beginning for him. If his behaviour does change for any reason, look at yourself first and try to work out when things changed. And then go back to basics for a bit to "reboot" your puppy to get him behaving the way you want him to again.

It's not the end of the world if he develops some bad habits in the home. It is your home, after all, and it is up to you to decide what rules apply to your dog. Bringing you an offering of dirty socks every time you come home is not going to cause anyone any harm, if that is all he is doing, but if he is destroying those socks or, worse, eating them, that is another matter! The things you should insist on relate to safety in the home and annoyance to others, including your neighbours. Use common sense and be considerate. Outside of your home, you have a duty to ensure that you have control of the way your dog behaves. We may be a nation of dog lovers, but not everyone likes dogs and there are plenty people who are scared of them. Again, use your common sense and be considerate to others.

Having a dog is a joy and I hope that this book has been a useful guide for your first year as a puppy owner. I hope you have learnt that, as well as being able to influence a dog's behaviour using commands, rewards or particular equipment, it is also possible to influence it with your relationship. This is what dogs themselves do. Your relationship with your puppy from the very beginning is key to how he will behave throughout his life. He will willingly do what you ask him, whenever you ask him, if you cement the foundations of that relationship at the outset and base that relationship on trust and respect, rather than dictatorship and fear. Respect the fact that he, like other animals, communicates in a different way to you. Understand *how* he communicates and you can massively speed up the way he learns by replicating these methods. But do always remember to rein in your OWN human instincts when communicating with him as they can often get in the way and confuse things! Remember, use your head not your heart first! Never forget that he is a dog and not a human!

Remember those important "Cs" – be calm, consistent, confident, commanding and take charge when need be. Take the lead and he will follow!

Acknowledgments

I would like to take this opportunity to thank all those who helped me in the writing of this book. Big thanks to all my clients past and present for the opportunity to work with their dogs. Many of them have gone on to become friends, so also fall into the next category of people to thank! Thank you to all the friends who have supported and encouraged me throughout this foray into the publishing world. Thank you to my family for putting up with my endless musings on dogs and their behaviour and for enduring the mess I inevitably create when setting up a space somewhere in the house to work on my book. A special thanks goes out to the kind people who helped with the proofing and editing of my manuscript – you know who you are!